POSSESSED VOICES

SUNY SERIES IN CONTEMPORARY JEWISH LITERATURE AND CULTURE

EZRA CAPPELL, EDITOR

POSSESSED VOICES

Aural Remains from
Modernist Hebrew Theater

Ruthie Abeliovich

Cover image: Nachum Zamach as the peddler-prophet, from *Habima*'s 1923 production of *The Eternal Jew*. Courtesy of *Habima* National Theater and the Israeli Center for the Documentation of the Performing Arts.

Author photo: Shahar Tamir

Published by State University of New York Press, Albany

For information, contact State University of New York Press, Albany, NY
www.sunypress.edu

Library of Congress Cataloging-in-Publication Data

Names: Abeliovich, Ruthie, 1978– author.
Title: Possessed voices : aural remains from modernist Hebrew theater /
　Ruthie Abeliovich.
Description: Albany : State University of New York, [2019] | Series: SUNY
　series in contemporary Jewish literature and culture | Includes
　bibliographical references and index.
Identifiers: LCCN 2018033265 | ISBN 9781438474434 (hardcover : alk. paper) |
　ISBN 9781438474441 (pbk. : alk. paper) | ISBN 9781438474458 (ebook)
Subjects: LCSH: Theater—Israel. | Jewish theater.
Classification: LCC PN2919.4 .A24 2019 | DDC 792.095694—dc23
LC record available at https://lccn.loc.gov/2018033265

10 9 8 7 6 5 4 3 2 1

In loving memory of my father,
Aharon Abeliovich

Contents

Illustrations

Acknowledgments

This book is about itinerant voices that resonate from bodies in which they do not originate. To fully experience this book, readers are invited to listen: to play the audio files documenting performances of the Modernist Hebrew theater at https://www.ruthieabeliovich.com/possessed-voices, and to tune in to the myriad voices embedded in the text. During the writing of this book many colleagues and friends offered insights, remarks, comments, and assistance that contributed to the configuration of my voice in various ways. I would like to express my gratitude to all the individuals who have helped me during the research, writing, and publishing process of this book.

I am grateful to Shelly Zer-Zion, that a few years ago, then as the head of the Israeli Center for the Documentation of the Performing Arts, generously handed to me *Habima*'s audio files and invited me to join a research group on historiography of theater in Mandatory Palestine (2011–12), in which I began to formulate the current study. Throughout the research and writing of this book I have benefited immeasurably from illuminating insights and radiant intellectual thoughts of three special people, it is a great pleasure to thank them. Ruth HaCohen, a model scholar, did not spare her valuable time to read, comment, and contribute from her expertise with inimitable sensitivity, imaginative wisdom, and pioneering studies on Jewish music and culture. I am extremely thankful to Edwin Seroussi for his friendship, superb critical acumen, for sharing with me his vast knowledge, and for his ongoing prolonged supportive and fruitful engagement with my work. I am deeply indebted to my PhD supervisor, Freddie Rokem, an admirable teacher, innovative scholar of the highest caliber, and most of all, an inspiring human being, whose stimulating intellectual presence continues to have profound bearings on my thought.

I would like to acknowledge the "Daat Hamakom" ICORE Center at the Hebrew University for providing much-appreciated support that enabled me to launch this project. During the research and writing of this book I was exceptionally privileged to benefit from the generous postdoctoral scholarship granted by the Martin Buber Society of Fellows in the Humanities and Social Sciences, also located at the Hebrew University. I owe a huge debt to the Martin Buber Society, for enabling me the optimal conditions one could possibly ask for, and especially for providing an incredibly rich and invigorating interdisciplinary scholarly environment. My special thanks go to Yigal Bronner, its brilliant academic head, and to Yael Baron, its admirable administrative director, for making this hub the paradise it is. My dear friends and fellows at the Buber society—the most exquisite fraternity one could possibly imagine—offered their insights in reading groups, seminars, and conversations, talking me through impasses, reading drafts, and furnishing their big-hearted support in many other ways. I am especially grateful to Moshe Blidstein, Maurice Ebileeni, Oded Erez, Orit Gazit, Eitan Grossman, Liat Hasenfratz, Laura Jockush, Nadeem Karkabi, Renana Keydar, Jan Kuehne, Limor Meoded Danon, Yifat Monnickendam, Yonatan Moss, Assaf Nativ, Yakir Paz, Shai Secunda, Nitzan Rothem, and Evelyn Runge.

Many thanks are also due to my dialogue partners—teachers, close friends, and colleagues—who, wittingly or otherwise, provided knowledgeable trenchant comments and constructive assistance: The historiography working group at the IFTR (Stockholm, 2016), the ASTR "Listening to the Sonic Subaltern working group" (Atlanta, GA, 2017) convened by Marci R. McMahon and Caitlin Marshall, Sharon Aronson-Lehavi, Chen Alon, Linda Ben-Zvi, Marcy Brink-Danan, Hans Ulrich (Sepp) Gumbrecht, Michal Grover-Friedlander, Ilit Ferber, Galit Hasan-Rokem, Brandon Labelle, David Levin, Yair Lipshitz, Peter W. Marx, Amit Pinchevski, Diego Rotman, Dani Schrire, and Dorit Yerushalmi.

Research for this book was conducted in numerous libraries and archives. I wish to acknowledge the wonderful professional staff of the Israeli Sound Archive at the National Library in Jerusalem, especially Gila Flam and Matan Wygoda; Olga Levitan from the Israeli Center for the Documentation of the Performing Arts at Tel Aviv University, Rami Semo and Ruth Tonn Mendelson from *Habima* archive, Yael Diner from Beit Ariella Theater Archive, the staff at the Gur Theater Archive at the Hebrew University of Jerusalem, Michelle Klein from the Photo Archive at the Hebrew University, and Rachel Laufer from the Israel Museum.

Many people were involved across the long path of preparing the manuscript for this book. I am grateful to Talia Trainin, who read and edited the manuscript with perspicacity and intellectual acuity. I wish to thank Rafael Chaiken, Ezra Cappell, and the devoted SUNY Press staff for their extremely professional and efficient work bringing the book to realization. Sections from chapter 1 were previously published in *Borderlines: Essays on Mapping and the*

Logic of Place (ed. Ruthie Abeliovich and Edwin Seroussi, De Gruyter Press, 2019); parts of the introduction and chapter 4 were previously published in a chapter published in *The Methuen Drama Handbook to Theater History and Historiography* (ed. Claire Cochrane and Joanna Robinson, 2019). I am thankful to Bloomsbury Methuen Drama for permitting me to reprint these sections. I wish to thank the University of Haifa for their generous assistance. This book is published with the support of the Israeli Science Foundation.

My innermost gratitude goes to Amos Gur for his sympathy and patience throughout our endless conversations, by which I gained better understanding of both myself and the world surrounding me. I thank him for joining me in my quest to find my voice, and for being a voice without a body. My dear family has been an unending source of love and support. I thank Yael and Haim Ben-Shahar for welcoming me with gracious warmth into their family, and for their abiding faith and support. My mother, Dvorah Abeliovich and my sister Nomi Abeliovich, thank you so much for always being there for me, for providing me a sounding board, for your unconditional and limitless affection—I love you both so much.

Danny—the man of my life, my best friend, my love, and my life partner—thank you for your sustaining presence, unsparing intellectual and emotional support, for the joy and for the exciting adventure, well . . . for everything. Our two sons, Yuval and Adam, have opened for me turbulent emotional worlds I did not know of. Thank you for being an infinite source of happiness, and for granting me invaluable powers. This book is dedicated to the loving memory of my father, Aharon Abeliovich (1935–2003), whose disembodied voice resonates in my work in profound ways I have not yet been able to fully articulate.

Preface

In the Synagogue

In one of his last short stories—the only one to take place in a recognizable Jewish world—Franz Kafka presents us with an image of the innards of an old synagogue in which "lives an animal about the size of a marten."[1] In this fragment, written in 1922 during the last stages of his ever-worsening tuberculosis, Kafka zooms in on a declining Jewish congregation that dwells in a small mountain town. There, in the shabby synagogue, an undefined, strange animal has been squatting for more than "the three generations of those who are gathered together in the synagogue."[2] As in Kafka's other bestiary stories, this animal provides the prism through which the reciprocal production of aesthesis in the make-believe world is depicted. The animal in the synagogue perceives the world through its sharp listening to the orchestrated sounds of a diluted community. I open this book with Kafka's story "The Animal in the Synagogue" in order to introduce the performative paradigm of *Possessed Voices*: listening to disembodied voices that resonate the cyclic synagogal sonic world that perished along with the demise of the European Jewry, at the calamitous aftermath of World War II.

Placing ethnography at the core of the synagogal fictional realm, Kafka's story pictures some of the central themes at the focus of this book, alluding to the theatrical logic and poetic properties of mediated vocalities, the visceral nature of listening, the imaginations subsumed in social constellations, and the multiple, sometimes overlapping, meanings attributed to the performative aural gestures, conveyed by various generations and interpreted each time anew.

Always timid, always nervous, the strange animal of Kafka's synagogue prefers to withdraw from the public eye and remain solitary in its hiding shack—evidently, some unknown hole in one of the synagogue's upper walls, near the women's compartment. During the ceremony, however, this uncommonly quiet animal creeps out of its hiding shack, onto its "favorite haunt,"[3] sinking its claws into the separating lattice near the women's gallery, stretching itself on the netted wall and gazing down at the main chamber. Occasionally, as Kafka tells us, when the animal is barred from this spot, it traverses imaginary and physical borderlines of the synagogue space. Sometimes it curls up on a certain spot on a very narrow ledge, on the wall opposite the women's section; at other times, it sneaks down, lured by the shining brass rod on which the curtain of the Ark hangs. The presence of the beast in the synagogue diverts the full focus of the congregation from the religious ritual. Its conspicuous, if silent, presence carves a new visible focal point in the synagogal space, drawing attention to its peripheral, usually unnoticed parts. In this spatial scheme, the liturgy and prayers that furnish the main event of the synagogal ritual recede to the backstage, transforming the participatory community into a chorus of ephemeral voices, sounding and fading away.

From its viewpoint on the fringes of the space, this animal stares intently at the congregation "with its bright, unwinking, and perhaps lidless eyes." Yet, as Kafka explicitly notes, it is certainly not looking at anybody but "it is only facing the dangers by which it feels itself threatened."[4] Its ears pricked, this timid animal quietly listens, attempting to intercept and decipher the rhythms, tones, and timbres of the sounds and voices emerging from the ritual. "It is only when prayers begin that it appears, startled by the noise,"[5] Kafka writes, denoting the way this quiet animal fabricates the space of the synagogue as a locus configured by the auditory faculty.

Whereas the space of the synagogue is visually fraught with boundaries and separations—the divisions between the upper balcony and the ground floor, men and women, animal and human—from the perspective of the beast this synagogue is a place rendered by the properties of sound as porous and permeable. Moving across the vertical axis of the synagogal space, we can fathom the hearkening of this animal—following J. L Austine—as a performative "listening act."

There are different modes of auditory attention: Listening, as Michel Chion argues, may be immersive or distracted, intentional or accidental; it can be causal, semantic, or reduced. Listening may vary in intensity, in emotiveness, or in signification.[6] In contemporary usage, listening is also employed in a way that transcends auditory substance and meaning, denoting a certain form of relational attention. These various modes of attention all share the positioning of the body as a resonating site, in which some kind of rhythmic beat flows and circulates inside, affectively shaping it. How, through the experience of listening, does the animal in the synagogue constitute itself? How does the penetration into and reverberation of the voices and sounds of the liturgy within its body structure and propel the animal's movement in space?

The synagogue is a quiet place; silence is disrupted by loud events that erupt and fill its space. We do not know the nature of the sounds resonating in the synagogue. Mediated through the animal's reactions, Kafka only accounts for how the voices of the liturgy act upon its timid listener. Alarmed by the noise, yet remaining persistently attentive throughout the entire service, the animal's listening involves its entire body; it foregrounds its physicality through the fullness of its responses to the sounds. Guided by its wide auditory range and its hypersensitive hearing, the marten-like animal has gained, through time, a profound affective understanding of the liturgical rhythms and sounds, of typical lamenting cries and preaches delivered in the synagogue; it intuitively encodes the sounds, and predictively responds to them as if it were a good Pavlovian subject. Thus, as Kafka writes, "though divine service, with all its noise, may be very frightening for the animal, still, it does recur, on a modest scale daily and on a grander scale during the festivals, always regularly and without ever a break; and so even the most timid of animals could by now have got used to it, particularly when it sees that this is not the noise of pursuers, but some noise that it cannot understand at all."[7]

When the prayer in the synagogue begins, the timbres of the ceremony stimulate this animal. Though the extent of its actual grasp of the ceremony is unclear, the animal responds to the affectivity of the performed sonority; it tunes in to its timbres, tones, intonations, and to the very force of their utterances, acquiring the ability to sort the pleasant sounds from those suggesting potential dangers for the beast. This animal seems to be trained in listening to the synagogue; to sensuously comprehend the typical sounds of the synagogue irrespective of their semiotic content. For this strange animal, the sounds of the synagogue act as an acoustic outflow; as sounds resonating without forcing upon them the burden of signification. The "light touch" of the voices of the synagogue vibrate its flesh; their resonance waves reverberate inside the body of the small animal, titillating its muscles, projecting imaginations into its present being, and engaging its instincts. The reactions of this animal in the synagogue, thus, demonstrate the affective transmission of the act of listening.

Through its reactive listening, the animal amalgamates the sounds of the prayers with its instinctive impulses. Paying close attention to the dynamic rhythms and tones of the praying congregation, this animal recognizes the service through its phonic substrata, and identifies its cyclic repetition throughout the Jewish calender year. Yet, even though it has adapted to the calendar of the synagogue, it is constantly gripped by fear. The sounds of the synagogue invoke anxiety, and anxiety permeates the animal's listening; its attention is divided between listening and imagining. Thus, this nervous animal in the synagogue is constantly positioned in a place which is not a place; besieged in the liminal position of inside-outside the social field of listening. Relying on the affective impulse of sound, the animal in the synagogue sets auricular experience as the pivot through which it comes to know its environment in ways that suggest an inextricable, inseparable subjective linkage to its world.

"What danger has this marten-like animal to fear, anyway?" Kafka asks, "Who intends to harm this animal that has been left entirely to itself for so many years?" What is it in the voices of the congregation that conjure anxieties stemming from memories of times long past, or, perhaps, incite intuitions about forthcoming calamities? Upon the disintegration of the traditional Jewish life dovetailing the migratory movement issuing at the outset of the long 1920s, Kafka's story provides an image of a deep sense of angst generated by an attenuating community in its twilight. "Does this old animal perhaps know more than the three generations of those who are gathered together in the synagogue?" Kafka suggestively asks, thus placing this strange animal as a presence removed from the flow of time, rendering the sounds of the Jewish community bearers of a mnemonic function.

From this perspective, this is a story about the lingering echoes of a fading congregation, whose voices we can no longer hear, as it is "becoming smaller every year and that it is already having trouble in raising the money for the upkeep of the synagogue."[8] Like the fur of this animal, which is matted by "dust and mortar" making it assimilate in the "paint inside the synagogue,"[9] the voices of the congregation manifest their diluting. The dwindling voices of the Jewish community enable us, the readers, to "dwell in loss," as Jonathan Boyarin puts it, and experience the uprooting Modernist reality of the 1920s that threatened the traditional structure of Jewish congregations.[10]

An "Other" to the Jewish community—often regarded among Europe's various Others—the animal in this synagogue is a creature of its time; a citizen of its place. At the turn of the twentieth century, it strides on narrow bars and slippery slopes, overlooking from above at the Jewish congregation, trapped in the relapses and transformations dictated by modernization. The liminal spaces this undefined animal occupies are reflective of the personal predicament and cultural fault lines under which Kafka writes: on a personal level, there looms his severe illness; on a social level, the outset of the 1920s marks the beginning of a massive Jewish migration movement around Europe. Thus, from its position hovering in between life and death, an inside-outsider of modernizing Europe, the animal becomes a figurative expression—an allegory—of the cultural conditions in which it partakes.

Positioned in between places, and constantly in fear, this animal diverts attention from the main ceremony unfolding at the synagogue, creating a fissure in space, opening it to secondary focal points materialized in its acrobatics along the synagogue walls, or in the fear of the women sitting in the upper compartments. It is never fully in the very place of its being, as it is always ready to challenge potential threats. The synagogue, with its ongoing cyclic repetitions, is itself a nontemporal place, rupturing historical time and cracking quotidian space. While the congregation of the synagogue practices its liturgical routine, the animal observes the ceremonial events from its metaperspective, overhearing the voices straining throughout three generations. In this sense, we could, perhaps, think of this animal as a sort of sonic repository that contains and stores the sounds of the past and the voices of the present. Its continuing presence on the unstable limen conveys its ability to actually hold a presence that is both integrated within the community yet suspended from participation in its linear temporality. Its whole being depends upon the gap in between, upon the ability to be (and not to be) in both places.

Listening hard, the marten-like animal turns into a reflecting witness, not by "resorting a lost world to our vision," as Boyarin points out, but by reminding us "that we are not the first generation to find loss is the heart of our connection."[11] The recurring experience of rupture and loss is expressed in the animal's position in the undefined space between the men and the women, as an audience to the ritual or as a participant in it, behind the curtain of the Ark or above it. The animal keeps distance from the action taking place on the synagogue floor; however, its voices and sounds constantly draw it into the communal event; its detachment from the performance and its impartial participation enable it to connect its present being to its overarching perspective of the past. And yet, the past, in this scene, is not granted a voice, as both the animal and the synagogal space seem to equally defy both the past and the present, and so, it is only upon the narrator's contemplation that history enters the story.

Kafka's short story is discussed here as a paradigmatic topos by which I outline the Modernist performative episteme of *possessed voices*. "The Animal in the Synagogue" opens for us the structure of listening from the position of the marten-like animal—as both listeners and participants in our aural cultural performances. Listening to the resonance of the space, we seek to learn of the past from its current performances. Listening, as Kafka shows here, entails stirring the body around and inside the visceral materiality of our world, opening it up to invisible reverberations. Like the animal in the synagogue, we might, perhaps, tune into the space as if it were an echo chamber, replacing our visual focal points in space and tuning into its climate through our listening. Accordingly, we can think of the voices absent from the local synagogue as an enduring resonance. These voices are not ephemeral because they constitute the synagogue space, construing it through their all-encompassing, continuing presence, even after they have separated from their bodies. Thus, notwithstanding the ability of disembodied voices to actually sound in space, their rhythms pulse in the bodies of their communities and we are summoned to listen to them—can we hear them? This book is an attempt to do so.

Introduction

Possessed Voices is a study of theatrical manifestations of the Hebrew language during the interwar period. It narrates the intriguing story of a largely unknown collection of sound recordings, produced throughout 1931–1965, preserving traces from the sounds and voices played in the early repertoire of the Modernist Hebrew theater (1919–1928).

The new political and social reality spanning across Europe during the 1920s, in the aftermath of the Great War, was formative for the Jewish national movement and, especially, for its endeavor to renew the Hebrew language and root it as the colloquial language of the Zionist enterprise. Between the pending demand of Zionism for a cultural reform, the accelerated processes of modernization, acculturation, and secularization, the traditional sociolinguistic structure of the European Jewry underwent dramatic transformations. The Ashkenazi multilingual province—which was comprised from an alloy of Yiddish as a vernacular language, Hebrew (*leshon-ha-kodesh*) and Aramaic as a medium for religion and cultural heritage, and the imperial languages (mainly Russian or German) as the official "state language"—began to fall apart. With the advent of modern Jewish nationalism, the language of religious creativity and prayer—Hebrew—gradually deviated from its traditional assignments. This process paralleled groundbreaking artistic and literary explorations, which reconfigured the cultural function of Hebrew in relation to its traditional qualities.

This book probes into the performativity of the Hebrew language played on Modernist stages in Europe between the two world wars, and examines the resonance of these voices in commercial sound recordings and radio programs broadcast during the first two decades of the State of Israel (established in 1948). The study examines four recordings of theater performances: three case studies from *Habima*'s formative repertoire, created when the theater was based in Moscow—a 1931 commercial recording of *The Eternal Jew* (premiered in 1919 and revised in 1923); a 1965 commercial recording of *The Dybbuk*

(1922); a 1961 recording of a radio adaptation to *The Golem* (1925)—and one case study from the repertoire of the *Ohel* Theater—a 1952 radio recording of the theater production of *Yaakov and Rachel* (1928).[1] These sound recordings enable access to aural traces from the voices engaged in hallmark productions of the Modernist Hebrew theater, all withstanding a prolonged presence of two decades and more on stages around the globe. The recordings document the performances featuring many of the original cohort of actors, and following—as much as possible—their original directing scheme. Analyzing the sonorities employed in theater performances, and the imaginations engrained in them, this book explores the shaping of the Hebrew language—how the theatrical enactment of the Hebrew plays conveys the emotive dimension of the dramas, and the manner in which the vocal rendering of the language binds its listeners together, creating a temporary *communitas*.

Basing my arguments upon the analysis of sound recordings, this study scrutinizes the theatricalization of the Hebrew language as a reflection of transformation processes in the multilingual Jewish cultural sphere in Europe. My main argument in this book is that in the early Modernist Hebrew theater, the recitation style, vocal delivery, and musicality of speech served as central components in the process of decoding the signs connoted by the spoken language. In other words, the intense semiotics of the musicality of the Hebrew as recited on the theater stage connected the mythical and biblical drama to the lives and affairs of the East European Jewry during the 1920s, transcending the semantic or lexical values of its utterances. This study proposes to apprehend the audible traces from this complex sonority, perpetuated and transmitted through acoustic media during the formative decades of the State of Israel, as a treasure repository providing Jewish immigrants, refugees, and survivors of anti-Semitic atrocities in Europe, with a venue for lamenting the decline of their home communities, and for creating a memory continuum that reconnects their diasporic past to their migratory present.

Modernist Hebrew Theater

Habima, the Modernist Hebrew theater collective whose performances constitute the subject matter of this book, was founded in Moscow in 1917.[2] Conceived as a dramatic studio under the auspices of the Moscow Art Theater (founded in 1898 by Konstantin Stanislavsky and Vladimir Nemirovich-Danchenko), *Habima* was established in the atmosphere permeated with the lingering afterechoes of World War I, under the long looming shadows of the Bolshevik revolution. It was founded by Menachem Gnessin, an educator and an amateur actor, Hanna Rovina, a kindergarten teacher, and Nachum Zemach, a Hebrew teacher who envisioned the establishment of an artistic Hebrew theater. During the first five years, its prominent cohort of actors was formed, when it was joined by figures such as David Vardi, Aharon Meskin, Yehoshua Bertonov, Shoshana Avivit, Miriam Elias, Miriam Goldina, Tamar Robins, Fanny Lubitsch, Raikin Ben-Ari, Baruch Chemerinsky, Chayale Grober, Raphael Klatchkin, Zvi Friedland, Ari Warshaver, and Moshe Halevy—who later resigned from the troupe, immigrated to Palestine and established the *Ohel* theater.[3]

As Joseph Stalin was centralizing his political power after the death of Vladimir Lenin (in January 1924), the theater encountered increasing persecution by the Soviet Communist Party, and especially by the Yevsektsia—the Jewish division of the Soviet Communist Party—that prevented the troupe from pursuing its artistic agenda in Moscow. In 1926, *Habima* left Mosow and set off on a global tour through Europe and the United States, spending almost a year in Tel Aviv (1928–29), and making Berlin its temporary home for an additional year (1930–31). The theater finally settled in Tel Aviv in 1931, becoming Israel's National Theater in 1958, on the tenth anniversary of the state of Israel.

Aiming to express the cultural energies of its time, from its inception *Habima* was committed to creating a Hebrew national theater that would demonstrate the fundamental principles of the Zionist enterprise. Prominently, it sought to infuse their audience with the ideals of the Hebrew revival movement. These tenets, as Gad Kaynar points out, included the regeneration of the Hebrew language, the renewal of artistic interest in biblical and Jewish heritage as dramatic substances, and the wishful aspiration to settle in Palestine and establish it as a national homeland for the Jewish people.[4] This ideological scheme entailed the establishment of a somewhat artificial differentiation between the new Hebrew theater and the Yiddish theater— ייִדיש טעאַטער literally meaning Jewish theater—by contesting diasporic Ashkenazi representation models. Aspiring to untangle the rooted symbiosis between Jewish culture and Yiddish culture, *Habima* wished to disconnect itself from the prevailing Jewish theatrical tradition, and specifically to obscure its profound artistic roots in the Modernist Yiddish theater.[5] *Habima*'s performances rendered Jewish myths, Biblical dramas, and folklore plots familiar from the repertoire of the Yiddish theater, however, the troupe performed in the Hebrew language, adopting the Russian avant-garde theater as its main aesthetic inspiration and working method.[6]

From its first public stage endeavor in *Neshef Bereshit* (literally meaning "Genesis Gala"), which premiered in Moscow on October 8, 1918, *Habima*'s performances were praised for their vocal rendering of the Hebrew language. The evening was also commended by significant authorities on theater in Moscow, as exemplified in a review by the theater critic Sergei Glagolin: "The young Hebrew theater knows how to fashion the sounds of words so that the expressed idea becomes clear even when one does not understand the meaning."[7]

Indeed, during the 1920s, many of the theatergoers that attended *Habima*'s performances held across Europe before a broad range of audiences did not comprehend the Hebrew language uttered on stage. In addition to the issue of language proficiency, *Habima*'s Hebrew was, from the beginning, rendered in the Sephardic (modern Israeli) dialect, which was alien even to those conversant in Hebrew, who mostly were of Ashkenazi origin.[8] Yet, during its formative years in Europe and after immigrating to Palestine in 1931, *Habima* flourished, enjoying admiration around the globe, becoming the epitome and agent of the spiritual tenacity inherent in the reviving Hebrew culture and language. How, then, did *Habima*'s audience understand the Hebrew drama played on the stage? In order to clarify this question, one is compelled to examine the kind of considerations that informed the shaping of the language in the Modernist Hebrew theater: What sort of connection did this theater wish their audience to experience by listening to the Hebrew language? What sort of cultural associations, imaginings, and memories did the theater imbue its spoken language with in order for it to act upon the audience? What was the emotional and communal impact generated by the pronunciation style, rhythm, tempo, accent, and melodies enacted on stage?

The musicality of the Modernist Hebrew theater looms large in its sound recordings. Besides the accompanying musical score, rooted in Jewish folklore, the recordings reveal the thick East European accents of the actors—who were familiar public figures in the Jewish communities, both in the Diaspora and in Mandatory Palestine—and the bountiful rhythmic nuances *Habima* was famous for. The vocal timbres of those renowned actors reveal their unique sonic signatures and manifest a central aspect of their theatrical aura. Finally, the orchestration of the aural drama emphasizes the communal ritualized experience issuing from the sound on the stage: at times, the texts are recited in choral form, while at others, a leading actor chanting the dramatic text in a distinct musical recitation guides the dialogue.

Tracing the performed vocalities in the Modernist Hebrew theater through rhythmic structures, aural gestures, and themes, this study aims to understand the affecting qualities embedded in the Hebrew language. By analyzing four case studies, I will shed light on the various cultural and aural references through which the staged Hebrew was performed. The sonority of the language, I argue, did not generate an autonomous semiotics, but rather created sounds that charged the drama with profound communal emotive dimensions.

Hebrew, in this book, refers to a specific language attributed—politically, ethnically, mythically, and historically—to Jews, and constitutes an aesthetic declaration through which national, prototypical representations are rendered. It is, by and large, through theatrical iterations that the convergence of these categories transpires. Despite its cultural specificity, this study should not be mistakenly regarded as circumscribed within an analysis of the exclusive sociolinguistic and historical circumstances under which the Hebrew language was renewed at the beginning of the twentieth century. Rather than operating as a semantic vehicle, Hebrew presents here a paradigmatic example for the analysis of language performance through its phonetic and musical enactments.

As I will demonstrate in the following chapters, by mobilizing synagogal vocal practices on the stage, the Modernist Hebrew theater created a precise and concise language that took into account the vernacular diasporic Jewish communities, borrowing regional Jewish dialects and shared speech habits. The theatrical manifestation of the Hebrew language displays the aural virtues of language performances, substantiating the ability of the language to reach the hearts and minds of its audience. This book, thus, frames the spoken language in the Modernist Hebrew theater as grounded on multiple modalities of expressive practices, such as spoken Hebrew and Jewish liturgical sensibilities supplemented by Yiddish intonation and other vernacular accents, and positions it vis-à-vis prevalent theatrical practices.

Melodies of the Hebrew Language

At the core of this book there lies a particular historical moment whereby Jewish sonority converged with Modernist theatrical recitation techniques. The Zionist cultural enterprise entailing the renewal of the Hebrew language presupposed that in order for Hebrew to gain "life" as a colloquial language, it must become a language of game and play; its semantic structure and phonetic properties were the pliable materials necessary for its frisky activation. This understanding fostered artistic explorations with the Hebrew language and its elocution, experimenting with existing and novel creative models.[9] *Habima*'s recitation style, vocal delivery, and musicality of speech demonstrate the innovative theatricalization of the language.

Initially established as one of the ethnic theater studios directed by Konstantin Stanislavsky and Vladimir Nemirovich-Danchenko, *Habima* studied and worked with some of the most important theater professionals within the network of the Moscow Art Theater.[10] The most significant voice and recitation classes delivered in *Habima*'s training studio that contributed to *Habima*'s forming of their professional artistic identity were taught by Prince Sergei Mikhailovitch Volkonsky (1860–1937), the director of the Imperial Theaters from 1899 to 1902. Volkonsky's lessons with *Habima*, which took place approximately between February and December 1919, included both theoretical lessons and practical workshops on stage speech and language diction.[11] These lessons were based upon two of Volkonsky's publications that derived from the theories of François Delsarte (1811–1871)—a French performance theorist and pedagogue—entitled *The Expressive Word* and *The Expressive Person* (1913).[12] Thus, in order to understand the guiding principle of *Habima*'s vocal training we must briefly venture into Delsartism—a theatrical approach that gained popularity between 1880 and 1920.

The father of Delsartism, François Delsarte, designated a philosophy and technique of animated movements that developed from "mythic posing," in Carrie J. Preston's terms.[13] Like many key Modernist artists, writers, and thinkers, Delsarte retreated into mythical tropes, biblical typology, and ritualistic modes of expression.[14] The centrality of myth to Modernist art, Preston explains, is an appeal to the ahistoric, and the foundational at a time of social fragmentation.[15] The Delsarte voice system seemed especially appropriate for *Habima*, which based its initial repertoire upon Jewish myths, performing biblical stories, legends, and tales in Hebrew, and utilizing them for reflecting and propagating the Jewish national revival.

Although Delsarte is mostly remembered for his method of actor training, his early research was primarily devoted to voice and speech.[16] Julia A. Walker describes the main innovation Delsarte introduced in his work on voice and speech. According to Walker, Delsarte "redefined the ruling paradigm of vocal instruction, shifting its emphasis away from a concern with vocal technique per se to an interest in the use of such techniques to engage the audience's understanding and emotional experience of the dramatic or musical piece."[17]

The Delsarte musical training method provided a way of analyzing the aural features of the performed drama, from inflection and intonation to rhythm and phrasing, and of assessing their effect upon auditors. In this way, Walker writes, actors wishing to represent with "scientific accuracy" the various emotional states of their characters could appeal to the natural laws of expression recorded by Delsarte.[18] As E. T. Kirby writes, vocal gestures, thus, were codified in terms of a simple, extensive, highly unified tripartite system: a neutral state was contrasted with the eccentric (active or forward) and with the concentric (passive or backward).[19] Walker explains that in tandem with his mythical gestural scheme, singers who trained with Delsarte were taught to sustain the most dissonant or unresolved note (for instance, the subdominant fourth) in the musical phrase.[20] As Walker writes,

> Realizing that the effect of a sustained emphasis in a musical phrase might be comparable to sustained emphasis of a spoken phrase, he [Delsarte] postulated rhetorical effects that could enhance an audience's engagement with spoken language. Intonation, for example, indicated which words were to receive emphasis—whether by vocal force or, as Delsarte was fond of pointing out, by a softness which elicited the audience's desire to hear more (both literally and figuratively).[21]

Thus, similarly to music, emphasis could be used in speech to linger on a phrase in order to increase the audience's desire to hear it to conclusion. Paraphrasing Archibald MacLeish's famous poem "Ars Poetica" (first published in June 1926), we could say that voice, according to the Delsarte method, should "not mean but *be*."[22] In other words, meaning is to reside as much in the way words were declaimed as in the semantic content of the words.

The Delsarte voice method, as interpreted and taught by Volkonsky, informed both Stanislavsky, who invited Volkonsky in 1912 to teach oratory and rhythmic recitation at the Bolshoi Opera and the MAT studios, and Yevgeny Vakhtangov—the renowned Armenian Russian director who worked with *Habima* and attended Volkonsky's workshops at the Moscow Art Theater. However, for *Habima*, Volkonsky's lesson had an additional impact. As Elena Tartakovsky explains, Volkonsky, like many of the teachers in *Habima's* dramatic studio, did not understand the enacted Hebrew, and often could not grasp the cultural and national signification of the actions. And yet, *Habima* nonetheless managed to produce professional actors who would enrich the artistic harvest of the theater.[23] The dramatic recitation classes in *Habima's* dramatic studio therefore demonstrate the poetic potential of Volkonsky's recitation technique.

Volkonsky's stage recitation method, which was taught in Russian, was supposed to train the actors to perform the plays in Hebrew. Despite the profound sonorous and lingual differences between these languages, Volkonsky trained *Habima's* actors to move their facial muscles and to articulate words as if they were reciting Russian texts, thus omitting many characteristic sounds of Hebrew speech. Lacking the aural knowledge of the Hebrew language, Volkonsky could not teach *Habima's* actors the correct pronunciation of the

Hebrew vowels and consonants; however, he could—and probably did—correct their speech according to the rules of articulation of the Russian language. *Habima*'s actors, according to Tartakovsky, articulated the Hebrew texts using the consonants and vowels of Russian speech.[24]

As I demonstrate throughout this book, the theatrical vocalization of the Hebrew language dramatized the Jewish myths taking into consideration the contemporaneous sociohistorical conditions of its creation. Accordingly, the amalgamation of Volkonsky's classic recitation style and Jewish substrata manifest an immanent paradox embedded in Zionism: established in the liminal turn of the century, Zionism was entrapped in between the progressive stream that grafted the Industrial Revolution, the development of science and technology, and the regressive impulse to return to the national past, articulated in modern mythopoetic terms. This foundational Modernist paradox—defined by Theodor Adorno and Max Horkheimer as the dialectical relationship between myth and enlightenment—engendered a culture that was in myriad ways novel; however, it concomitantly gestured toward its traditional pasts.[25]

One of the paradigmatic examples for this ingrained temporal contradiction is the decision to adopt the Sephardic pronunciation. Notwithstanding the fact that Ashkenazi Jews were the majority in the *Yishuv* at the beginning of the twentieth century, and in spite of their difficulty in mastering it, the desire to return to the Land of the Fathers and to the ancient Hebrew language motivated their decision to adopt the Sephardic pronunciation.[26] For *Habima*, the decision to recite the drama in the Sephardic Hebrew meant leaving behind the familiar rhythmic speech patterns of the Ashkenazi dialect. As this study demonstrates, in order to manifest its nationalistic incantatory function, and support the performance of memory, *Habima*'s dramatic recitation replaced the measured Ashkenazi dialect with a melodious speech rooted in the vocal practices of the East European synagogues. Thus, the audience, who were largely unfamiliar with the musicality of the Sephardic speech, could understand the drama through its familiar religious rhythmic manifestations.

Possessed Voices

Deeply embedded in the scopic regimes of modernity,[27] the Jewish body—its representation, visibility, and gender signification—has been the focus of myriad studies, within and beyond Jewish exegetical and literary traditions.[28] Against the "corporeal turn" in Jewish studies, this book traces the trajectory of voices migrating from their acting bodies—from the theater stage to the disembodied voices aired on the radio.

Habima's theater productions on Israeli radio devised its staged performances as voices suspended by the radio waves, permeating domestic and public
spaces through acoustic capacities. The voices of *Habima*'s leading actors—familiar on account of their staged performances—gained prominence in the Jewish
cultural life, and especially in Mandatory Palestine. Bearing the epithet of "the
mother of the nation," Hanna Rovina, often considered the first lady of the
Hebrew theater, epitomized the flow of iconic voices from the fictional theater
sphere into the public domain. Rovina's vocal qualities were enhanced in all of
her stage appearances, and her vocal signature became a well-known acoustic
token. The admiration that Rovina's memorable performance received led to her
participation at the opening ceremony of the first Hebrew radio station—then
named Kol Yerushalayim—on March 30, 1936, in which she recited Chaim
Nachman Bialik's prose poem "Megilat Ha-esh" (Scroll of Fire).[29] Thus, although
the medium of the radio severs broadcasted voices from their corporeal anchor,
in the case of theater voices, it does not generate disembodied voices. Rather,
the body of the performing speaker transduces into a metaphysical spectacle
conjured by the act of listening and the force of memory.

Kol Yisrael (the Voice of Israel) was, from its inauguration (as Kol
Yerushalayim), and up until 1968, the only electronic mass media active in
Israel. As such, it operated as a central vehicle for the implementation of
the renewing Hebrew language, providing a virtual shared space in which
the language was publicly actualized, aimed at "inducing public memories,"
as Tamar Liebes points out.[30] The daily address in Hebrew strengthened the
linguistic infrastructure of the Zionist community, which was, at the time,
only partial and fragile, updating the language to fit the colloquial needs of
its speakers. On a cultural level, the broadcast was an essential contribution
to the fashioning of the identity of the Zionist revolution, connecting the
Yishuv in Palestine with the Zionist movement in the Diaspora.[31]

Furthermore, the Hebrew division of the radio served as a laboratory
for the development of new expressions and for experimenting with various
lingual registers and styles of speech. Most importantly, the radio had the
power to disseminate the new spoken Hebrew throughout the country, as part
of the Zionist aspiration for sovereignty. In tracing the complex interplay of
cultural, political, and linguistic factors influencing the radio audience, I wish
to study the dynamic relationship between membership in an audience and
membership in a community and ask how the radio extended the structure
of feeling among Jewish immigrants. Analyzing radio recordings of theater
productions, I examine how the bilingual factors break down into detailed
sonic associations, through accent, speech cadence, rhythm, melody, and
tempo that partake in the shaping of a national identity.

Along with the media transformation, dramatic leitmotifs altered. The focus on the transfiguration of *Habima*'s performances from staged corporeality into vocal reproduction enables us to understand the rupture in Jewish life and culture in the face of body-language severance. The transfiguration of the performing bodies into an invisible, yet essential vocal form, is central not only to the understanding of the language-experience of *Habima*'s performances, but also for understanding the idea of the body as a medium in post-Holocaust Israeli culture. Implicit in this argument is the analysis of voice not only as a force that animates the poetics of drama, but also as a bodily corpus: the way sound engages and manipulates its listeners through auricular participation, its incantatory function and effect, the sort of conjured presence it summons.

Thus, if theater (in)spirited the Hebrew language, the radio medium transformed the Holy Tongue into a present living memory subsumed within its listener's corporeality. We must not confuse such presence with haunting voices of the dead, as the performance of the Hebrew language was far more tangible and feasible than the volatility of ghosts. The transformation of theater performances into radio dramas entails the loss of the material body, rendering it an ambiguous gesture, shifting between hope and despair. On the radio, the voices permeate into radio waves, becoming ethereal and uprooted; at the same time, the un-bodied voices enter the domestic and public sphere through radio broadcasting, and take up animation supremacies. They are voices possessed by their former embodiments, and they themselves acquire the ability to possess.

In this book I argue that the theater voices recorded and broadcast on the radio served as a fundamental venue not only for assimilating language, but also for opening up a path for social lamentation over the annihilated European Jewry.[32] I suggest that while the drama enacted in the Modernist Hebrew theater depicted a fictional world populated by fictional characters, the voices and sounds it staged were structured as a sign system familiar to its listeners from Jewish religious vocal practices (such as cantillation or liturgical singing).[33] In other words, the vocalities in these performances transgressed the imaginary threshold of the fictional, verging on a social ritual. A more general claim lies here—which follows a venerable tradition, advocated by Jean-Jacques Rousseau in his writings on the emotive role of melody within speech delivery—that the vocal has no fourth wall; it forays from the fictional sphere into the so-called reality, and when the listeners are able to encode its sounds, it draws them into a shared affective communal experience.

Possessed Voices gravitates between two distinct historical periods and narratives: the 1920s theatrical manifestations of the Hebrew language, and their audio reproductions at times in which the processing of the Holocaust and World War II traumas had not yet come to pass publicly. In this sense, this book challenges Jewish and Israeli historiographical narratives aimed at the "negation of the Diaspora," in the face of the apparent rupture between pre- and post-Diasporic Jewish existence and the public silencing during the 1950s and early 1960s of the abovementioned atrocious experiences. Rather than provide fixed points of temporal or cultural orientation, the recordings I study enable the infiltration of the past into the present.

The present, as Hans Ulrich Gumbrecht argues, has turned through technological media into a dimension of expanding simultaneities—a "broad present" that juggles concurrent worlds, assuming elusive identities, lacking clear contours. Gumbrecht defines an essential tension that inhabits such an expansive present: on one side lies an insistence on the concreteness, corpo-reality, and presence of human life. On the other side, however, technology projects a radical virtualization which abstracts the body and sensory contact with the world.[34]

Between these two powerful vectors, our new present began to unfold. For this reason, digital technologies require critical acts that address the separation of the time and place of the live performance in 1920s from its recording date and the circumstances of its much later audio reproduction and performance. This gap insinuates that the recordings preserve within their sonority the strata accumulated during the ongoing repertoire of their performance. The firming of theatrical knowledge by technological media creates a performative construct by which the "show" could, theoretically and acoustically, be played and replayed. The continuing resonance within the aural cultural sphere poses some fundamental issues vis-à-vis the analysis of the performance: What sort of vocal images did *Habima*'s performances stage in the 1920s? How did this stage language evolve? And, how were these images perceived years later, in their audio reproductions?

Nostalgic "Sound Souvenirs"

Habima's audio files reiterate aural instantiations that bear an affinity to the staged experiences of the theater. Yet, one cannot avoid asking, is it the live-ness that we are listening to, or are those, perhaps, the disembodied voices of the dead that resound through the recordings? Reproduced years later on the radio, *Habima*'s voices bespeak the world "before." Their cries, lamentations, and prayers belong to a world obliterated in World War II. In that sense, they manifest, through nostalgia, the rupture from a vanished culture.

Nostalgia, as Svetlana Boym explains, expresses a yearning for a different place and time, often one that has passed long ago, or, perhaps, never existed. Coined in 1688 by Johannes Hofer as a medical term, "nostalgia" was said to confuse the present with the past, the imaginary with the real.[35] The aural traces from the Modernist Hebrew theater, I argue, are objects of nostalgia, as they evoke imaginary affective experiences by intimating a memory of a fictional place and time through sounding iconic dramatic voices, reverberating with a rhetorical topos based upon Jewish sonority.[36] Thus, the language and melodies presented in these recordings do not only act as remains from theater productions but also as mnemonic signs of afflicted imaginations from the eclipsed Jewish culture in Eastern Europe.

Friedrich Kittler depicts the ability of sound technologies to retrieve residues from a sonic world, and thus to constitute a cultural repository of audible "souvenirs" from a specific reality.[37] The recordings of the Hebrew Modernist theater performances, all produced three decades or more after their original stage debut, indeed present traces of voices distinctly recognized as belonging to a concrete historical and artistic realm, created before the decay of East European Jewry in the Holocaust. These recordings are remnants from voices that belong to a declined world and will, therefore, be explored in this study as artifacts of "communal nostalgia" that conjured up memories among the European immigrants in Mandatory Palestine and Israel, enabling them to process and lament their lost pasts.

The conceptualization of the ways whereby voice reproduction assumes an ambiguous position in between the theatrical tradition in which it was formed and a space of nostalgic reflection outside it, is effected mainly through the notion of "vocal imagination," extrapolated from Jonathan Sterne's synaesthetic concept of "sonic imagination."[38] The vocal imagination, it is proposed here, heals the temporal and spatial discontinuity between the voice and its experience in the past, negotiating its reproduction as a creative force for developing a retrospective cultural understanding, and the experiential ground of the interpreter in the present time. The recording of *Habima*'s theater voices reflects a wish to incorporate these voices into the soundscape, underlying the passion for producing their presence, even as disembodied entities.

Probing into the vocal imaginations of theater performance, this book is grounded on performative listening, as delineated in Kafka's short story "The Animal in the Synagogue," discussed in the preface. In its modernist context, this form of listening was constructed through its increasing domestication, first by the gramophone industry and later through the radio. This study is thus premised on the idea that listening cannot be detached from the subjective identity of its listener and the surrounding material and social conditions.

Without attempting to essentialize hearing, this study probes into listening as a hermeneutical action that coincides with Theodor Adorno's attribution of recorded sound as one that "belongs to the pregnant stillness of individuals."[39] Adorno, in this citation, highlights the temporality of a listening that always awaits a future site for becoming. Performative listening to *Habima's* sound recordings, thus, stems from their capacity to satiate the nostalgic desires of the newly displaced and dispersed immigrant populations for those imagined communities left behind in their homelands, and to reinforce their connection to their mythical past.

Listening to Theater

Ephemerality is the fundamental performative paradigm that theater historiography grapples with. Given the impossibility of overcoming the fleeting nature of the theatrical event, the challenge to access the past is often mitigated through the claim that performance actually "becomes itself through disappearance," as Peggy Phelan convincingly suggested.[40] Hoping to recuperate something from the experiential dimension of the live event, historians cling onto any remaining or fragmentary relics related to the performance. The scarcity of visual documents renders the attempt to retrieve the sensuous elements of the performance as speculative and, hence, as incomplete. Thus, bringing the past into the present summons attentiveness to hidden dimensions of "performance remains," in Rebecca Schneider's prolific term;[41] to listen carefully to stratified timbres entombed in them. The voices and sounds of the stage that have been preserved may account for such latent strata.[42]

The sounds of the past are, by their ontological nature, doomed to phenomenological loss, immersing into the permanence of the eerily mute archive. The emergence of recording technologies at the end of the nineteenth century succeeded in recuperating both the fantasy and aspiration to listen to bygone iterations. Recorded voices pierce our present, enabling us to experience, once again, idiosyncratic, specific expressions. In this sense, digital technologies skewed the stringent disjunctions that separated the material vestiges from the "authentic" experience of the performance, producing new kinds of remains, inviting us to reformulate our historiographical approaches to the theater archive.

In this book, I listen to past voices out of their aural remains. This quest resonates historical sound studies in its basic tenets, while proposing another method: within the extensive literature on sound studies and historiography, theater sound is unique in its transmedia focus, namely (1) the recording and reproduction of the live event; (2) the significance of place to the listening experience and to the formation of a theatrical community; and (3) the ideological aspects of vocal dramatic recitation on the theater stage and on the medium that preserves and broadcasts it.

Recent scholarship on theater history has investigated aurality within the theatrical apparatus. In stark contrast to works that necessitate a filling of the aural void by reimagining the voices that were played at the Wooden O in Elizabethan London, or to those of renowned actors such as David Garrick or Sarah Siddons, this book distinguishes itself from other sources in the materials it explores.[43] It presents and studies evidence from the aural aesthetics of the Modernist Hebrew theater, and analyzes them in their artistic, cultural, and ideological contexts.

What does it mean to listen to theater? Theater, as we learn from its etymological roots in the Greek word *theatron,* literally "a place for viewing" (from *theasthai* "to behold"), is defined primarily as a visual event: when we go to the theater we ask for good seats so that we can *watch* the action. However, as an audience, we are equally engaged in the act of *listening* and occupied with the acoustics of the performance space. The etymological roots of the word *audience* reside in the Latin *audentia,* which literally means hearing or listening, and points toward the significance of sonic aspects in the configuration of the shared experience. An audience's reaction to the mise-en-scène depends equally upon the aural dimension, which includes factors such as sound reproduction, reinforcement, and resonance. Listening to theatrical drama enables us to focus on the dramaturgical interpretation implied by the connotative space and the metaphorical meanings that are created by speech intonation and vocal execution.

"Listening," as Jonathan Sterne maintains, "requires hearing but is not simply reducible to hearing." "Listening is a directed, learned activity: it is a definite cultural practice," according to Sterne. Addressing Modernity's turn toward listening, Sterne credits listening with the development of "audible technique" or a "set of practices of listening that were articulated to science, reason, and instrumentality and that encouraged the coding and rationalization of what was heard."[44] Listening is thus distinguished from hearing as a dynamic faculty of perception that is learned, and that is historically and culturally variable.

Following Sterne, I analyze audio recordings of theater productions as a site of cultural production as well as a locus that promotes the accumulation of cultural capital through aurality. I engage with both the spatial production of a unique sonority and the embodied specificity of a vocal phenomenology. The concept of listening is therefore developed in this study as a historical method and theory through which aural strata are incorporated into the subject. I read sound as a representational medium but, more specifically, I narrow in on the capacity of sounds to materially structure social relations between subjects.

Centering on the extralinguistic performance of the Hebrew language in the theater and on the semiotic shaping of this language to imbue signs eliciting affection, this book undertakes Michael Bull and Les Back's invitation to regard sound as a modality of knowing, as expressed in their edited collection *The Auditory Culture Reader*. Like numerous other resourceful writers in the prolific field of sound studies, such as those assembled in Trevor Pinch and Karin Bijsterveld's *The Oxford Handbook for Sound Studies*, Back and Bull advance their core notion of "deep listening," calling for an auditory attention that would trace a myriad of meanings embedded in a distinct sound.[45] However, the disinclination of these studies to address the visual trajectories inherent in sonic practices and discourses potentially replicates the ocular bias, and eventually reflects an incomplete cultural sensory understanding.

In *The Sound Studies Reader*, Jonathan Sterne defines this sensory partiality as an important identification of sound studies. He argues that this partiality stems from the key terms employed to describe and analyze sounds belonging to multiple traditions and are constantly problematized under academic exchange.[46] This book aims to overcome this bias by approaching sound within its performative context, and by applying a comparative approach to transmission media. It will show the interaction between voice, identity, and presence on the theater stage and in sound recordings, examining, at every phase, the tools that create exuberant sonic imaginations.

As an analytical historical method, listening is premised on the inextricable reciprocity of subject and object; thus, sound recording sets the historian's physical sensibilities as a central vehicle in the affective understanding of the performance. Approaching sound reproduction technologies from a theatrical perspective implies the reclaiming of the corporeal within the auditory and scholarly experiences, and sets the voice as a dynamic expression that bypasses the barrier of presence and absence, transcending the fictional to tap into the real. This book shows how the ghostlike resonance of the voices staged in the Modernist Hebrew theater resurrected the Jewish diasporic vocal imagination as an integral component in the Israeli soundscape.

This endeavor, however, meets profound methodological intricacies. Despite the awareness of the central role played by the spoken word in dramatic arts, theater and performance scholarship have not hitherto developed a critical vocabulary that would capture how actors sounded. Regina Bendix points to the exclusivism of musicology, prompted by its resorting to an esoteric system of notation for the study of voice and aural performances. She argues that an interdisciplinary approach to sonority of performances was, until recently, sporadic, as anyone not conversant with musicological terms and notation would hesitate to participate in the discourse, or would, rather, defer to the authority of an expert in the field.[47] This book attempts to contribute to the fashioning of a terminology that might aptly describe and analyze the theatrical aspects of dramatic vocal recitation.

However, listening to theater on sound recordings generates a completely different experience than that of listening inside a theater house. In stark contrast to the ephemeral performative experience in the theater, in the case of recorded sound, digital and analogue technologies preserve and reiterate ad infinitum transient instantiations. Yet, due to the transient nature of the performative event, we don't know how close the audio recordings are to the live performances they document. The art and manner whereby deploying sound technologies mediate, translate, intervene in, and alter modes of performance and listening are often neglected. This book aims to contribute to the consolidation of a methodology that poses the digital audio collection as a dynamic, fluid repertoire subject to continuous transformation over time. It examines the fluctuation and bifurcation between the time and place of the live performances and their recorded reproduction in order to understand the reverberation of these Jewish vocalities vis-à-vis the immigrant society in the Israeli cultural sphere.

At the core of this research there lies an extensive archival fieldwork conducted in theater and sound archives in Israel and Europe, from which visual and textual evidences related to the scenography, creation processes, and critical reactions to the performances are studied. Each audio recording is examined in relation to three dimensions of resonance: (1) as a trace of theater performances produced during the 1920s, each audio recording is analyzed in both its theatrical and its social-historical context; (2) as sound reproductions of a theater events, this study considers how the perception of the performed voices, and of the Hebrew enacted on stage, is altered by their transformation from a staged performance into reproduced, apparently disembodied, recorded voices; (3) the study examines the resonance of the staged voices in relation to their much-later audio recording circumstances. Befitting a cross-media study, this work applies a comparative approach to its subject matter. Its primary interest is the reverberations and alterations in the vocal imagination echoing on the stages in Europe and (pre-state) Palestine during the 1920s vis-à-vis its replication, nostalgic enactment, and perception on the radio as disembodied sound reproductions made during the 1950s and 1960s, within a different cultural orbit.

In listening, as Deborah Kapchan writes, "method *involves* practice," in which the scholar becomes a resonating instrument letting his sources permeate him, much as in the case of spirit possession.[48] Listening positions the subject simultaneously as connected with the performed sounds and as distant from them. Accordingly, my listening is aimed not only at studying the source—the voices of the theater performances—but also at making it a resource. The audio recordings are, hence, examined as vestiges of the theater performance created in a specific sociohistorical context; as sonic instantiations, manifesting a distinct vocal aesthetics; and, as artifacts of nostalgia.

The four chapters comprising this book are devoted to four case studies, unfolding according to the chronological order of the productions. Each chapter tells a different fragment of the story and, together, they comprise a melodious plot line entangled in the twentieth-century catastrophe that befell the European Jewry. The first chapter focuses on a 1931 commercial recording—produced in London during *Habima*'s years as an itinerant theater troupe—of Hanna Rovina performing the Messiah's mother lamentation from *The Eternal Jew* (1919/1923), a dramatic legend by David Pinski. This play is based on an ancient Jewish legend according to which on the very day of the destruction of the Temple by the Romans, the Messiah was born. The recording sounds Hanna Rovina delivering a lamentation over her son in a trembling voice which evokes sonic associations to synagogal liturgies. Specifically, this lamentation mostly draws on the synagogue service of the Ninth of Av (Tish'a' b'Av), commemorating the destruction of the first and second Temples.

This chapter focuses on the vocal representation of grief as an essential phase in the national path of redemption. Probing into Rovina's aural sensibility, the opening chapter asks how it resonated with the roving experiences of *Habima* in tandem with the wanderings of Jewish immigrants. It examines how the syntax of decline and revitalization in the mythical drama crosses the fictional threshold and penetrates, through liturgical vocalization, the Modernist Jewish realm of territorial displacement and cultural uprooting. The trajectory of this chapter follows three performative occasions in which Rovina performed the lamentation in fluctuating historical circumstances: *Habima*'s staging of Pinski's play in Moscow; Rovina's recitation before the German Jewish theologian and philosopher Franz Rosenzweig at his Frankfurt residence in mid-January 1928, during *Habima*'s German tour; and as issuing from the 1931 commercial record, delinked from the *Habima*'s theater performances. The chapter posits that the liturgical melodies woven into this monologue endow the drama with communal and national meanings that bind the audience through their religious communality.

The second chapter focuses on the creation of the Jewish community by the enactment of a shared rhythmic pattern, as manifested in a 1965 sound recording depicting *Habima*'s third staged production: a performance based on *The Dybbuk*, or *Between Two Worlds*, written in Russian (between 1914–18) by folklorist and ethnographer Shloyme-Zanvl Rappoport (1863–1920) under the pen name S. An-sky, and translated into Hebrew by Chaim Nachman Bialik. *Habima*'s 1922 production of An-sky's play was renowned for its use of the materials collected in his ethnographic expeditions (1912–14). Its dramatic scenes feature religious rituals, folk songs, tunes, local stories, and social habits customary to the Jewish life that, within two decades, would vanish forever from the European cultural scene. This chapter charts the trajectory of the adaptation of voices and sounds associated with Jewish communities to the theater stage, and finally, of their transmutation into disembodied acousmatic voices in the 1965 audio recording. At the center of this chapter lies the recurring melodious rhythmic pattern governed by dynamics of "rise-fall" as a reflection of the messianic politico-theological idea whereby redemption may only emerge after it passes through despair, grief, failure, and calamity.

Probing into shared rhythmic speech patterns, this chapter explores the mode whereby the shift from the stage to the radio reflects and propagates the conceptual and performative alteration in the notion of "community." Following Freddie Rokem, this chapter proposes that the dramatic rendering of the communities documented by S. An-sky and utilized by *Habima* in 1922, metamorphoses, in the 1965 radio reproduction, into a public lamentation—a *communitas* of mourning—over these demised communities.[49] In this sense, we could, perhaps, suggest an interpretation according to which many Jewish immigrants, mostly refugees from Europe and survivors of the Nazi atrocities, were, in this sense, possessed by nostalgia for these sounds.

The third chapter of the book discusses a 1961 recording of a radio adaptation of *Habima*'s 1925 performance of Halpern Leivick's play *The Golem*, directed by Boris Illich Vershilov. In this chapter, I focus on the aural materialization of the emptied interval that amalgamates the "rise" with the "fall." Regarding the creation of the golem as a figuration of "the revival of the Hebrew language," I argue that *Habima*'s theatrical shaping of Hebrew in *The Golem* marks a paradigm shift in their approach to dramatic recitation that reflects transformation processes entailed in the troupe's experiences of immigration and displacement. Furthermore, as I demonstrate in this chapter, when mediated as ethereal voices broadcast on the radio, the aural reproduction of *The Golem* subsumes a nostalgic reflection on the revival of the Hebrew language, this time as the medium that resuscitates the obliterated European Jewry.

The Golem was broadcast on the Israeli national radio during the Jewish New Year holiday in September 1961, a few weeks after the denouement of the Eichmann Trial in Jerusalem—an event that was extensively covered by the Israeli radio.[50] During the course of the trial, Israel's national radio broadcast hours of testimonies by Holocaust survivors who, for the first time, unfettered their silence to bear witness of what befell "there," thus metamorphosing from mute living bodies in the Israeli public sphere into broadcast "disembodied" speech. This chapter analyzes the sound recording of *The Golem* as a fictional reaction to the radio mediation of the Eichmann Trial, and to the representation of trauma on the radio, by underlying the split between voice and body, and pondering on the moral justification of physical retribution.

The fourth chapter presents a 1952 radio recording of a 1928 theater production of the Russian biblical play *Yaakov and Rachel* by Nikolai Aleksandrovich Krasheninnikov, translated into Hebrew by Avraham Shlonsky. This play was adapted to the stage and directed by former *Habima* member Moshe Halevy, and performed by the *Ohel* theater—an amateur theater troupe that worked under the patronage of the General Labor Federation of Jewish Workers in Mandatory Palestine (*Histadrut*). The vocal aesthetics in this recording are intriguing: despite the fact that all the participants in this production were Jews of Ashkenazi origin—mostly newcomers from Eastern Europe—the actors' speech imitates an Oriental accent and intonation. More specifically, they perform their text in a melodious, rhythmic, dramatic declamation that alludes to the liturgical cantillation of Yemenite and Sephardic Jewish traditions.

Unlike the previous chapters, this chapter presents sounds and rhythms that were new, foreign, and unfamiliar to the *Ohel* actors who performed them. Probing into the experience and meaning of performing sounds imported from Arab cultures, this chapter examines how Jewish immigrants perceived and performed Hebrew against the backdrop of the Zionist diachronic historical narrative of the Jews' "return" to their origins in the Promised Land. The idea of nostalgia is articulated here as the longing for an imagined biblical land that portrays the roots of Jewish immigrants in Palestine. Analyzing recorded fragments from *Yaakov and Rachel*'s radio adaptation, I describe the symbolic aural gesture of the "return" to the mythical homeland—the experience of source—as one that brings to the stage the migratory experience; namely, a sense of displacement, alienation, and estrangement as central tokens of this movement. *The experience of source* is explored throughout this chapter across its various materializations in the *Ohel*'s audio recording: (1) by questioning the ability of the archival recorded source to conjure theatrical performances; (2) through the embodiment of the Hebrew biblical source; (3) in the vocal invocation of the imagery that nurtured the Hebrew performance; and (4) through aural dynamics manifesting indigenous dispossession.

Through the practice of "cross-temporal" listening, this book proposes to redeem the voices of the past from their performative ephemerality. It argues that the adaptation of the live drama from the stage to the radio conveys a lament over the lost expressions of the East European Jewry, invoking them as aired voices resurrecting from the decayed Jewish diasporic culture, perceived by prevalent Zionist thinkers as a disembodied existence.

CHAPTER ONE

The Messiah's Mother Lamentation

The Sonic Imagination of *The Eternal Jew*

In 1931 *Habima*'s years as a roaming theater troupe came to an end when the theater reached its final destination—the shores of Palestine—establishing its permanent residence in the bourgeois center of the Jewish community in Mandatory Palestine—Tel Aviv. *Habima* left Moscow in 1926; during five years of traveling, the troupe was based in Berlin, from which it set off to tour—among other places—Poland, Latvia, Lithuania, Austria, Germany, France, Italy, Switzerland, and the United States.[1] They spent almost a year in Tel Aviv (1928–29), making Berlin their home for an additional year (throughout 1930–31).[2]

For East European Jewry, entangled in the agonist relapses of ascending ethnocentric nationalism across the European orbit, *Habima*'s tour and its performances in various locations around the globe were of great significance. In times of renovation of the Jewish culture, dovetailing increasing anti-Semitism, *Habima* was perceived among Zionist circles as a symbol for the tenacity and resilience of the Hebrew culture.[3] However, despite the financial and organizational support the theater received from leading figures of Jewish communities, at the beginning of 1931 the gates of Europe began to close for the nascent theater troupe, which experienced substantial difficulties in attaining visas and other documents needed for touring Europe, as well as to encounter anti-Semitic violent incidents.[4] In addition, as if these difficulties were not burdening enough, during *Habima*'s stay in Konstanz, Germany, the theater faced severe financial difficulties that imperiled the troupe's ability to continue its operation, leading its members to the final decision to leave Europe and head for Palestine.

Their last station before heading to Palestine was London, where they performed at the small West End Phoenix Theater, owned by Jewish media producer Sidney Bernstein. Their performances in London received enthusiastic reviews from the local critics and from leading figures in London. The theater company was especially praised for its staged language. In one newspaper, for example, the reviewer stated:

> Although you may not understand a single word uttered by the *Habima* players, it is impossible, once you have fallen under the spell of their particular method, which seems to aim at a subtle orchestration of emotions through rhythmical speech and gesture, to divert your attention from them for a moment.[5]

During their time in London, members of the troupe recorded a commercial record album under the *Magic Notes* (78 rpm) international label of *Columbia Gramophones* for ethnic music from around the world. On one side this record features a recording of Hanna Rovina's lamentation—an extract from her role as the Messiah's mother played in *Habima*'s 1923 performance *The Eternal Jew*—labeled as "Bei'm Klages Mauer, Yerusholayim" (The Wailing Wall lamentation, Jerusalem); on the other side, the opening choral song from *Habima*'s 1925 performance *The Golem*, labeled as "Eliyahu Hanovvi" (Elijah the Prophet),[6] which features a *piyyut* (liturgical poem) traditionally sung at the end of the Shabbat.[7]

There is no evidence—documentations or written personal stories—unfolding the circumstances under which this recording was made. Only the actual recorded object exists and can be played in various archives, as well as purchased in public auctions of collectors' items forums (even on eBay shopping website). The matrix number indicates that it was recorded in January 1931, just a few weeks before *Habima* left Europe to settle in Mandatory Palestine.[8] Thus, although the conditions of its production remain obscure, we can presume that this record was made as memorabilia from *Habima*'s remarkable vocal moments and for commercial distribution.

What was the rationale behind the production of this record? Perhaps it was produced in order to grant *Habima* a lingering resonance in the European sphere that would remain after its departure. Alternatively, perhaps the record was made in order to enhance the troupe's cosmopolitan allure among the Jewish audience in Palestine. These questions remain unanswered. Nevertheless, the decision to include in this commercial record these two dramatic moments, two short specimens of the entire repertoire of *Habima*'s performances, which, evidently, produced many poignant musical moments, is intriguing and calls for further investigation of this record. In the following chapter, I center on Rovina's performance of the Messiah's mother's lamentation and identify it as the most memorable musical moment of the performance. I observe this recording to be an agent participating in the manifestation of the Hebrew language, and reflecting through its themes the liminal Diasporic condition of European Jewry in 1931, and of *Habima*'s members in particular. Thus, Rovina's vocal performance operates here as a hook by which the sonority of Jewish mourning is unfolded in its cultural and social dimensions.

Before delving into Rovina's lamentation, I would like to address the decision to place "Eliyahu Hanovvi" song and "The Wailing Wall Lamentation" together. These two recorded dramatic moments are thematically associated. Hanna Rovina's lamentation originates in a monologue she performed in David Pinski's play *The Eternal Jew*, which is based on a Jewish legend about the birth and disappearance of the Messiah on the day the Temple in Jerusalem was destroyed (AD 70).[9] The song presented on the reverse side of the record is the recurring musical motif in *Habima*'s production of *The Golem* (1925), performed in harmonious choral strains that herald the soon-to-come Eliyahu the prophet. The various tales of Eliyahu, a prophet who is considered to possess immortality, and the legend of the (wandering) Eternal Jew share many thematic strands: like the Messiah in the legend of the Eternal Jew, Eliyahu the prophet departs from earth by a whirlwind that transports him to heaven.[10] From that point, he does not commence an angelic existence, but rather is said to come back to earth, living a life of continuous roving disguised as a beggar, thus resonating the figure of the peddler in *The Eternal Jew*.

The two sides of the record present different modes of anticipation to the Messiah: *The Eternal Jew* tells the story of the birth and disappearance of the Messiah when the Temple in Jerusalem was destroyed. Eliyahu Hanavie's song praises the forthcoming arrival of the prophet who, according to Jewish legend, is supposed to be a precursor of the Messiah and announce his near arrival.[11] One side of the record features a dirge over a personal and national calamity; the other celebrates a grand expression of hope vis-à-vis the impending future. One side of the record features a feminine monologue; the other side presents harmonious choral strains.

The contrasting emotional expressions, represented in the two sides of the record, are also evident from the circumstances of the broadcasting of these two musical numbers: Rovina's lamentation was usually played in the context of the Ninth of Av, the Day of Atonement commemorating the destruction of the first and second Temples in Jerusalem. The "Eliyahu Hanavie" liturgical song, on the other hand, was played on Saturday evening—the closing of the Shabbat and the promising outset of the coming week. Therefore, I propose to consider these two musical fragments as two units that coalesce to compose the sonic imagination of the messianic idea by which redemption can only emerge when it passes through despair, grief, failure, and calamity. The following chapter focuses on the aural representation of grief in Rovina's lamentation. Later on, in this book, I will discuss *Habima*'s performance of *The Golem* (1925), and specifically the "Eliyahu Hanavie" choral song.

Examining Hanna Rovina's lamentation, I probe into how the syntax of decline and revitalization in the mythical drama crosses the fictional threshold and accesses, through vocal aesthetics and technological mediation, the Modernist Jewish realm of territorial displacement and cultural uprooting from their homes. I ask how Rovina's vocality elicits imaginations relating to the legend of the Eternal Jew, and how this legend is framed in the geopolitical context in which *Habima* performed, between Europe of 1931 and Mandatory Palestine.

The Messiah's Mother Lamentation

David Pinski's dramatic poem *The Eternal Jew* was initially written in Yiddish in 1906 under the title *The Stranger*, then translated into Hebrew by Zionist pioneer, teacher, and translator Mordechai Ezrahi (Krichevsky) for its debut performance by the Yaffo theater group—the Hebrew-speaking amateur theater established in Palestine. Menachem Gnessin, a leading actor in the Yaffo troupe, introduced the play to *Habima*'s actors at the beginning of 1919, after the rehearsals for *The Dybbuk* had been suspended due to Vaktangov's grave illness. The Georgian Russian director Vakhtang Levanovich Mchedelov (1884–1924), a follower of Stanislavsky, was assigned to direct *Habima* in this play, together with the scenographer Georgy Yakulov and the composer Alexander Krein.

This production was staged in two versions: the first premiered in December 1919 in Moscow, presenting a short dramatic poem that amalgamates catastrophe with redemption, describing the day of the destruction of the Temple as the day of consolation in which the Messiah was born.[12] The second version of the play, staged in 1923, presented a developed version of the play that emphasized expressions of agony in the legend by including in the performance a scene of the masses in the bazaar mourning, a chanting chorus, and an elaboration of the role of the Messiah's mother, and within it, the lamentation performed by Rovina.[13] *Habima* staged *The Eternal Jew* approximately 304 times between 1919 and 1958, in different venues around the globe, and Rovina's lamentation became one of her most memorable vocal performances.

The following analysis will focus on the second version of Pinski's play as it unfolded in a prologue and two acts. The drama of *The Eternal Jew* depicts a crowded oriental bazaar in the small town of Beris Arva at the time of the destruction of the Second Temple in Jerusalem. Along with rumors reaching town about the siege of Jerusalem by the Romans, a man disguised as a peddler of clothes enters the bazaar. He seeks for a child that was born at the very same hour in which the Temple in Jerusalem fell. This child, according to the stranger, is destined to become the Messiah, who will bring redemption to his people. The peddler's message incites rage and aggression among the people in the bazaar, who accuse him of spreading false hearsay. At that moment, an enraged crying young mother enters the bazaar, telling the people of the massacre and destruction that occurred in Jerusalem, thus corroborating the peddler's message. At the center of the noisy bazaar, with its many customers as her witnessing audience, this young mother laments her child's birth at the accursed hour in which the Temple was destroyed, at a time when her people experienced the most terrible and grievous of all dooms. Along with her mournful vocal performance, some more messengers enter the bazaar, fugitives arriving from Jerusalem, bearing testimonials of the calamities devastating the destroyed city. The local bazaar crowd gradually transforms into a woeful congregation when its members begin to grieve in sorrow. The peddler then reminds them of the second part of his prophesy, according to which the newborn child of the lamenting woman is destined to become the Messiah. When the people search for the one bound to bring them redemption, a servant comes in crying out that the child has vanished in a whirlwind. The play ends with the peddler walking out from the astonished crowd, declaring that from now on he will be committed to follow a life of wandering, devoted to finding the lost Messiah.

Pinski's drama ends in a hopeful note, opening the possibility for future redemption, signified by the quest for the lost Messiah. The Messiah's mother lamentation, however, presents a pure melancholic vocal gesture in which she communicates her sorrow through a dialogue with the stranger. The audio recording condenses the dialogue into one extensive and climactic monologue that brings together the powerful link between the vocal and bodily performance of the maternal lamentation, and the national calamity brought about by the destruction of the Temple in Jerusalem.[14]

Let's approach the recording.[15] Rovina begins the lamentation with a dramatic declamation that accelerates in rhythm and tempo with every word she recites:

Oh, how I prayed not to have him on that day. I entreated God not to open my womb, that my child should not have to go through life with the consciousness that on the day of his birth his people were visited with the most terrible and grievous of disasters—that he should not be to me as an eternal tombstone over the grave of my nation and its faith. And when God did not give ear to me, and the pangs of my labor increased, I wished to oppose the Lord and work my own will. I bit my lips and held in my breath. I wanted to keep my child in my womb. And when the pains grew stronger and I gasped for air, losing the strength of my will—and when I saw that the child would be born despite all I prayed to God that it be born dead.

It was the third hour after mid-day. The last walls of the Temple had collapsed in the flames and the late heroes were slain and in that selfsame moment my son's cries filled the house.[16]

In her dramatic recitation, Rovina parallels the ineffable agony of her people due to the abandonment by their God to the unbearable separation of her son from her body, mourning his birth that paralyzed her ability to act on the cursed moments of the calamity in Jerusalem. She emphasizes her sorrowful expression through the dynamic vocal inflection that gradually moves in a glissando from heightened speech into an enduring and sweeping expression of grief materialized in mere vocal exclamation.

The musicality of Rovina's recitation creates sonic associations to liturgies performed in the synagogue. Specifically, this lamentation informs from several significant liturgical gestures: the first musical gesture in Rovina's singing derives from a common trope in the Kol Nidrei prayer that features in one of the most emotionally poignant moments of the Yom Kippur service. Then, the next musical trope may be associated with a common motif that can be heard, among other occasions, during the performance of the "Kaddish" at funerals.[17] The common denominator between these ceremonies is the weeping and mourning tone of the prayers. Within the fictional world, these melodies of grieving enhance the sorrow over the destruction of the First and Second Temples in Jerusalem. However, for the audience that attended *Habima*'s performance of *The Eternal Jew* in 1923, or listened to the recording later on, these wailing sounds were associated with the communal mourning services of the synagogue. As I show in what follows, Rovina's performance specifically related to the Ninth of Av (Tish'a' b'Av) prayers, commemorating the destruction of the First and Second Temples. The title of Rovina's monologue—"The Wailing Wall"—explicitly refers to the residual section of the wall surrounding the Temple, which endured its destruction as a memorial for generations.

As her wailing accelerates, Rovina's voice intensifies in heft, when she inserts into Pinski's text the reverberating cries *Oy li-Alelai* (אֲלָלִי לִי אוֹי)— Hebrew for *O my God*—to express the unbearable personal pain caused by the national catastrophe. The interjection *Alelai* (אֲלָלִי), iconic of the Ninth of Av synagogal public lamentations, parallels the opening of the book of Lamentation *Eikhah* (How /אֵיךְ) and is further repeated in the other versicles. These vocal gestures of sorrow, according to Galit Hasan-Rokem, are emblematic of the performance of lamentations, featuring in many cultural variations. Hasan-Rokem mentions, for instance, the *aiai* sound, identified by Nicole Loraux as a key cadence in ancient Greek laments, signifying the cry of all cries, materialized in a generic vocal emission, and containing the entire range of expressions of sorrow.[18] In a similar fashion, Rovina's cry *Oy li-Ale-lai*, which phonetically resembles the Hebrew verb *Yalel* (wail /יְלֵל), is an immediate, unmediated vocal gesture of grief.

The insertion of pure vocal introjections into the dramatic text enhances the pathos embodied by Rovina's body and vocal language; however, it also stages an explicit reference to the Ninth of Av (Tish'a' b'Av) synagogue ceremony. The *Alelai* (אֲלָלִי) parallels the typical introjection *Alalai-li* ("Woe is me!") familiar from the elegies (*Kinot*) for the Ninth of Av. The Ninth of Av compendium is comprised from the prayer services, the book of lamentations (*Eikhah*), and a collection of elegies composed in response to various pogroms and persecutions of the Jews, especially in Russia and Ukraine. The verbal motif *Alalai-li* commonly appears in relation to such tragedies. For example, it also features in written dirges for Tish'a' b'Av by R. Menahem ben Jacob of Worms, entitled "Alalai li" referring to outbreaks of anti-Jewish violence in the Rhineland town of Boppard (1179, 1196); and in "E-vel a-o-rer," ascribed to the eleventh-century German liturgist Menachem bar Machir of Regensburg, composed after the 1096 pogroms in the Jewish communities of Worms and Mainz. A far earlier example featuring the reoccurring motif of this introjection appears in a dirge written by Rabbi Elazar HaKallir, a Galilean liturgical poet of the late sixth–early seventh century who has the congregants respond *Alala li* in twenty-one verses throughout his Ninth of Av lamentation. This dirge, included in the Ashkenazi book of prayers and traditionally recited on the morning of the Ninth of Av, addresses the theme of mothers disavowing their children during the calamities of the war against the armies of Babylon (appearing in the Book of Lamentations 2, 20)—a leitmotif also in Rovina's lamentation.

Habima's veteran actor Shimon Finkel mentions in his memoirs that the decision to perform the monologue of the Messiah's mother in this specific melodious evocation of liturgy was made during the rehearsals of this scene.[19] Rovina was not a musician and did not follow a written musical score. When associating the Messiah's mother lamentation with those performed during the Ninth of Av synagogue service, Rovina probably drew on her sonic memories from her Hasidic home in Minsk, and on her formal religious education.[20] Thus, the synagogal wails presumably acted, for Rovina, as well as for other members of the theater troupe and for significant parts of its audience, as an accessible repository in which past sonic memories lingered, breeding sustaining aesthetic resources. By mobilizing the melodies of the synagogue onto the theater stage, Rovina relocated a sonic sphere rooted in a Jewish communal practice into the dramatic mythical sphere of the theater stage. This mixture, infusing the mythical with a religious sonority, personal as it may be, entails underlying ideology.

By rendering the lamentation in relation to the Ninth of Av ceremony Rovina intertwined the legend with the communal vocalities commemorating the event within the synagogal space in which the public mourns for various tragedies and pogroms befalling different places and times. The audience could thus recognize itself, through the staged sounds of the synagogue, as

Figure 1.1. "Bei'm Klages Mauer, Yerusholayim" (The Wailing Wall lamentation, Jerusalem): the cover of *Habima*'s Columbia record.

belonging to the same cultural and religious cluster, which offered a compelling, if ambiguous, image of the destruction of the Temple as reflecting on current atrocities.[21] Consequently, Rovina transforms a millenary religious practice into a Modernist performance. This constellation amalgamates the two apparently distinct realms of theater and synagogue. Theatrical, fictional make-believe and devotional congregation coalesce into one event that subsequently envelops together the listeners—both the fictional crowd of the play and the actual audience—into a community that faces the catastrophic portents of the dramatic events and looks for the future possibilities they behold.

Franz Rosenzweig's Cry: What Does Melodious Recitation Do?

When Rovina recorded the lamentation during *Habima*'s London tour, her vocal delivery was already renowned as one of the great dramatic moments conceived by the Hebrew theater. One of the most captivating anecdotes surrounding the performance of this lamentation is of Rovina's recitation before the German Jewish theologian and philosopher Franz Rosenzweig at his Frankfurt residence in mid-January 1928, during *Habima*'s German tour.[22] Rovina, then a young and promising actress, was invited by Eugen Mayer, a leading member of the local Jewish community in Frankfurt, to visit Rosenzweig, who was severely afflicted by a muscular degenerative disease that confined him to his armchair, depriving him even of the ability to speak. Bereft of costumes, lighting, or scenery, Rovina delivered her dramatic recitation of the Messiah's mother lamentation while Rosenzweig sat listening, paralyzed on his couch, with his six-year-old son Rafael beside him.

That evening of that day, Mayer wrote a letter to his wife Hebe narrating the event in detail: "I just had the most extraordinary experience," he wrote, "Her recitation was deeply moving . . . and Rosenzweig was aroused to tears. . . . Rosenzwig was so grateful he gave her his favorite old Bible and managed to tell her:[23] 'you had never recited (*vorlesung*) in front of an audience that generated so much joy as I had. Not even in the biggest auditorium.'"[24] Years later, in June 1972, Rafael Rosenzweig, who ran out of the room upon hearing the exhilarating voice that filled it, shared with Rovina his memory from that day. He wrote: "It was my first encounter not only with the vivid Hebrew word but also with the art of the stage and I benefited from my attempt to escape from the two as much as Jonah benefited from his attempt to run away."[25] What was it about Rovina's performance that aroused Rosenzweig's deepest feelings, and eventually lured him from his mutism?[26]

This question informs a wider account regarding the divergent ways by which sound, accent, and melody of speech affect the individual listener, and furthermore, the way in which the individual emotive dimension binds the listening community. In the specific Jewish historical moment, as Paul Mendes-Flohr explains, the link between melody and emotion formed part of Rosenzweig's broader endeavor to transform the ancient Hebrew language, mostly practiced in its textual uses and in religious contexts, into a language of the heart, a language that speaks to and for the soul.[27]

These ideas reach back to Jean-Jacques Rousseau's notions regarding the modes by which the verbal expression of language can come to signify emotional abundance. Rousseau writes his reflections in his *Essay on the Origin of Languages* (*in which Melody and Musical Imitation are Treated*), published posthumously in 1781, in the context of eighteenth-century aesthetic debates on the interplay between nature, culture, and social forces. His essay identifies the essential and original function of the spoken language in communicating social and moral drives and emotion. Amplifying this idea, Rovina's performance seeks to reclaim the emotive dimension of the ancient Hebrew language by charging it with melodious tropes of Jewish lamentations familiar from the communal setting of the synagogue.

Rousseau conceptualizes the dynamics of speech and melody in terms of the necessity to communicate emotion: "To repulse an unjust aggressor nature dictates accents, cries, pleas: here are the most ancient words invented."[28] Thus, within the heightened speech, melodic rendering, vocal inflections, and noticeable accent, one is able to unleash the true colors of emotions. However, as Julia Simon argues in her study of music and politics in Rousseau's work, it is not the sounds themselves that move the listener but rather the expression signified by them.[29] Rousseau conceives melody as a system that operates like a language of which, in order to decode it, one is required to master its formal building blocks. He argues: "Sounds in melody act on us not only as sounds, but as signs of our affections, of our feelings; it is in this way that they excite in us the movements that they express and of which we recognize the image in them."[30]

To continue this train of thought, we thus could say that in order for Rovina's melody to operate as an emotive expression, the sounds she performed need to be anchored in a structured sonic system, familiar, in some degree, to her listeners. Perhaps this argument could also explain the different reactions of contemporary listeners to the recording of the lamentation. Over the past years, I have played this recording many times, in both academic and nonacademic venues, to a culturally diverse audience. Every time it was intriguing to experience the dividing of the room upon listening to Rovina's lamentation: for those listeners who do not share the particular cultural and historical context of this performance, Rovina's lamentation seemed an overdone expression of sorrow that ridicules, in its grandiose gestures, this tradition. However, those listeners who did "get it" decoded the melodious signifying system and could, therefore, be profoundly moved by Rovina's vocal performance.

For Rousseau, the vocal is an apparatus of the language—operated by phonetic pronunciation, melody inherent in speech, tempo, and rhythm—crucial for shaping its emotive capacities on an individual level, but also for engaging with ethical and political realms. Rovina's lamentation seems to follow this notion. At a time of national revival, the Hebrew language was animated by imbuing it with woeful liturgical melodies. Rovina accentuates the inflections of her voice in order to connect her listeners not only to the Hebrew language, but also to the emotive dimension in which it is rooted.

Assuming that Rovina, indeed, followed her acclaimed live lamentation from *The Eternal Jew* in a similar fashion to that registered in the audio

Figure 1.2. Hanna Rovina as the Messiah's mother in *The Eternal Jew*. Courtesy of *Habima* National Theater and the Israeli Center for the Documentation of the Performing Arts.

recording, I suggest that Rosenzweig's emotional reaction was an outcome of his sonic memory from a highly emotional moment he had experienced at the synagogue, incorporated with that which he identified as a live demonstration of his pedagogical approach to the Hebrew language. At those moments, his deep love of Hebrew interfused with the Jewish sonority familiar from the dirges performed in the synagogue.[31]

One of the legendary stories about Rosenzweig relates to his decision to return to Judaism as a pious Jew after converting to Christianity. During the Yom Kippur prayer in September 1913, at a small synagogue in Berlin, Rosenzweig understood, as Eugen Rosenstock-Huessy writes, "that he would have to remain a Jew—but on a different basis than before."[32] Paul Mendes-Flohr describes the unique event:

> Having witnessed, perhaps for the first time, a traditional Day of
> Atonement service, Rosenzweig concluded that Judaism was not
> spiritually moribund as he and his friends assumed. Reversing his
> decision to enter the Church, he thus affirmed that a meaningful
> life of faith may be pursued within the precincts, as he put it, of
> the Synagogue.[33]

Something happened to Rosenzweig during that September day at the synagogue; he experienced some kind of revelation emanating from the vibrant Jewish congregation engaged in the liturgical ceremony.[34] Among the devoted praying congregation and the liturgical sounds of prayer, Rosenzweig experienced a meaningful, perhaps transformative, moment.

Rosenzweig addresses the centrality of the community in the Yom Kippur liturgical service in *The Star of Redemption* (1921), identifying the Day of Atonement as the climatic point of the Jewish liturgical year and as the instance whereby the Jewish community experiences eternity within its shared togetherness. During the Yom Kippur service, Rosenzweig adds, "The individual is directly judged. He stands in the community. He says *We*."[35] Each member in this congregation, according to Rosenzweig, stands by himself and experiences the event; however, their shared being in the synagogue, and their mode of participation in the service—their immersion in the sounds of the prayer—binds them in the acute moment of repentance, the unstructured community of equal members pounding their chests in front of God. Following this vein, we could, perhaps, understand Rosenzweig's emotional response to Rovina's performance as triggered by her use of melodious tropes from the Kol Nidrei service, an encoded sonic memory that reminded him, consciously or subconsciously, of those significant sentimental moments at that small synagogue in which he felt part of the intense "togetherness" of the congregants.[36]

Yet, there is another aspect to Rosenzweig's deep emotional elevation during Rovina's performance. Eugen Mayer adds, in his letter to his wife, that when the former complimented Rovina for her performance in his private house, he referred to the lamentation using the German noun *vorlesung*, most commonly translated as a "lecture," referring to the practice of knowledge instruction or demonstration in front of an audience. Rosenzweig, thus, identifies a didactic element in Rovina's lamentation that relates to the recharging of the Hebrew language with its neglected emotive dimensions.

Mendes-Flohr explains that Rosenzweig "regarded the revival of Hebrew—of the Jew's active knowledge of the language—as essential to the renewal of Judaism as a spiritual and religious culture." He viewed, according to Mendes-Flohr, the Hebrew language as a vehicle, a medium, to access the entire content of Judaism.[37] However, as Galili Shahar contends, despite his views regarding the necessity to renew and practice the spoken Hebrew language, Rosenzweig was dubious concerning the Zionist attempt to engender a new kind of spoken secularized Hebrew that would be released from its theological tradition and that would function as a territorial language bound to soil and race.[38] Shahar contends that Rosenzweig perceived the essence of Hebrew in its traditional Holiness and in its "ability to receive and to gather words, motifs, and names from the spoken languages of the nations. . . . Hebrew is thus always in a process of renewal."[39] By tying Hebrew to the land of Palestine, it gives up its original sources and alienates its historical depth and spiritual virtues.

Upon recommitting to Judaism, Rosenzweig devoted himself to gaining proficiency in Hebrew. In his essay "It is Time: Concerning the Study of Judaism" (1917),[40] Rosenzweig argued for a far-reaching reform in German Jewish education. He claimed that the instauration of the Hebrew language should be foregrounded not only through attaining proficiency in grammar and vocabulary, but also through active recitation of fundamental Jewish religious texts. Rovina's performance of the lamentation seems to implement this vision. The prayer in the synagogue is recited in Hebrew, and delivered, much like Rovina's lamentation, with a melodious recitation, thus stratifying it with the related communal and ceremonial layers of meanings.

The Hebrew language, according to Rosenzweig, is the mode of expression essential to the Jewish culture and people that heals a fundamental rupture within its diasporic existence. In his essay "The Jewish People" he argues: "So far as his language is concerned, the Jew feels always he is in a foreign land,

and knows the home of his language is in the region of the holy language, a region everyday speech can never invade."[41] From this perspective, the Hebrew language keeps the Jews unsettled in their homes, preserving their state of wandering. Rovina's lamentation in Hebrew illustrates this idea through the alienating effect created from the merging of the conversant liturgical musicality and the new Sephardic pronunciation of the Hebrew language. By blending Modern Hebrew language recited in the Sephardic pronunciation with the liturgical melody, Rovina's performance reformulates the familiar connection between words and music, while, simultaneously, epitomizing the lamentation over the destruction of Jerusalem vis-à-vis the Jewish existence in Europe during the interwar period.

Habima Imagining Grief

The recording of Rovina's lamentation apparently introduces us to the possibility of experiencing her unique vocal signature, which manifested a substantial dimension of her theatrical allure, and sensing aspects of her magnifying vocal effect on the listener, as narrated, for example, in the Rosenzweig anecdote. But then—is it really so? Rovina's performance was recorded in a studio in 1931, years after the original debut of the show, in a different geographical and cultural setting. Hence, it is problematic to deduce from it how Rovina's voice reverberated in the theater houses at the time, and how the audiences might have reacted to the aural drama in its staged context. It occurs to me that when I am listening to Rovina's recording I am actually listening to her performance, adapted from the vast theater stage of the '20s into the intimate recording studio in the '30s, and then, once more, converted from an analogue format to a digital MP3 format. How do these technological adaptations affect Rovina's voice, and what can be learned about her aural performance from these recordings? In other words, I ask: What is preserved from Rovina's voice and from her physical performance in this adaptation/transformation/ translation process, and what is lost?

This audio recording disengages Rovina's stage performance from her voice, and thus obliterates indications of visual staging aspects, or of the audiences' reaction to the aural drama. In his extensive study on the cultural history of the disembodied voice, *Dumbstruck: A Cultural History of Ventriloquism* (2000), Steven Connor argues for a cognitive bias that systematically assigns voices to bodies. And when there is no body? Connor contends that the listener supplies one by means of superimposing imagination on the heard voice. The body then becomes, according to Connor, a mental construct affected by various epistemological factors such as the time, place, and circumstances of its attentive listener.[42] I would like to further extend Connor's argument and suggest that it is not merely the speaking body that we imagine, but also the contingent world to which it refers. In other words, both the visual anchor of the voice and its semiotics are actualized as imaginings according to the configuration of the interplay between the voice, its transmission, and the experiential circumstances surrounding its audition.

Rovina first performed the role of the Messiah's mother in 1923 in Moscow as a young exuberant actress. By 1931, when recording this lamentation, Rovina, as well as the other members of the troupe, was facing the end of their wandering days before reaching their destination in Palestine. Just before leaving the familiar European sphere, Rovina recorded her voice and symbolically disentangled it from her corporeal performance and from its theatrical setting. These circumstances enable her voice to facilitate different historical scenes. In order to reflect upon the ambiguous dynamics undergone by the lamentation, and the transformation in its position between the aural culture and its perception, I turn to explaining the sonic imagination of place engrained in Rovina's recording of the Messiah's mother lamentation.

The vocal imagination embedded in Rovina's lamentation centers on the aural representation of the mourning over the destruction of the Temple that doomed the Jew to a wandering existence. The idea of a homeless nomadic Jew preoccupied *Habima*'s members, and was apparent in their ambivalent attitude toward the Zionist territorial vocation and, especially, to the idea of immigrating to Palestine. Some members adopted the idea of becoming a wandering transnational troupe of Hebrew players. However, the dominant thrust among its founding members was to establish *Habima* as a national theater in the national symbolic center of Jerusalem. David Vardi, one of *Habima*'s prominent members, articulated this vision in his memoirs from the formative days of the theater:

> In the long, cold winter nights, when we sat frozen in *Habima*'s foyer . . . Nachum Zemach, standing near the cold radiator and warming it, would gaze up and vision. Craning his lips, and supporting his chin with his thumb and left finger, he articulated his vision:
>
>> . . . and now we are in Jerusalem, the *Habima* edifice rising in splendor on Mount Scopus . . . and all the people living in Zion come to us pilgrims from all corners of the land.[43]

Vardi's recollection of Zemach, as Gad Kaynar points, alludes here to the passage in Isaiah that refers to "the end of days" when "the mountain of the Lord's house shall be established as the top of the mountains . . . and all nations shall flow unto it."[44] Despite this eschatological vision, in 1931 the company settled in Tel Aviv, not in Jerusalem.

Zemach, who had left the troupe in early 1927 to settle in New York City, fantasized on Mount Scopus as the natural setting for *Habima*'s sounds and voices. Nearly a century later, I sit at my office desk at the Hebrew University, overlooking the open-theater located in the eastern slopes of Mount Scopus, bordering the Judean Desert. I hear the recorded voice of the Muezzin arising from the Palestinian village Issawia, and imagine Zemach's unrealized vision of Rovina performing the Messiah's mother lamentation in Mount Scopus. I imagine her expressionistic acting style, and her exaggerated makeup; I picture in my mind the oriental colors of the bazaar contrasting with the monochromatic sandy colors of the Judean desert in the backdrop.

These imaginings elicit an immediate association to the ancient Greek tragedies, in which the pathos of the recited drama was enhanced by the natural scenery.[45] It animates Rovina's catastrophic vocal gestures on the backdrop of

Figure 1.3. The open-theater at Mount Scopus campus, overlooking the Judean Desert and the Hills of Moab (east), January 1, 1930. Photographer: Alfred Bernheim. Courtesy of the Israel Museum, Jerusalem.

the politically charged landscape of Eastern Jerusalem. This sonic imagination, however, is radically different from *Habima*'s staging of *The Eternal Jew* at the theater house in Moscow where it was originally performed.

Rovina's vocal performance does not belong to the landscape of Jerusalem. It was formed in the context of the Zionist ideal of the national return to the Jewish homeland. As such, it expresses the continuous anxiety from lurking threats that compelled the wandering impulse, and the longing for a yet-to-be realized aspiration that leads the indefatigable search for redemption. In order to figure out the sonic imagination entrenched in this performance, and the dynamics between the spectacle and the aural qualities of the drama, I thus survey reviews and photographs that depict the stage and the action performed and compare these with Rovina's recitation praxis.

The Jewish strata of the folkloristic legend of the Eternal Jew, set at the core of Pinski's play, did not inform the dramaturgical interpretation of Mchedelov, the director who worked with the troupe.[46] Moshe Halevy writes about the 1919 version:

> Mchedelov . . . did not grasp the spirit of *The Eternal Jew* and the Messianic idea imbued in it, nor did he feel the tragedy of the Temple's destruction and the Diaspora. . . . The designer . . . although of oriental origin, also failed to understand the Hebrew spirit, and his work reflected a Caucasian view, rather than the landscape of the Land of Israel.[47]

In the context of post–World War I, and in the wake of the Bolshevist revolution, the 1919 production of *The Eternal Jew* has widely been interpreted as an allegory reacting to relevant European transformation processes. Kaynar explicates the scheme arising from this frame of reference, by which the lost Messiah becomes a representative of the "New Man" who could save the masses from the spiritual apocalypse, as well as from soulless bourgeois corruption.[48]

In the second version of the play, the communist allegory, as Moshe Halevy writes, was enhanced by presenting the class struggle between the older generation and the peasants, thus rendering the play a showcase for Bolshevist theater.[49] Carmit Guy, Rovina's biographer, notes that the absence of familiar visual representations of the landscape of Palestine and the lack of a typical Hebrew character led *Habima*'s members to consider this production a performance that subjugated a Jewish legend to Modernist concerns and Soviet themes. Some members of the troupe, as Guy notes, were outraged at Mchedelov's inclination to undermine the Jewish national dramatic potential.[50]

Kaynar maintains that the Modernist stage design, created by Yakulov, confirms the Bolshevist reference in Mchedelov's interpretation. The center of the stage featured a constructivist pyramid, rising from within a round construction. This stage hosted a noisy oriental bazaar. The actors wore colorful draperies, and makeup that underscored their facial features according to the expressionistic tradition. One of the most famous images from this performance is of Nachum Zemach, who played the prophet—the figure that would bring redemption when his search for the Messiah was completed—bearing the Jewish stereotypical feature of the Semitic crooked nose.[51]

While the photos and reviews of the stage depict its scenography as almost lacking Jewish features, theater reviews and personal memoirs that depict the sounds arising from the stage portray a production governed by sonic religiosity. The stage of *The Eternal Jew* presented scenes of public mourning and communal grief that reverberated in Krein's music. The Messiah's mother lamentation marks the peak sonic moment of this production. Her arrival onto the stage while lamenting the birth of her son brings about a turning point in the plot of the play, and changes the mindset of the crowd atmosphere of the hectic colorful bazaar. Prior to her lamentation, the people of Beris Arva have refused to believe the rumors about the destruction of the

Figure 1.4. The stage design by Georgy Yakulov in *Habima*'s 1923 production. Courtesy of *Habima* National Theater and the Israeli Center for the Documentation of the Performing Arts.

Figure 1.5. The Bazaar scene from *Habima*'s 1923 production of *The Eternal Jew*. Courtesy of *Habima* National Theater and the Israeli Center for the Documentation of the Performing Arts.

Temple. Rovina's lamentation signifies the moment of public acknowledgment of the calamities befalling Jerusalem. Following the lamentation, the whole stage begins to weep. Moreover, as Carmit Guy writes, the fictional sounds of communal grief arising from the rehearsals during work on *The Eternal Jew* suffused the soundscapes outside the room:

> They got on stage and narrated the destruction of the Temple with grieving voices; several actors practiced the lamentation so loudly that they caused Mchedelov to freeze, as if he had just witnessed the actual destruction of the Temple. The lamenters reached a climax, so that the passers-by from the street outside that heard their voices were certain that someone was taking heavy blows there, inside. Once militiamen were sent to check on what was going on, and did not believe it was a theater rehearsal.[52]

This account frames the public mourning on the stage as based on a sonority that exploited the intense semiotics of the Jewish grief. Theater critic Akim

Figure 1.6. Nachum Zemach as the peddler-prophet, from *Habima*'s 1923 production of *The Eternal Jew*. Courtesy of *Habima* National Theater and the Israeli Center for the Documentation of the Performing Arts.

Lvovich Volynsky articulated the Jewish dimension embedded in the cries iterated on the stage:

> No other nation cries like the Jews cry. . . . [T]his is, as one could say, a historical cry . . . something that cannot be phrased into words, something monumental, Psalm-like.[53]

Ruth HaCohen depicts the historical and cultural attribution of noisy, loud weeping to the synagogue, as reflected from the German phrase *ein Lärm wie in einer Judenschule* (noise as in the synagogue, or as loud and disorderly as in the synagogue) which originates in the Middle Ages.[54] This phrase, according to HaCohen, depicts the bustling yelling and cries of the praying Jews in the synagogue as a paradigmatic category of noise. The descriptions of the staged soundscape of the oriental bazaar follow this cultural attribution of the noisy synagogue, thus conflating the fictional stage of the legendary Beris Arva with the cultural category of the Jewish commotion.

Maxim Gorky, who attended *Habima*'s production of *The Eternal Jew* three times, also underscored the sonority of Jewish anguish. He wrote:

> Without understanding the language and only by pleasure of listening to the sound and rhythm did I feel all the anguish of the prophet who was not understood by his people he loved so dearly. . . . But it was not the play that made the deep impression. No, the impression was created by the harmony of performance, by the musical unity of the performance at large and each individual in and for himself.[55]

The depiction of communal grief presented in *Habima*'s production of *The Eternal Jew* indeed alludes to a dominant musical mode of the synagogal ritual. Thus, while the mise-en-scène of the colorful bazaar lacked the depiction of Jewish elements, the voices crying on the stage were shaped as distinctly Jewish. By deciphering the gap between the visual elements of the spectacle and the nonverbal sonic properties of the performance, the audience could comprehend the drama.

Within the explicit vocal religious reference, the delivery of the lamentation in Modern Hebrew, with a Sephardic pronunciation, created a sense of incongruity. The Sephardic intonation and pronunciation related to the Zionist endeavor to redefine Hebrew as a colloquial language; however, for *Habima*'s contemporaries it was not yet naturalized as a spoken dialect. In this sense, we could consider the spoken language in this lamentation as a factor that brings forth the social context of European Jewry in Moscow during the liminal 1920s, when Rovina first performed the lamentation, in Rosenzweig's residence in Frankfurt in 1928, or in the recording of this performance in 1931. Thus, the sounds of mourning were configured as unsettled voices in constant flux, much like the legendary figure of the Eternal (wandering) Jew, *Habima*'s Hebrew theater, or the Jewish communities in the soaring anti-Semitic atmosphere in Europe of the 1930s.

When *Habima* played these scenes of public mourning in Europe in 1923 or 1931, in Mandatory Palestine, or after the formation of the Israeli state, the mythical representation of the drama overlapped with the sonic experiential basis of the listening audiences. In the same manner, every time *Habima* performed these public lamentations, the actors' weeping voices reverberated with different social and political circumstances. Thus, when Rovina recorded the lamentation in London in 1931, her sorrow referred to the fictional realm of the dispersion of the Israelites and the Judahites from their ancestral homeland, but it also bespoke *Habima*'s farewell from their homeland continent.

During the 1930s, after having settled in Palestine, and throughout the 1940s, *Habima* made it a tradition to perform this play in the week prior

Figure 1.7. The Messiah's mother (Hanna Rovina) and the peddler-prophet (Zvi Friedland). Courtesy of *Habima* National Theater and the Israeli Center for the Documentation of the Performing Arts.

to the Ninth of Av (Tish'a' b'Av).[56] In these performances, Rovina performed a sonic instantiation familiar to the audience from the synagogal mourning ritual within the social and artistic framing of the theater-house, as if the assembly in the theater supplemented the gathering in the synagogue. Thus, although her voice-act referred to the specific fictional world of the legend, it was harnessed as a liminal "moment in and out of time"—in Victor Turner's words.[57] In other words, Rovina's association to the Ninth of Av lamentation expressed a generic cry, aggregating several catastrophes, such as the pogroms against the European Jewry, the bloody attacks on Jewish populations in Palestine, the Holocaust, and the Zionist call for redemption in the Holy Land.[58]

Rovina's recorded lamentation thus constructed a collective performance through an individual speech-act. Her dirge served as a vocal reaction to the disastrous events of the first century, fluctuating from the destruction of the Temple in Jerusalem to increasing violence against Jews in early-twentieth-century Russia and Ukraine, from the horrifying slaughter fields of the Great War that were still burning at the time, to the Arab revolt in 1929 and others. In this sense, Rovina marks, through her distinctive mournful Jewish sonority, a linear Jewish expression shaped to draw continuity from pre-exilic Jerusalem to the Jewish settlements in 1931 Mandatory Palestine. Under such circumstances, this lamentation capitalized on a religious mode of communication and on a mythical narrative, in order to respond to novel vicissitudes, and thus structure the past as quasi-compulsorily repetitive. The grief and sorrow reflected in Rovina's 1923 lamentation varies from its ensuing recording, and its much later appearances. However, one melodious line knits them together across their different temporalities, and configures them as belonging to the same cultural realm.

The Liminality of Voice

Rovina's lamentation brings together different cultural realms and modes of expression through its aural shaping as a liminal condition. Within this under-three-minutes monologue, she passes through various imagined vocal borderlines, much like the incessant traveling of the eternal (wandering) Jew. Gershom Scholem articulated the idea of language emission as a liminal border crossing in his 1917 essay "On Lament and Lamentation" ("Über Klage und Klagelied"), in which he defines the language of the border:

> [W]hereas every language is always a positive expression of a being, and its infinity resides in the two bordering lands of the

revealed and the silenced [*Verschwiegenen*], such that it actually stretches out over both realms, this language is different from any other language in that it remains throughout on the border [*Grenze*], exactly on the border between these two realms. This language reveals nothing, because the being that reveals itself in it has no content (and for that reason one can also say that it reveals everything) and conceals [*verschweigt*] nothing, because its entire existence is based on a revolution of silence. It is not symbolic, but only points toward the symbol; it is not concrete [*gegenständlich*], but annihilates the object. This language is lament.[59]

Scholem's essay, written as an epilogue to his translations of the biblical Book of Lamentations into German, depicts two lands: one signifies the language of revelation, the other—the language of silence; the border between the lands intersects with what Scholem describes as the language of lament.[60] Lament, young Scholem argues, is neither speech nor silence; it negates content and thus reveals nothing. Following these assertions, Ilit Ferber defines Scholem's theory of lament as a linguistic structure that is essentially bound to a precarious position on the border.[61] In this sense, Rovina's lamentation stages, through its very expression, the notion of transgression of apparent boundaries.

The vocal crossing that Rovina performs between the verbal recitation and the pure vocal emission of grief and sorrow, and between the languages and the melody of her delivery, marks the imagined borderlines contravened in the Messiah's mother lamentation. She manifests a borderline between the Hebrew language and, particularly, its Sephardic pronunciation, and the traditional synagogue melodies that express the profound traditional sonic sediments of the Jewish communities of the Eastern European Diaspora. Enacting this borderline, Rovina challenges the fine line separating these two realms, positing the sonic memory as representative of the recognition of belonging to a place characterized by its dynamic fluidity. Thus, the spoken and sung melodies within Rovina's lamentation, despite their representing two different realms, wove cultural associations that *Habima*'s audience could assemble into a cohesive interpretation of the drama. Rovina's heightened speech and melody enabled listeners to imagine the function of the religious vocabulary in a national context.

Throughout the lamentation, Rovina's language gradually deteriorates, as she transforms eloquent speech into pure vocal expression. By doing so, she gives voice to another transgression structured within the genre of lament, which, as Galit Hasan-Rokem argues, expresses the limits of verbal reference.[62] Mikhail Gnessin, an influential figure in the Russian Jewish nationalist school of music, developed a theory conceptualizing *The Musical Interpretation of Drama* (1912–13): a rhythmic recitation that enhances the poignancy by inserting into the drama musical patterns derived from the internal logic of the Hebrew language and its religious practices in liturgy. In an essay entitled "*Habima and Musical Possibilities Entailed in its Performances*," Gnessin manifests his artistic ideas regarding the dramatic musical recitation he developed:

> The musical recitation marks the border between mundane speech and recitative. This recitation style does not require a singing voice, as the voice is articulated much like ordinary stage speech. The emotional values of human speech are available to this voice; however, the tempo of this speech and intonation are rendered according to a certain musical melody.[63]

Gnessin mentions in his essay the artistic development that occurred in music at the beginning of the seventeenth century. Especially relevant to his essay are the musical ideas invented and practiced at the end of the sixteenth century by members of the Florentine Camerata, most notably by the performers and composers Jacopo Peri and Giulio Caccini. Peri and Caccini, according to Claude V. Palisca, invented a new kind of solo singing in the theater, termed Monody: a style of recitation in between speech and song. Inspired by the classical model of ancient Greek and Roman tragedy, they fostered a vocal performance that would enhance the expression of the recited drama by performing it with continuous music.[64] Peri defined the declamation he desired in dramatic music:

> [T]hat type of voice assigned to singing by the ancients which they called "diastematic" (as it were, sustained and suspended) could at times speed up and take an intermediate path between the suspended and slow movements of song and the fluent, rapid ones of speech . . . ,[65] approaching that other [species] of speech, which they called "continuous."

Gnessin's vision of the "musical possibilities" entailed in the new Hebraic theater follows the abovementioned model. Moreover, he poses that the intervallic motion of the singing voice should derive from the diverse repository of the Jewish sonority.

Rovina's glissando, moving from speech to singing, takes the lamentation away from the familiar sounds of the synagogue, charging it with a liminal, transgressive element. By performing the masculine synagogue cantor's "trope" with a feminine voice, an obstruction of the traditional hierarchy of gender roles takes place, contravening the normative spatial borderlines of the performed ritual. Lamenting is the realm of women traditionally performed in the open space. Hasan-Rokem contends that by articulating wailing as an act not of acquiescence or submission but rather as one of independence and even resistance before God, the book of Lamentations displays a tendency similar to that of many laments recorded in oral performances all over the world.[66]

The subversion of hierarchies, as expressed in laments, has been attributed to women. As Nicole Loraux has demonstrated with regard to laments in classical Athens, wailing is a strictly restrained and policed activity and representatives of the male hegemonic order have, in these and many other cases, instituted firm regulations stipulating where, when and for how long laments may be performed, and especially demarcating where and when they will not be tolerated. Rovina's lamentation crosses this borderline, and reverses the lamentation from a performance in the open space of the cemetery, where the feminine voice projects to masculine ears, into a theatrical performance of a feminine voice articulating the vocality attributed to the synagogal enclosed space, where, traditionally, the masculine voice projects onto the female ears.[67]

Such a reversal also appears in the dramatic shaping of Rovina's lamentation, problematizing the traditional theme of performative and textual traditions of lament: discontinuing ties between mothers and their offspring. Hasan-Rokem explains the pain expressed in the epicenter of lament as stemming from the harsh contrast between the intuitive, wished-for inseparability of the mother-child dyad and the unfortunate circumstances of mourning for the irreversible loss of a child.[68] However, rather than bewail the death of her son, Rovina—the Messiah's mother—mourns his birth.

Hasan-Rokem links the separation of the mother and child to prior possible separations in a child's life, beginning when the fetus implanted in the mother's womb begins to develop his separate pulse and will; continuing with the tearing apart of bodies in birth, after which the distance keeps growing. The Messiah's mother's lamentation, nevertheless, centers on the birth of her child as an affirmative inversion that parallels death. She grieves his survival, not his death; she cries about his demanding presence, not about his demise. This loaded moment takes an ironic turn when, at the end of the play, she discovers that her son, who is the Messiah, has disappeared.

The theme of transgression is central to the genre of lament, as a performance of resistance before God. In her performance, the Messiah's mother expresses her grievance toward God for the unfortunate birth time of her son that prevented her from joining the war, and for keeping him alive, thus burdening her with providing for her newborn son. In contrast to the central expressive formula of laments, the mother here does not address the deceased. Instead, she appeals directly to God, who brought her son into this world, against her will, at the very same hour in which the Temple was destroyed. Frustration, apparent in both text and tone of her lamentation (at some point she cries: "You provide him!"), is customary in the Ninth of Av ritual in the synagogue.

In many synagogues, several performative acts are executed to express not only deep grief but also grievance toward God for refraining from saving His people in times of calamities: many times the prayer is conducted under dim lights, the furniture is rearranged, and those praying stand either in felt shoes or in socks. On that day, perhaps as if to "act out" their despair, there is no Torah learning, and the *tallit* and *tefillin* are worn in the afternoon and not in the morning, as usually.[69] However, it is important to note that these symbolic acts conclude with the expression of public affirmation and trust in God's authority, and faith in the ultimate redemption of Israel. In a similar way, the aggravation expressed by the Messiah's mother within her lamentation constitutes her position of complaint, by which she implements the force of continuity as stemming from deep sorrow.

What, then, might be the signification of the liturgical borrowing into Rovina's dramatic monologue within the modern theatrical framework? Obviously, Nicole Loraux writes, no one actually dies on stage, and, essentially, no one laments. Yet, what remains fundamentally *real* in the theatrical event is its social setting. The liminality of Rovina's lament, further underscored by its liturgical delivery, alludes to specific mourning rituals performed in a distinct social situation. Theater, as Loraux explains, is a place of assembled collectivity, taking place in a civic space and at a time in which a community turns into a congregation by performing for itself its conflicts and values. In the process of its adaptation to the stage, the lamentation comes to emphasize not the uniting functions of social grief, but rather the conflicts at stake. These conflicts, as Loraux explains, are not between themes, but rather between the very elements constituting theater as a form of discourse endowed with meaning. Thus, in order to understand the conflicts arising in the performance, one must attune oneself to the articulation of the dialogue and lyric passages.[70] The use of sonic quotations from the synagogal soundscape evoked the radical communal changes that preoccupied the audience in 1923, marked imaginary cultural and geographical borderlines, and engaged the spectators as an emerging national community (however, not necessarily Zionist) undergoing transformative social processes.

In 1931, when this lamentation was recorded the threshold it signified was rather different. As the gates of Europe gradually began closing down, the ground underneath the Jews of Europe began moving. Facing the urgency to cross the territorial borders of their homelands, and leave behind their web of life, the European Jewry experienced the unstable condition of liminality as a mental and physical continuing situation. Rovina's recorded lamentation depicts an audible trace from the despondency of these years as a vocal act situated on the borderline between Jewish history and myth. On this borderline, *Habima* paradoxically anchored itself a virtual space for transmitting the traditional weeping sounds of their community.

CHAPTER TWO

The Rise and Fall

The Return of *The Dybbuk* and the Making of the Acoustic Community

During the long 1920s, when *Habima* was roaming in Europe, the United States, and Mandatory Palestine, millions of Jews around the world were intensively occupied in casting new identities, establishing new affiliations to social groups, and redefining their belonging to their local, according to identity categories the flux of Modernity produced: religion, ethnicity, nationhood. The interrelated flowering of urbanization and secularization, dovetailing the development of new communication and transportation technologies, destabilized the fixed boundaries of the traditional community. These processes paralleled the Zionist endeavor to reformulate the Jewish collectivity in modern social terms, and to transform it from a traditional subculture community into a nation-state. Under such circumstances, dynamics of apparent assimilation or homogenization of Jewish culture catalyzed the need to perpetuate and reassert emblematic features of the traditional tight-knit Jewish community. This entailed, among other things, preserving and recording the typical aural traits of Jewish vernaculars: recitation patterns of collective texts, common musical shapes, and mutual iterations of customary rhythmic modes. *Habima*'s Hebrew theater participated in the mediation of this cultural symbolism by evincing meaning, values, and significance relevant to its audiences.

This chapter focuses on the making of the Jewish community by the enactment and propagation of a shared rhythmic pattern—a symbolic and auditory beat that runs through social and fictional narratives—as manifested in a sound recording depicting *Habima*'s third staged production: a performance based on *The Dybbuk*, or *Between Two Worlds*, written in Russian between 1914–18 by folklorist and ethnographer Shloyme-Zanvl Rappoport (1863–1920), under the pen name S. An-sky, and translated into Hebrew by Chaim Nachman Bialik.

The world premiere of An-sky's play, performed in Yiddish by *The Vilna Troupe* under the artistic directing of Dovid Herman, preceded its Hebrew debut. This production was initially staged in Warsaw in December 1920, on the occasion of completing the thirty days of ritual mourning over An-sky's death.[1] Soon after its premiere, this production became *The Vilna Troupe's* most popular performance, and its most eminent artistic achievement. As Debra Caplan writes, "[D]uring the 1920s and 1930s nearly half a million theatergoers attended the Vilna Troupe's touring productions of *The Dybbuk* as 'Dybbuk' mania' swept across dozens of countries."[2] *Habima's* performance of *The Dybbuk*, as Shelly Zer-Zion contends, sustains a profound artistic inspiration from the Yiddish production that preceded it.[3]

Habima's production of *The Dybbuk* was directed by the Russian Armenian director Yevgeny Vakhtangov, with scenography by Nathan Altman and music by Yoel Engel. Following its debut in Moscow on January 13, 1922, this performance was considered the theater's signature show: praised for its stylistic merging of Jewish tradition and expressionistic spectacle. This artistic achievement was also translated into a box office success: *The Dybbuk* became the longest-running performance in the history of Israeli theater, staged for more than four decades, over 1,300 times.

In 1965, forty-three years after its theater debut, *Habima* recorded *The Dybbuk*, in a special staging that included many members of the iconic cast from the veteran troupe, accompanied by the Israeli Philharmonic Orchestra conducted by Moshe Vilensky. This grand staging was recorded and produced as a commercial vinyl record, also broadcast on the national radio station Kol Yisrael.[4] The recording of *The Dybbuk* presents the plot of the play as depicted on stage—the story of a Hasidic community in the town of Brinnitz, in which a young bride-to-be has been possessed by the dead spirit of her lover. Leah—the bride-to-be—is forced by her father to marry a wealthy man despite an earlier promise made by her father to the father of Hanan[5]—a Yeshiva student, an enthusiastic Kabbalah practitioner, and the object of Leah's affection. Tormented by his passion for Leah, Hanan dies while engaged in magic activity aimed to win back his beloved Leah. His death does not mark the end of the drama, but rather its inception: Hanan's spirit transmigrates into Leah's body in the form of a dybbuk—the Jewish cultural pattern for spirit possession. Leah's body becomes a vehicle for the voice of Hanan's spirit. The acting-out of her possession disrupts the wedding celebration, transforming the joyful, social atmosphere into a horrifying scene that affects the whole community, breeding fear and disorder. In order to restore peace within the community, the local rabbi performs an exorcism ritual. However, the outcome of this attempt proves as calamitous as the wedding ceremony: rather than reclaiming her body and reintegrating into the community, Leah, supposedly, unifies with her dead lover in the next world.

In this chapter, I engage with the shaping of the voices emerging from the recording of *The Dybbuk* as expressions of the East European Jewish community, sounding two distinct, however simultaneous, *Zeitgeists*: the Bolshevist revolution, and the emergence of Zionism. At the center of this chapter is the recurring melodious rhythmic pattern governed by the dynamics of "rise-fall," as evident from the aural, textual, symbolic, and theatrical aspects of *Habima's* audio performance. In the previous chapter I discussed the sonic imagination of the messianic idea by which redemption can only emerge when it passes through despair, grief, failure, and calamity. The "rise-fall" melodious pattern reverberates with this political-theological idea. As I show in this chapter, the aural dynamics of "rise-fall" transforms in *Habima's* production into a conceptual rhythmic model resonating both a historical perception and a fictional depiction of the Hasidic community represented in An-sky's play.

I perceive the aural rendering of "rise-fall" in the recording of *The Dybbuk* as a mode of experience that grounds collective speech and expressive patterns, and thus binds together those members who consider themselves part of this communal vocal world. First, I probe into the various aural layers of the symbolic construction of the rise and fall dynamics in the Hasidic community depicted on *Habima's* stage, and explore the dialectical interaction between the individual and the group as presented through the aural organization. Then, I turn to interrogate how the "rise-fall" aural pattern created in 1922 was perceived later, in 1965, when the actors performed as immigrants to a community mostly comprised of immigrants, in the state of Israel.

Alicia Schmidt Camacho articulates the notion of *migrant imaginaries* as a term that encompasses the world-making of immigrants whose mobility changes the character of national life. *Migrant imaginaries,* according to Schmidt Camacho, create fictions that produce forms of communal life and political organizations in keeping with their own fragile agency as mobile people.[6] Returning to *Habima's* manifestation of the Hebrew language, I ask: How did *Habima's* aural performance serve the social imagination of the transitioning Jewish communality in 1922, and what changed in these imagineries when the performance was altered from the stage to a commercial vinyl record in 1965?

I observe the process of medial adaptation undergone by *The Dybbuk* as a strong manifestation of Raymond Williams's conception of the "changing structure of feelings" (1983), which describes "the continuity of experience from a particular work, through its particular form, to its recognition as a general form, and then the relation of this general form to a period."[7] Williams traces a profound tension between the historical artifact—the fixed, finite, and, in the case of theater, receding work of art—and its active presence through its continuous enactments. *Habima*'s album exhibits its presence, evoking timely values and meanings of the 1922 production, as recorded, nevertheless, in 1965 and then, once again, as interpreted today. The "changing structure of feelings" therefore conceptualizes the connection between past cultural elements and the social present, and in relation to historical processes. In what follows, I grapple with the question of how the technological transformations *The Dybbuk* underwent instantiate "the structure of feeling" elicited from *Habima*'s performance of An-sky's play.

Between Two Worlds: Visual Imaginations and Aural Realms

The stage at the opening of *Habima*'s 1922 performance of *The Dybbuk* displayed an old synagogue.[8] In the middle of the stage, a preaching platform had been erected—in Hebrew, a *bima*—from which the liturgical ceremony and Bible reading in the synagogue take place. To the left, in the background, was the Holy Ark, whereby the Bible scrolls are kept. Over the proscenium two words were hanging—"Hear, Oh Israel" (*Shema Israel*)—denoting the first two words from the first prayer every Jewish child learns to recite, and the last words a pious Jew is supposed to utter before his death. In their theatrical context, these two words call the audience to listen to the aural manifestations of the Hebrew language enacted on the stage, emphasizing the central role played by the hearing faculty in this performance. Accordingly, I tune in to the voices emerging from the recording of the performance.

The 1965 commercial record reproduces the voices of *Habima*'s actors in a straightforward manner, without resorting to mediation by a narrator. Thus, in order to achieve a fuller understanding of the audio performance and contextualize the dramatic replicas as stemming from the visual and aural world of the East European Hasidic community, listeners must have relied, to some extent, on some previous knowledge, perhaps even on their memories, of the theatrical stylization of the characters in this performance. Indeed, this album enables its listeners to re-experience some of the most iconic dramatic lines, performed by familiar voices of the Hebrew stage, the most memorable of which is that of Hanna Rovina, who played the role of the possessed bride Leah in one of the best-known climactic declamatory moments of Israeli theater. When Rovina played the possessed bride, she manipulated her voice to lend it the low timbre of a male voice. "You are not my bridegroom!" she cried loudly in a lingering dense replica, as her body became a theatrical vessel that uncannily harbored and issued forth a male voice, obviously other than her own.

In the absence of a visual anchor, the vocal enactment of possession exclusively through sonic means might seem peculiar, if not absurd. What point is there in an aural performance that conjures a visual theatrical illusion? A glimpse into the global history of radio—the shared forms of radio programs that developed across cultures and geographical locations—reveals that radio performances of audio-visual illusions were prevalent in the middle of the twentieth century, especially by ventriloquists such as Peter Brough in Britain or Edgar Bergen in the United States. From 1937 to 1956, American listening audiences tuned in to hear the verbal battles between the vaudevillian couple Edgar Bergen and his witty dummy Charlie McCarthy. The success of this ventriloquist radio show is intriguing: ventriloquism wholly depends upon a visual illusion—the voice of the ventriloquist *seems* to issue from a source other than his body; however, radio, the aural medium par excellence, ostensibly casts off the visual elements of the show.

Steven Connor explains the popularity achieved by this radio ventriloquism on the grounds of the audience's previous acquaintance with the spectacle. "It is possible," Connor explains, "for the ear to borrow and internalize some of the substantiation powers of the eye, and to mold from them a kind of sonorous depth, a space sustained by and enacted through the experience of sound alone."[9] Connor's hypothesis may also account for the impact caused by Rovina's vocal performance of Leah's possession: following more than four decades of staging, the listeners were acquainted with Leah's pallid countenance, and with her expressionistic gestures as the possessed bride; they were conversant with the scenography of the old synagogue and the Jewish figures that populated the stage, and thus they could summon the theatrical vision from her recorded oral delivery.

Yet, the aural performance emerging from the vinyl record differs from the staged one. It crafts a domain that is largely illusory, while retaining a firm bond with the actual familiar Jewish diasporic sonority. It manifests the attempt to *listen* to theater, as a central mode of dramatic production. The recording of *The Dybbuk* foregrounds the performative scenario as a tracing not only from a staged production, but also from an aural environment, a sort of soundscape, in which voices and sounds gather up to create an extensive, mobile, virtual, and, to some extent, alternative vicinity. The fictional world summoned by the recorded performance falls under what Connor terms *sonorous autonomization*: "a world of sound functioning separately from and in excess of the visible world."[10] This alternative world, indeed, stems from the visual; however, it establishes a separate, largely illusive realm by leaving more room for the imagination.

Continuing this idea, the voices recorded in *Habima*'s 1965 album are prompted by two kinds of visual and aural sources: while they belong to the fictional staged realm, they also derive from the East European Jewish world represented on stage, a world that by 1965 had already been shattered. Accordingly, the sonority established in *Habima*'s album amplifies the social engagement with the act of possession that takes place within the evoked community. While the epicenter of An-sky's drama rests on Leah's possession, the myriad of voices and the sound organization in the recording sets the focal point within the imagination of the Jewish community, as it demands that the listeners recreate the play through sound alone. In this sense, we might perceive the 1965 resonance of *Habima*'s renowned performance as a late reflection on the sounds and voices associated with the sonic environment of East European Jewry, issuing both mundane and ritualized sonorities and speech patterns.

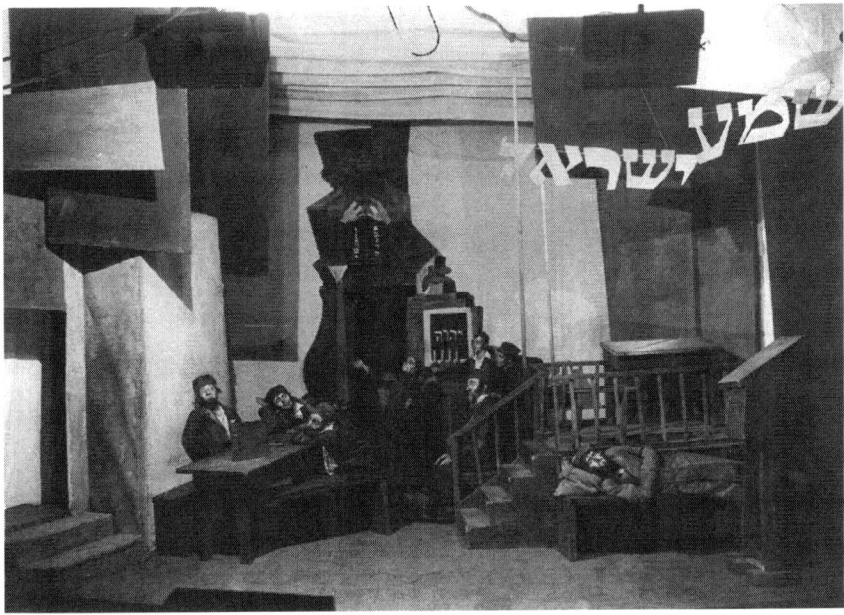

Figure 2.1. The stage of *Habima*'s 1922 performance of *The Dybbuk*. Courtesy of *Habima* National Theater and the Israeli Center for the Documentation of the Performing Arts.

The transformation of *The Dybbuk* from a theater performance into an audio drama redefines it as a cultural reproduction that corresponds to the qualities of its medium—disembodied sounds eligible for continuous repeated performances. It is in the hiatus between the staged and the recorded performances of *The Dybbuk* that we might, perhaps, find the key to understanding the changes of sensibilities generated by this metatext. Thus, if we could understand the exchange system by which the aural compensates for the lack of a visible scenario, we could, perhaps, also better understand the production and transformation of what may be called the cultural sensorium—that is, the cultural meanings of the relationships between the aural and the visible, voice and script.

Figure 2.2. Hanna Rovina as Leah in *Habima*'s production of *The Dybbuk*. Courtesy of *Habima* National Theater and the Israeli Center for the Documentation of the Performing Arts.

The Haunting Archive and the Voices of the Dead

An-sky's play revolves around the theatrical manifestations of three social rituals—the synagogue prayer, the Jewish wedding, and the exorcism of the dybbuk from the body of the possessed bride. The rendering of the rites, customs, and ceremonies in *Habima*'s performance was based upon the materials collected in the ethnographic expeditions An-sky led during three consecutive summers throughout the period of 1912–14 to the Jewish communities in the Pale of Settlement, in which Jews were allowed permanent residence.[11] The expedition members transcribed and chronicled the everyday life and customs of these communities.[12] They collected Judaica items and photographed the places and people of the Jewish communities; most importantly for our current interest, they recorded with a phonograph the songs, melodies, and parables of the communities they visited.

An-sky, as Gabriella Safran points out, fostered an ethnographic vision that fused cutting-edge documentation technologies with folkloristics.[13] This approach made its mark in *The Dybbuk*: when Leah speaks in Ḥanan's voice, she enacts both the position of the phonograph and of the singer whose recorded voice it reproduces. It may be, as Safran suggests, "that An-sky was so fascinated with dybbuk stories, in which the voice lives on transgressively after the death of its owner, because they recalled his own work with the gramophone. The fantasy of conquering death was prominent in the early history of sound recording, and An-sky recorded the people of the shtetl, sometimes willingly and sometimes against their will, preserving their voices so that they might be heard long after their death."[14] Similarly, *Habima*'s recording of *The Dybbuk* gives presence to the "bygone" East European Jewish communities by transforming them into disembodied theatricalized recorded voices.[15] In other words, the recording converts the absence of the long-gone agents of Jewish folklore into vocal performances that establish their presence "here and now" through aural reproduction.

The recording of the folklore items gleaned by An-sky and his peers was not intended to be confined to historical documentation, but rather, as part of an educational doctrine, to enhance traces from Jewish heritage by animation and continuing dissemination. The same logic follows *The Dybbuk*, a play written in the aftermath of the ethnographic expeditions in order to foster the reenactment of the traditional Jewish world. Chaim Nachman Bialik, the translator of *The Dybbuk*, made a derogatory comment on An-sky's play: "I have the impression that, as a collector of folklore, you combed through the garbage dumps. You picked out your little fragments of folklore and pieced together the remnants of all sorts of clothing into patches and took those patches and sewed them together into a sort of crazy quilt."[16] Bialik refers to the eclectic quality of the play, which brings together pieces of folklore, and fragments from the social and cultural texture that gave dimension to life in the communities An-sky and his peers visited.

An-sky's attempt to bring Jewish folklore onto the theater stage should be read in the context of the nineteenth- and early-twentieth-century impulse to retrieve selective aspects of Jewish tradition and culture in order to retain the connection to an endangered world.[17] Throughout the play, Safran writes, the characters explain to each other customs or landmarks; they perform songs, dances, and rituals, dramatizing over and over "the encounter between a loquacious storyteller and an eager listener."[18] *Habima*'s recording of An-sky's drama resonates with this kind of engagement between narrator and listener. It reconstructs the experience of listening to talkative voices at the core of drama, while also granting the reproduced voices an autonomous afterlife by detaching their apparent linkage to their corporeality, and presenting them, much like the voice of the dybbuk, as issuing from a surrogate medium. By granting Jewish folklore, religion, and culture a recorded afterlife through their theatrical presence, *Habima*'s performance reconstructs the traditional, organic, close-knit community—in sociologist Ferdinand Tönnies's term, the *Gemeinshcaft*—that at the time of An-sky's ethnographic expeditions, was already enveloped with a nostalgic allure.[19]

The theatrical enactment of An-sky's play elevated the ethnographic materials to become a communal performative experience.[20] This observation seems to capture a central theme in An-sky's play: the tension between individual and societal forces as materialized through the regulation of Leah's body during the wedding and its related rituals performed by the community and its representative agents. This tension is also evident from the design of *Habima*'s album: the cover of the album features a photo (by Shraga Friedman) from the concluding scene of the second act when the guests at the wedding realize that the bride—Leah—has been possessed by a dybbuk. In this photo, a group of men and women extend their right arms upward in the air with a straightened hand in a symbolic gesture that indicates the expulsion of the dybbuk. Inside the album's box was a booklet with the program of the show. On both covers of the booklet a photographed image of Leah's ghostlike countenance appears.

Through the theatrical representation of mass, and the enactment of the tension between community and individual, *Habima*'s recorded album, as well as its staged performance, manifests different kinds of fusions between theater and ritual and the way religious rituals, in their modern context, reshape the dynamics between individual and community. In other words, the engagement with ritual on *Habima*'s theater stage could be formulated as part of an attempt to redefine the Jewish community as a social assembly in which the individual re-affiliates with his traditional origins. As an audio performance, the recording of *The Dybbuk* sounds a religous realm beyond the fictional. It resonates a "vocal community," in Ruth HaCohen's terms, referring to the shared cherished corpus of sounds and melodies, the molding of vocal practices, the orchestration and controlling of the sounds upon which the community is established.[21] By replaying the voices, tones, and rhythms associated with East European Jewry, *Habima*'s audio recording enfolded its listeners with the aural traces of a perished world and its bygone ritual practices.

In what ways does the interweaving of typical traditional Jewish sonority in the recording affirm the diffusion of the past into the present? And, to what degree does it attest to an experience of a cultural rupture in its transmission that brings forth the necessity of igniting lost feelings, a nostalgic allure of tradition? The recording of *The Dybbuk* presents a sonority distilled from the European soundscape, singled out for theatrical preservation, thus intended to grant this vanished aural culture an afterlife. In what follows, I would like to explore the aural rendering of the afterlife of *Habima*'s performance of *The Dybbuk* as issued in the 1965 commercial recording.

As sonic memorabilia from a legendary performance, the recording recycled the sonorities *Habima* performed in 1922 into its present 1965 moment of production. The record generates the illusion of a performance that enacts the play "here and now" to its listeners, through its canonical sounds and voices. But, then, is it really so? Are the sounds of 1965 the same as those performed in 1922? By 1965, the first generation of *Habima*'s actors were firmly assimilated among the Jewish society in Israel. The *shtetl* realm depicted in *The Dybbuk* was miles away from their world, remote from their cultural orbit, and, thus, could only be re-experienced through theatrical imagination. It only makes sense that after more than four decades of life in Israel, their Russian accents would subside, their Yiddish speech intonation would lose its edge, and their proficiency in Hebrew would increase. The recording, therefore, does not summon "authentic" voices, but an amalgamation of a nostalgic apprehension of *Habima*'s legendary performance and the memory from the typical sonorities of the Hasidic community.

Nostalgia is also built into the dramatic structure of An-sky's play. As Naomi Seidman argues, at the center of An-sky's play lies the mashup of two temporal realms: strands from Haskala (the Jewish Enlightenment), romantic narratives of resistance to the elderly generations that are considered progressive, are woven into a contradictory set of traditional Jewish folk beliefs. The dybbuk itself, Seidman maintains, embodies the dialectic between progress and tradition: a figure drawn from the repository of the premodern occult that also attests to the modern creed regarding the inalienability of romantic choice.[22]

The attempt to capture voices and sounds in an audio recording and channel them through memorabilia demonstrates the paradoxical ability of recording media to animate an ephemeral "living" presence through acts of preservation. In this sense, the endeavor to restore the Jewish sonority through the audio recording enhances the idea of the return of the haunted spirit of the dead in the guise of the dybbuk—coming back from esoteric premodern times and speaking through a surrogate body, as Rachel Elior articulates, "from the mouth of the person possessed as a distinct personality."[23] The album, therefore, tells the story of the manifold cultural strata layered by the long process of canonization.

Habima acknowledged its unique artistic and commercial achievement in *The Dybbuk*, and thus was motivated to preserve it. Following Vakhtangov's premature death, the task of controllling all the elements in the production, in keeping with its original detailed stage directions and energy, was of the essence. A special supervisor from the troupe was appointed to be in charge of all aspects of the theatrical production—guiding the second generation of actors to perform in the spirit of Vakhtangov's artistic vision, and meticulously following the original stage directions and accuracy of the tone and intonation of the dramatic utterance.[24] Thus, what began as an apprehension of dynamic cultural forces transformed into a reified commercial product.

In 1965 *Habima*, by then an established cultural institution, no longer reflected the nascent spirit it had manifested when staging An-sky's *Dybbuk* in 1922. As the performance aged, along with its iconicity, apparent signs of ossification became evident, as it gradually lost its artistic vividness. In its debuts during European tours throughout 1937–38, *Habima* was praised for the artistic achievement of the *Dybbuk*, and, especially, for preserving Vakhtangov's legacy.[25] However, as the years passed by, the theater began to be criticized for allowing the rigid format to overcome all other elements of the performance. For example, during *Habima*'s 1954 tour in Paris, theater critic André-Paul Antoine stated that, according to his impression, the performance no longer generated astonishment with its artistic tidings.[26]

As Elena Tartakovsky writes, *The Dybbuk*'s final international tours were held in the United States in 1964 and in the UK in 1965, around the time the performance was recorded. Theater critics who attended these performances expressed their disappointment at the deterioration of its initial artistic values and the evidence of "signs of petrification, stagnation displacing the rhythmic live actions."[27] In the local arena, the responses of the audience also reflected the aging of this production, as critics called for the exorcism of *The Dybbuk* from the national theater's repertoire, and urged the company to pull down the curtain on this production.

The strongest testimony to the obsolescence of the production was expressed in the aging of the veteran generation of *Habima*'s actors. Throughout the years, many members of the original cast had either died or left the theater; others could no longer enact young characters. In the final performances, only five out of twenty-four actors were survivors of the original cast. This included Hanna Rovina. *Habima*'s managers considered Rovina to be an essential part of the production, and felt that replacing her would harm the already-diminished reputation of the performance. In 1965 Rovina was seventy-seven years old, and her unsuitability to enact the part of Leah, the young bride, was evident to all. The theater company, nevertheless, insisted that she remain in the leading role, as her public persona had become identified with the role of Leah.[28] This physical mismatch is absent from the audio recording: although a person's voice is subject to gradual aging over time, in the absence of a point of reference or comparison to previous recordings this change would be imperceptible to the auditors of the album.

Freddie Rokem explains the lingering presence of An-sky's play in the repertoire of the Hebrew theater as necessary in the aftermath of the Nazi genocide and the catastrophic consequences of World War II. The rupture of Jewish life in Europe, Rokem argues, generated a vital need to grapple with the concrete outcome of death and the longing for all that had perished. This explanation is premised on the sonic and visual traces *Habima*'s performance presented of the vibrant world that had existed prior to the rupture that befell European Jewish communities following World War II. The assessment of *The Dybbuk* as a highly relevant theatrical text may explain, according to Rokem, its ability to generate different timely performative manifestations, and to attract audiences over a remarkably long period of time.[29] The enactment of voices and melodies associated with this extinct world offers the possibility, or the illusion, of bridging this breakup.

Barbara Kirshenblatt-Gimblett problematizes this linear metanarrative by alluding to the principle of anachronism, which operates via its unsettling temporal direction. She explains: "There is no dramatic rupture, no simple sequence of life, death, and rebirth, as the term *revival* would imply. Instead, old and new are in a perpetually equivocal relationship. The future precedes the past, the new precedes the old, the revival precedes its historical models."[30] Following Kirshenblatt-Gimblett's argument, we could thus suggest that as an object triggering nostalgia, the recording of *The Dybbuk* is anachronistic, rendering the imagination of the past as determined by the necessities of the present, but mostly by presenting a departure from the deterministic narrative of history by resurrecting the voices of the dead.

The recording of *The Dybbuk* enabled the sonorities of the traditional Jewish communities recorded by An-sky in his ethnographic journeys to gain a performative afterlife, enabling these sounds to return over and over again. The voices performing in this recording assume the haunting presence of their staged manifestation, thus reflecting the basic structural gesture of the dybbuk: the recorded or broadcast voice disengages from its corporeal anchor while retaining the aural signature produced by its medium.

The idea of audio media as enabling an uncanny form of disembodiment that grants the subject the power, real or imagined, to leave the body and transport his or her consciousness to another location has been linked with recording technologies from the early days of its inception. Thomas Alva Edison articulated such a position in his vision: "I am building an apparatus," he declared, "to see if it is possible for personalities which have left this earth to communicate with us."[31] Edison's venture was premised on the aspiration of granting the modern subject an afterlife, from which the dead could communicate with the living. Jeffrey Sconce explains that the idea that machines could be devised to transmit spectral sounds and contact with the dead was not preposterous among scientists and artists. Sconce cites British electrical researcher Mark Dyne who, as late as 1962, argued that "just as ordinary radio and TV signals are unseen vibrations through the air, so I believe there are disturbances in the ether caused by the spirit world. . . . All we have to do is to find the wave length and frequency and we shall be able to pick them up,"[32] thus demonstrating the perception of technology as a means to bridge "between two worlds"—in the phrase bearing the subtitle of An-sky's play.

Habima's recording of *The Dybbuk* presents a most explicit manifestation of the association between the mechanical and the magical, between the "media" and spiritual "mediums." The unification of Leah and Ḥanan, in the form of the dybbuk possession, renders a body set in between the worlds of the dead and the mortal. Motivated by his affection for Leah, the voice of the dybbuk operates in line with the role of love as portrayed in Plato's *Symposium*, by Diotima, who is ventriloquized—like a dybbuk—through Socrates's mouth. Diotima explains that love is "the mediator who spans the chasm which divides them, and therefore in him all is bound together, and through him the arts of the prophet and the priest, their sacrifices and mysteries and charms, and all prophecy and incantation, find their way."[33] Dwelling in between two worlds, the recording of the dybbuk, much like the dybbuk itself, mediates between the bygone diasporic social structure and culture and the new "homeland."

Thus, while the drama in this recording presents a fictional world in which fictional characters enact, the voices and sounds it stages belong to a concrete historical moment of Eastern European Jewry at the turn of the twentieth century, manifesting traces of a Jewish world that, when recorded, had long been obliterated. In this sense, this recording reflects the endeavor for cultural continuity in light of the sharp rupture in the diasporic Jewish existence, and the nostalgic aspiration to revive these cultural roots. This explanation regards *The Dybbuk* as a mode of communication that transmits an abstract—perhaps even imagined—perception of a community stitched together by sharing sounds and voices. This community, it is important to add, not only performs its own traditions per se, but also the echoes of the cultural knowledge inherent to its later reenactments.

The nostalgic resurrection of the pre–World War II Hasidic sonority through the Israeli radio soundscape displaced the dramatic voices and sounds from their concrete historical and temporal context. In this respect, the recording demonstrates how an archive participates in the production and dissemination of knowledge by sounding and re-sounding the voices of the past. Interweaving An-sky's archival documentation with the *presencing* of a cultural repertoire, *The Dybbuk*'s recording imbued the voices of the actors, and the vocalities of the perished communities, with a sense of liveliness that traversed the fictional threshold of the theater space, conquering the shared invisible, electronically generated, sphere of the radio listeners. The typical Jewish sonorities of the Hasidic community of Brinnitz were endowed with a tangible autonomy in which the "real" had, in effect, been eroded by its theatrical, analogous performance. What is, then, created, is a technological turbulence whereby a mediated and ultimate ghostly community is revealed within the unfolding diegesis of the actual world.

"Mipnei Ma?" An Oratorical Moment of Participatory Singing

The title of *Habima*'s performance and album—*The Dybbuk*—has a double meaning: Firstly, as Yoram Bilu points out, it refers to the Jewish variant of the dissociative conditions of altered consciousness in the form of a haunted spirit that penetrates a surrogate medium and speaks from within it;[34] Secondly, the term *dybbuk* is extrapolated from the notion of "Dvekut" (attaching, binding, or, literally, sticking), that has been identified by Gershom Scholem as a central expression of the Hasidic practice: an immersive mystical devotion to God that is essential for redemption. As Seth L. Wolitz argues, although the idea of *Dvekut* relates to an individual spiritual experience, the attachment to the community is paramount, because elevation can be achieved only by adherence to the spiritual leader that guides his flock to holiness.[35] The Mishna phrase "dybbuk of friends" ("בדיבוק חברים") refers to the clinging together of friends as a necessity for the attainment of Torah wisdom.[36] In what follows, I focus on the ways *Habima*'s audio performance expands this semantic ambiguity, presenting the transmogrifying of the dead soul in the form of a dybbuk as central to the formation of the community. I observe the multilayered representation of the Jewish community through the theatrical paradigm of the chorus as a model for the communal, as a medium for connecting the past with the present, and, consequently, as means for establishing a social aesthetic experience grounded on shared sonority.

The first depiction of the community appears in the opening of the album, with the harmonious choral strains of the *Batlonim*—a group of men humming the tune of the Hasidic song "*Mipnei Ma*" (translated into English as "because of why"), a three-note melody that is played several times throughout the performance, setting the keynote sound of the production.[37] The words of this song, which both opens and closes the play, are:

> To what and why
> did the soul descend
> from the heights to the depths
> the descent is on account of the ascent
> the descent is on account of the ascent.[38]

The *Batlonim* chorus chants this song twice, initially humming in slow tempo that gradually transforms into singing. The contrasting middle part reworks and distorts the idea of the tune with declamations. The concluding section functions as a climax that reverses the arch of the tune by posing the "*Mipnei Ma*" tunes before and after the declamatory music. The short paradoxical phrase in this song—"the descent is on account of the ascent"—is chanted twice, in a melodic curve that counterpoints the meaning of the words: when the words affirm the exalted elevation, the tune falls to its lowest point; when the words pronounce the profoundest depth into which the soul has fallen, the melody reaches its highest peak. Thus, the choral singing provides a structural replica of the Hasidic motif of the fall-rise route the soul must undergo in order to achieve redemption.

"*Mipnei Ma*" is one of the many melodies gleaned by the musical division of An-sky's expeditions, which explored mainly in Volhynia and Podolia, and included, among others, composer and musicologist Yoel Engel, who was commissioned to compose the music for Vakhtangov's production of the play.[39]

According to Wolitz, this song was collected by Alter Kacyzne in Vitebsk, An-sky's hometown, from Hasidim who sang it according to the traditional way of the Sorotshiner Rebbe.[40] Engel, according to An-sky's vision, did not interpolate into the performance the melodies the expedition documented as a neutral "ready-made." Rather, as Albert Weisser explains, he reworked the melodies, especially those played in the Vitebsk region and in the Polish Lithuanian area of the Jewish oral tradition.[41] Such an adaptation is evident, for example, in the singing of the *Batlonim* chorus that perform a sorrowful version of the Ukrainian Hasidic *nigun*, which traditionally used to be performed rather cheerfully.

Habima's 1922 stage performance began in the dark before the curtain opened and the traditional synagogue scenography was revealed to the spectators. The space of the theater-house was filled with soft choral strains humming the song "*Mipnei Ma*." Unable to connect these voices to a visible source, during these moments the audience listened to these acousmatic voices emerging from behind the stage screen. The unseen choir vocally represented the condition of the dybbuk—suspended in between two worlds: fictional and real, revealed and mystified, past and present, living and dead.

The in-between, liminal, position of the chorus is enhanced by charging their voices with beings from another time. Menachem Gnessin, one of the founding members of *Habima*, portrays in his memoirs a moment that charges the singing in the opening act of the play with the energies of Jewish national revival prevailing in Moscow during the February revolution of 1917.[42] Gnessin recalls An-sky reading from the play on a winter evening, in the living room of Hillel Zlatopolsky, an influential middleman (or, more accurately, a *macher* in Yiddish), involved in all aspects of the Jewish community. The guests crowded the room, and An-sky, who sat in the corner of the murky room, read out loud from his play. The several gold-framed paintings hanging on the walls of the room served as the backdrop for the listeners that packed the room, among them, Gnessin mentions, Nachum Zemach, the founding member of *Habima*.

When An-sky completed his reading, the audience, mesmerized by his intense verbal performance, remained sitting silent for a long time. They too, Gnessing explains, wished to prolong their immersion in that long-gone world, unwilling to open their eyes and return to mundane reality. The silence broke when Zlatopolsky began to whisper the Hasidic song "*Mipnei Ma*." Gradually, the singing began spreading and growing around the room. Soon enough, the entire room was singing loudly and in unison, enthusiastically raising their voices as if they themselves had been a group of Hasidim gathering in the Rabbi's home. Even when An-sky and Zlatopolsky had left the room, the stimulation did not subside. The joint singing, Gnessin points out, had opened the hearts and minds of the gatherers, who began recalling and telling Jewish parables of righteous persons and miracle makers, as a natural dovetailing to An-sky's reading. When Zlatopolsky returned into the room, he brought with him news: he had bought the play from An-sky for *Habima,* under the condition that Bialik would translate it into Hebrew.

Gnessin's depiction of the participatory communal singing of the Hasidic *nigun* "*Mipnei Ma*" frames the opening of *Habima*'s staged performance and, later, in the aperture of the audio recording. This instance falls under Ruth HaCohen's term "an oratorical *moment*"—depicting the "enrichment of the present with voices and beings of other times."[43] This definition resonates with the essence of the disembodied voice of the dybbuk that expresses itself despite prevailing temporal, spatial, and ontological boundaries. The participatory singing at the beginning of the play sets up a vast range of correspondences between realities. It interweaves parallel meanings, referring both to the traditional Hasidic religious community from which this song emerges, to the uplifting moments of the joint singing at Zlatopolsky's home during the exciting days of the Bolshevist revolution of 1917, and to *Habima*'s celebrated performance of *The Dybbuk* in 1922. The singing of the chorus at the opening of the audio recording coalesces these four different places and times into one "oratorical moment," like the very voices participating in the act of shared singing.

The spectators who attended the performance in 1922 or later could join the chorus, intoning this familiar keynote, becoming part and parcel of the cultural represented world. This experience transformed the audience, for the time span of its occurrence, into a theatrical congregation bound together through shared singing. Such a momentary community, as Erika Fischer-Lichte contends, is not based upon common beliefs or shared ideologies, but on the bodily co-presence of actors and spectators, thereby assembled for a particu- lar duration in a particular space, with singing as the constitutive element that welds them together.[44] As long as the performance lasts, it is capable of establishing a bond between individuals who come from the most diverse biographical, social, ideological, religious, political backgrounds and remain discrete individuals who have associations of their own and generate their own, quite different meanings.

The recurrence of the musical motif "*Mipnei Ma*" throughout the performance enveloped the audience, so that by the end of the performance the spectators could all chant it. This participatory dimension of the wider community in the theater—that includes both actors and audience—is further enhanced by the different meanings attributed to the linguistic Hebrew root of *Kahal* (קהל), used to identify a congregation, a social get-together, and an audience, be it in the theater or in a religious assembly. This term seems especially relevant for studying vocal images of Jewish community due to the derivation of the Hebrew word for chorus—in Hebrew, *Makhela* (מקהלה)—from the linguistic root *Kahal*. Furthermore, as Anke Hilbrenner explains, the term *Kahal* also has some concrete historical association with the Hasidic world recreated on *The Dybbuk* stage.

During the second half of the nineteenth century, the term *Kahal* became a keyword within the discourse of the larger "Jewish question," namely, the segregation of the Jews dwelling in the Pale of Settlement from the governmental institutions, and the commissions of the Russian Empire.[45] The term *Kahal,* a word that signified in the late Russian Empire (up until 1844) the internal legal autonomous governments of Jewish communities, unfolds, in the context of the beginning of the twentieth century, a negative overtone vis-à-vis the isolation of the Jewish communities from the all-Russian public sphere, and an anti-Semitic perception of the Jews as a subversive entity that was forming "a state within a state" while exploiting the Empire's resources.[46]

Simon Dubnow, the founding director of The Jewish Historical-Ethnographic Society, to which An-sky was affiliated, took up components from the anti-Semitic argument, and interpreted the idea of the *Kahal* within the Jewish national context as one of the building blocks of liberated Jewish self-government in the spheres of social and national life, as well as in the fields of cultural activity. Dubnow focused on the social history of Hasidism as an example of a successful social and institutional organization, and as a model for organic "togetherness," through which he developed his concept of a community that is established on values of accountability and solidarity, and as a paragon of Jewish diasporic nationalism.[47]

When put on stage, the Hasidic community transcends the Jewish context and relates to the Modernist tradition of mass spectacles, prevalent between the two world wars, as described by Fischer-Lichte.[48] From this perspective, the community on *Habima*'s stage may also be considered as part of the renewed interest in theatrical forms of the chorus on theater stages in Europe during the early decades of the twentieth century, during times in which various emancipating social movements reconceptualized the idea of the civic public. Specifically, *Habima*'s staged community could reflect the revolutionary communist ideologies that both An-sky and Vakhtangov sought to promote.[49] In this respect, the representation of the community as a chorus may also be related to extant notions of solidarity among the Jewish revival movement. At a time of accelerated processes of acculturation and assimilation, Zionist and communist ideologies met at a contact point that stressed the urgency of creating a tightly knit, and apparently unified, community. We can describe this move as an endeavor to resist the inclination toward the large-scale, urban, anonymous, competitive society, and to reassemble around the nostalgic image of the tribal, family-oriented, close-knit, cooperative society.

In contrast to the traditional Jewish sonority issuing from *Habima*'s audio recording, photographs from the staged production documenting the visual *mise-en-scène* of the stage reveal a Modernist theatrical aesthetics, stemming from the expressionistic scenography, the distorted choreography and (symbolic) movement, the tragic body language, exaggerated costumes and masklike makeup of the actors.[50] Alexander Kugel defines the cultural references of Vakhtangov's production: "With all his talent and depth, Vakhtangov deviates from the Jewish spirit . . . the beggars and cripples and monsters belong to the world of Hoffman, Poe, Andreyev. . . . [it is] pouring strange wine in Jewish bottles."[51]

I suppose the "Jewish bottles" that Kugel refers to are the sounds, and the Jewish lore emerging from the stage. Together, the audio-visual spectacle thus conjured a hybrid performance, bringing together modernity and tradition, affection and reflection interwoven to create temporal ambivalence. The Jewish community staged in 1922 depicted a grotesque, distorted image of the Jews: from the beggars and the poor, to the possessed bride. As I show in the following, these sinister, sometimes exaggerated, depictions can also be found in *Habima*'s album, which portrays the Jewish community by aural means as a collective that shares melodic contours and speech patterns.

The Speech Community:
The Rise-Fall Contour in Speech and Melody

When the curtain opened at the beginning of the performance, it revealed a group of "*Batlonim*," literally "beggars," that represent the comic stereotype of the Jewish layabout who spends most of his time in the synagogue, always available for making up the number (*minyan*) required for religious services or for prayer.[52] On stage, some *Batlonim* gathered around a table in an old synagogue; others were dozing into sleep while allegedly reading *Gemarah*; in the forefront of the stage three beggars sang and conversed. In the recording, the choral singing of the *Batlonim* transforms, in a kind of glissando, into vivid storytelling that unfolds in the form of dialogue. Three *Batlonim* recount parables about renowned Hasidic figures, such as, Reb Shmelke of Nikolsburg, and Reb Dovidl of Talna. They complete each other's stories, by adding details and by inserting vocal interjections in reaction to the parables.

Their dialogue, I argue, transcends its evident dramatic function, becoming a theatrical enactment of local Jewish oral traditions. The speech patterns that were performed on the stage, according to An-sky's written stage directions, mime various typical Jewish pitches often attributed to the Ashkenazi communities in the *shtetls* of the Russian Pale of Settlement.

The rendering of a specific cultural orbit through phonic enactment of language falls within Dell Hymes's term "speech community," broadly defined as the shared rules for the conduct and interpretation of speech.[53] The following dialogue from the opening of the play exemplifies some of the audible elements of the Jewish "speech community":

> FIRST BATLON: [*in the manner of a storyteller*] Reb Dovidl of Talna, may his merits protect us, had a golden chair on which was carved: "David, King of Israel, lives forever." [*pause*]

> SECOND BATLON: [*in the same manner*] Reb Yisroel of Rizhin, of blessed memory lived like a monarch an orchestra of twenty-four musicians played at his table and when he traveled his carriage never had less than six horses.

> THIRD BATLON: [*with enthusiasm*] And they say that Reb Shmuel of Kaminaka wore golden slippers. [*Entranced*] Golden slippers![54]

This dramatic text manifests some perceptible features of the typical Jewish speech style, namely, the use of anecdote to lead off an argument, citations of significant Rabbis, and energetic speech gestures. Other elements of Jewish speech unfold as the dialogue progresses—the repetition of rhetorical questions ("That's obvious! Who can't see that for himself?"), and argumentative stances ("you are mistaken! True greatness must be suitable bedecked"). The typical Jewish speech is also apparent in the way the *Batlonim* prolong the last syllables of heightened words, as customary in Talmudic chants. Occasionally, the *Batlonim* insert vocal interjections, characteristic of spoken Yiddish, such as *ayi-yai-yai*! In between spoken replicas the beggars interject as a chorus intoning wordless Hasidic tunes in nonverbal syllables such as "Ya-ba-bam," "Aah-aah-aah!," or "Doy-doy-doy." The *Batlonim* repeat certain phrases in their text ("Who knows! Who knows!") in order to emphasize the rhythm of the text; finally, they recite the text in a "rise-fall" spoken melodic contour, characteristic of Yiddish, and discussed extensively later in this subchapter.

As Hymes's idea of the "speech community" suggests, the speech of the *Batlonim* defines a community, not in terms of a single language used, but of a repertoire—a set of ways of speaking that infuses speech styles, phonology, and discourse patterns. The *Batlonim* in *Habima*'s opening act spoke Hebrew infused with Russian Yiddish accents that connected them to the trilingual culture and the Ashkenazic vernacular of the *shtetl* represented on stage.

The vivid dialogue of the *Batlonim* in the recording demonstrates the incorporation of residues from the East European multilingual environment within the Hebrew language. Yiddish, as Ken Friedman notices, is like a dybbuk; it haunted the evolution of Modern Hebrew.[55] Friedman terms the appropriation of the musicality of Yiddish colloquial speech by Hebrew "innovation by translation." Such appropriation, according to him, involves a cross-linguistic adaptation that creates Hebrew performances permeated by Yiddish speech contours. Indeed, the actors in the recording present the absorption of phonological and grammatical elements from Yiddish.

From this perspective, the Hebrew enactment of the drama stages vocal residues, ghosts of Ashkenazi culture. The *Batlonim*—liminal characters of layabouts—embody this hybrid, in-between phonological performance that reflects the multilingual realm of its time. As a theatrical chorus of mendicants, they stage a debased being in the form of a diasporic phonology that cannot be attributed to a cohesive corpus, but is constantly depicted as dynamic repertoire of sounds in between two worlds: Yiddish and Hebrew. In *Habima*'s audio performance, this notion is manifested by the constant shift performed by the *Batlonim* from declamatory speech to melodious singing.

The transition from recitation to singing was typical of itinerant Jewish entertainers—known as *Badkhonim*—who used to perform at weddings, holidays, and other festivities that hosted folk entertainment. Recitation and singing—or, in Yiddish, *Tsu zingen un tsu zogn* (צו זינגען און צו זאָגן)—lay at the core of their performative poetics. The flux between singing and declamation, and the transformation of speech into melody, was one of the dominant features of their performance. The tradition of the *Badkhn* goes back to the Second Temple in Jerusalem (530 BCE–70 CE), whereby their performative recitation practices followed the reading of the Torah, stratifying the liturgy with an exegetic textual layer in the form of melodious speech. The melodies attributed to the text correlated with the recited lyrics, thus becoming an essential part of their enactment, and, assisted the performers in memorizing the text. These melodies were often borrowed from familiar liturgies and prayers.[56] Much like *Habima*'s actors, the Jewish itinerant *Badkhn* was not informed by musical notations. The synagogue, the Jewish home, and the street furnished his sonic resources.

Vakhtangov adapted this Jewish tradition onto the Modernist theater stage. The *Batlonim*'s vocal theatrical approach amplifies the significance of the tones and melodic gestures in decoding their parables. They charge their speech with pace and meaning; explain the stories they recite through vocal expression and by accentuating their tonal range. Prince Sergei Volkonsky, a theater director at the Russian Imperial Theaters between 1899–1902 who taught theoretical lessons and practical workshops on stage speech and diction at *Habima*'s dramatic studio, articulated the mixture between Modernist and Jewish elements. With specific relation to *Habima*'s performance, Volkonsky asks: "How much of this is 'art' and how much is 'race'?"[57] What Volkonsky identifies as "race" are stereotypical Jewish elements that are rendered into the Modernist staged language.

The actors' stylized speech, indeed, turns out to be one of the most prominent loci whereby the combination of tradition and Modernist art reverberates. The actors in the recording deliver a melodic contour of speech that defines much of the musicality of Yiddish parole, and is usually referred to as "the rise-fall" intonation contour. Initially theorized by U. Weinreich, and then elaborated by Zelda Kahan-Newman, the rise-fall intonation contour may be assigned to a sentence, or even to one word that breaks into two units: the first receiving a rising pitch and the second taking a falling one. The rise-fall intonation, Kahan-Newman explains, transforms a declarative into an interrogatory sentence, thus giving it the meaning of a rhetorical question.[58]

The actors' rise-fall speech intonation conveys a prominent element in cosmic Hasidic thought, also reverberating in the choral singing of "*Mipnei Ma*": The theme of the descent of the Jewish individual soul and communal being as a necessary phase in the processes of its rising toward the infinite. This particular rhythm of speech, which characterizes significant Hasidic figures on the stage, renders the articulation of language, as well as its pauses and respiration, as a conceptual space of communality. How, then, does the spoken language on stage, and in the audio recording, define this locus of communality?

The recording of *The Dybbuk* emphasizes the theatricalizing of the rise-fall speech contour through its melodious enactment in Hebrew, pronounced in a modern Sephardic dialect. Thus, while the melody of the language associates the fictional world with the diasporic Ashkenazi (Hasidic) culture, the dialect of the characters clearly bespeaks the Zionist language renewal interfused with the envisioned homeland of the Jewish people in Israel. The tension between the two dialects provides an outlook on the transformation processes, and perhaps on the fault lines of the traditional Jewish multilingual stratification.

In 1965, when *Habima* recorded this sort of stylized diasporic speech, the actors were all well assimilated in Israel. While phonic residues of mother tongue tend to remain as indicators of immigrant identity, the salience of these sonic markers may vary in degree and intensiveness. *Habima* recorded *The*

Dybbuk forty-three years after its Moscow premier, and thirty-four years after joining the Jewish endeavor to create a monolingual Jewish community in Palestine/Israel. To what extent does the self-evident Jewish pitch presented in the audio recording reflect the cultural world depicted on stage, and to what degree did the actors theatricalize their pronunciation to evoke the cultural orbit from which they emerged? There is an element of anachronism in this query: while the Hebrew language in its (Israeli) Sephardic pronunciation portrayed *Habima* as part of the Zionist cultural enterprise, its later incarnation, as manifest in the 1965 enactment of *The Dybbuk*, compelled the actors to give voice to the sort of sonority associated with the Diaspora, from which they wished to distance themselves in order to conform with the "native" Israeli.

As Benjamin Harshav argues, modernizing Jews sought to dissociate themselves from their old identity, and this was also expressed through speech: "The individual tried to repress in his own emotions and behavior every manifestation of the negative 'we' (don't yell like a Jew, don't be pushy, don't talk with your hands etc.)."[59] Yet, elements from this distinct diasporic vocality can be heard in the 1965 recording. The evincing multilingual sound of *Habima*'s vocal performance stages the seemingly paradoxical feat in which the new Hebrew voice is traced through vestiges of the traditional diasporic Ashkenazi speech.

The Heterophonic Chorus: Noise and Disorder on Stage

In the recording, the theatrical choruses evolve as the play progresses: the first act of the play presents the *Batlonim* and the *minyan* in the synagogue; the second act of the play summons the village square before the anticipated wedding, in what seems to be a theatrical depiction of a typical noisy Ukrainian Jewish town. Sounds of dancing and Klezmer music, and the muffled racket of a hustle from Sender, the bride's father's, house permeate the stage. The community celebrating the oncoming wedding is further represented by the women competing among themselves to dance with the bride, begging to get closer to her. The bride is never alone on the stage; she is always accompanied by a group of women and, at times, by Reb Mendel and other members of the marital arrangement, who are celebrating in dance the forthcoming wedding and enveloping her with celebratory sounds. At the epicenter of this act lies the *Batlonim*'s dance with Leah, in which they ecstatically twirl the bride-to-be.

After the dybbuk invades the bride, and following his debut vocal performance among the community, the third act opens in the home of Reb

Azriel of Miropol. Around the table, a group of six or seven Hasidic men are gathered. Some of them sit and read Psalms, the others converse. Upon the entrance of the Rabbi, the group begins to harmonize its elocution by responding to his melodious speech with an affirmative response, and later by joining his singing of a Hasidic *nigun*; when he pauses his singing they also become silent; when he preaches or solemnly intones a tune, they all listen. The forth act of the play features Reb Azriel surrounded by the *Dayanim* (religious judges) Shimshon and Michael. In a vivid conversation, they all discuss how to tame and exorcise the dybbuk.

Volkonsky addresses the communal experience that is reflected from the chorus in *The Dybbuk*:

> I can still hear the lamenting and gloomy voices, the melodies of liturgy and dance; I can still visualize the rustling spinning dirty Caftans, while stomping and striking their finger up—what a magnificent adhesive chorus of the poor and miserable! . . . This vocal orchestration is unprecedented to anything we have yet seen here. In an inconceivable way the spoken word transforms by the force of emotion into a lamentation, and the lamentation—into *nigun* (melody).[60]

The different choruses prevalent in the performance, as Volkonsky writes, issue sounds that reflect a religious sonic repository that defines, by its very practice, a community that shares rituals, melodies, and speech patterns. In 1922, this sonority reproduced a community that materialized in the fictional theatrical depiction of the vocal organization in synagogues, and it yielded an image that resonated with the semblance of the masses suffused by the communist revolutionary atmosphere in Moscow at the time in which the performance was initially produced.

The community represented in *The Dybbuk* by the different choruses on stage presents various modes of sonic organization: within the space of the traditional synagogue rendered in the first act, the ingathering of the synagogue presents a coordinated, joint recitation as a chorus of men that upholds the sonic realm that prevails throughout the prayer. In addition to synchronized recitation and singing, there are many moments in the recording that manifest a heterophonic chorus, that is, simultaneous, disorganized melodies uttered by the participants in prayer, as well as jumbled exclamations and vocal interjections of the community in response to the main actions taking place on stage. In the cacophonous moments of nonsynchronized and discombobulated voices of the crowd, in which emotions are played out on stage, during prayer, or in reaction to the depicted dramatic occurrences, the sonority on the stage seems to correspond with the derogatory characterization of Jewish parole, as a speech style characterized by loudness, and prolixity. As Ruth HaCohen has demonstrated, when voicing their soundscape publicly, Jewish congregations were stereotypically depicted as raucous, in polar opposition to the Christian euphonious ones.[61]

These somewhat noisy voices can be heard, for example, when the men on stage retreat to recite individual prayers based on Psalms that are uttered within a shared space. In these moments, the vocal community on stage is formed by individual characters that join their voices together into a uniform expression in a concrete place and time, as part of a shared social doctrine. Whether sung or spoken, the vocal community represented on stage is premised on mutual listening, and coordination that entails not just the simultaneous movements of the vowels and syllables, but also the shared state of mind of the performers.

The group also functions as a chorus in its reaction to the parables told on stage. At times, they speak in one clear voice, at other moments each member of the choir on the stage answers individually, staging the plurality of voices in an allegedly spontaneous speech that imitates varied responses, such as those heard in any social gathering. The lively, uncoordinated discourse among the *Batlonim* is evident, especially when they utter the public prayers of the Psalms, each at his individual pace. At the end of the second act, following the traditional meal for the poor, when Leah is performing her possession, and the messenger declares, "A dybbuk has entered her," the entire community on stage reacts by uttering disorganized sounds, creating sonic turmoil.

In accordance with Vakhtangov's expressionistic theatrical approach, the choreographed group on the stage performs nonnaturalistic vocal gestures: their Jewish "noisy" sonority is accentuated in the performance. Volkonsky addresses this element in *The Dybbuk*: "Even the most exaggerated contortion does not reveal to be *ridiculous,* submerged in profound sincere emotion, as deep as past human generations. An ancient voice stems from these Caftans, a secret depth that ascends to our contemporary present."[62]

Deeply moved by the expressionistic stylization of Jewish sonority, Volkonsky is reacting to the pervading criticism of *Habima*'s expressionistic style. What is especially striking for me in this observation is Volkonsky's description of Jewish sonority as "ridiculous." When I played this recording to academic and nonacademic audiences (between 2014 and 2016), many listeners commented that this form of speech, as well as the theatricalizing of Jewish prayer, seems to render this recording as "an object of ridicule."

The fact that the same adjective was shared by Volkonsky in the 1920s and by contemporary listeners bespeaks a bathetic ethnic representation in Vakhtangov's performance. Perhaps the difference lies in the attitude toward what were considered as ridiculous vocal elements. During the 1920s, this typical sonority was part of a wider expressionistic artistic approach; however, nowadays this may seem as a travesty. And in 1965? When *Habima* recorded these voices, they had gathered a treasure house of a Jewish diasporic past, from which the dominant Zionist culture sought to distance itself. Do the actors in the recording express the Zionist rejection of this declined world? Did the listeners to the 1965 album perceive this sonority as ludicrous?

At this point, we must distinguish between the community issuing from the 1922 stage and that resounding in the 1965 vinyl record. Naomi Seidman identifies the ghostly figure of the dybbuk as a manifestation of the concrete semiotic crisis of East European Jewry at the beginning of the twentieth century. The dybbuk, Seidman explains, portrays the profound tension between the traditional world and modern creeds affected by the emancipatory and assimilatory processes that accompanied the urbanization and industrialization of Europe.[63] Under such circumstances, the accountability of the individual to communal institutions, and to national social structures, underwent a re-examination.

Habima staged the play at times in which there was a growing need among European Jewry to loosen the burdensome ties of individuals to their community, as well as great temptation to withdraw from the community of belonging altogether. Issues of integration, assimilation, and unification may also be identified in the vocal organization of the represented community. Volkonsky addresses the tension between community and individual: "Despite all the communal and the consolidated—how different they are from each other! Each one according to his shades and each one to himself—and yet, they are all together and are all as one."[64] Within the chaotic, varied reactions of the crowd, Volkonsky discerns a community in which individuals may express themselves in more than one voice, and yet form a social body.

In Plural Voice: Performing Dissociation

Until this point, we have engaged with aural manifestations of communality in *The Dybbuk*. In what follows, I would like to show how individual iterations are shaped in this recording as dissociative utterances that interject into the social sphere and disrupt its cohesiveness, in order to reaffirm and enhance social solidarity.

The tension between individual and community is translated in *The Dybbuk* into aural gender-based relations. Against the predominant male vocal community represented by the religious choruses, the play positions fundamentally opposite vocal instantiations embodied by three individual feminine aural performers: (1) Gnessia—the sorrowful woman lamenting in the first act, (2) Leah in her possessed state, and (3) Ḥanan, who was portrayed in the 1922 production by a female actress. I argue that in their few dramatic incarnations, these three voices do not speak for themselves, but are rather shaped as voices that function as vehicles for an identity other than their own. That is, rather than give voice to a fictional, idiosyncratic character, they perform a body-voice pattern that functions as a sonic repository and speaks in more than one voice.

In the early manifestations of *Habima*'s production, the role of Ḥanan was performed by Miriam Elias cross-dressed as a young Yeshiva student. As Yair Lipshitz writes, the casting of a female to play the role of Ḥanan is a prefiguration of one of the dominant attributes of the dybbuk: a masculine presence within a female body.[65] It underscores sexual differences and gender plurality through Ḥanan's theatrical identity. In the recording, Ḥanan's voice is played by Zvi Friedland. Although the gender ambiguity is not as salient when a man plays the role of Ḥanan, in the recording Ḥanan's voice is rendered as a gentle voice with an inner trembling that charges it with a sense of gender ambiguity.

The second female character to appear on stage is Gnessia, played in the 1922 production by Chayale Grober (1905–1964) and in the 1965 recording by Tamar Robins (1898–1984). Gnessia enters the synagogue weeping, lamenting over the illness of her dying daughter. The elevation of her pitch intensifies in tandem with her emotions, gradually shifting from dramatic recitation to heightened melodious speech. The woman approaches the Holy Ark with firm steps, pushes aside the curtain and, in a ritualistic cry, pours out her troubles. In an interview with actress and singer Chayale Grober, she reconstructed the creation of this scene.[66] She recalls Vakhtangov asking her to play the scene with no words but only through melodies that express the meaning of her words. Grober explains that she took inspiration for her part from the synagogal "Yom Kippur" prayer she remembered since childhood.[67] Gnessia's woeful lamentation is followed by a chorus praying Psalms in a distinct weeping and pleading tone, evoking an exaggerated heterophonic synagogue public prayer.

This recorded monologue demonstrates the kind of anachronism introduced by the audio recordings, especially with regard to the process of canonization: Grober's monologue, which featured in *Habima*'s 1922 production, apparently alluded to the melodious rendition of Rovina's lamentation in her role as the Messiah's mother in the second version of *The Eternal Jew* that premiered in 1923, discussed in the previous chapter. However, the question of which version took precedence seems to be marginal to the dominant aural image prevalent in these two performances: the feminine lamentation as a liminal intervention in the public sphere.

As discussed in the previous chapter, lamenting is considered a vocal practice predominantly carried out by women, who are considered not only to convey emotions but also to perform an action by which they come close to the world of the dead spirit. Galit Hasan-Rokem associates this risky position with feminine figures such as the Pythia at Delphi and the witch of Endor, who tread borderlands between the dead and the living, and communicate with voices from the afterlife.[68] In this sense, Gnessia's lamentation is a sonic precursor to Rovina's performance in her role as the possessed bride Leah.

Leah/Rovina's possession is vocally rendered through the depiction of her body that ventriloquizes a male voice, dissociated from its own female identity. With the spirit of Leah's dead lover occupying her body, the young bride-to-be becomes a mediator for an individual expression of a female constrained within patriarchal socialization rituals in women's lives. It underpins the profound tension between the need of the subject to take control over his actions and identity, and the controlling institutions of traditional social systems. Possessed by the lost spirit of the dybbuk, Leah submits her presence to storing its voice, surrendering her identity to becoming the mouthpiece for her dead beloved.

The Jewish variant for the dissociative trance pattern of identity disorder is manifested in legends of the dybbuk that most commonly ascribe the impregnation of a woman's body with the restless spirit of a deceased man.[69] Yoram Bilu argues for a psychological and sociological explanation of the dybbuk as a means of expressing individual deviance from the social order (particularly, though not solely, in the sexual sphere), and then the taming of this deviance and the reestablishment of social and religious control via exorcism.[70] Leah can reclaim her voice and express her frustration toward the patriarchal confinements only in someone else's voice.

Both Leah's and Gnessia's vocal performances fall under Steven Connor's definition of "the vocalic body," which cites "the idea—which can take the form of dream, fantasy, ideal, theological doctrine or hallucination—of a surrogate or secondary body, a projection of a new way of having or being a body, formed and sustained out of the autonomous operations of the voice."[71] The vocalic body functions as a container that resonates the sound system of the community depicted on the stage. When Leah becomes possessed she becomes a body with two voices; a body that functions as a site of an identity crisis. Furthermore, the vocalic body manifests the self-annihilation of the speaker in favor of an idea or a doctrine. This idea seems to be especially appropriate when discussing the Hasidic religious community depicted on the stage. The Hasidic liturgical practices demand the immersion of the worshipper in the act of prayer. Much like the state of possession, the Hasidic prayer involves the whole body, through vocal practices and dance. Connor's notion of the "vocalic body" defines Ḥanan's corporeality in terms of gender construction, as a capacious medium that archives and subverts this patrilineal textual and performative tradition. Thus, the vocalic body provides a general descriptive basis for the rhetorical function of the tensions between the performance of individual feminine voices, gender identity, and the community to which the performing body is tied.

Leah's vocalic body, however, does not merely serve as a vehicle for the dybbuk's voice, but also partakes in the act of possession.[72] When Leah speaks in Ḥanan's voice, she composes her presence as plural, and represents her stance against the confining social restrains of her community. Bilu explains that the phenomenon of the dybbuk emphasizes the collective (or controlling) level of the individual motivation that leads to the state of possession by the dybbuk. He contends that the implications of dybbuk possession and exorcism were too far-reaching to be exhausted by the aspect of the individual. The rectification of deviances often bore profound reverberations in the social world and contributed to its reorganization. In this manner, deviance is harnessed to enhance social control and conformity in the community. Symptoms representing aberrant wishes that, if directly expressed, would have threatened the very foundations of Jewish life were exorcised and subdued into a conformity-enhancing agency. This dialectical transformation could only have taken place in traditional communities that monitored and governed the entire living environment of their members. Since this process necessarily involves an elaborate, coordinated interplay between individuals and societal institutions, the analysis should encompass both levels.

The transgression of the impassable divide between the living and the dead, symbolized by Ḥanan's voice issuing from his beloved, proves fatal for Leah's body. In this respect, the plot of The Dybbuk does not present the viability of the communal institutions, but reflects the intolerance of the conservative Jewish community to deviance. The composition of communality entails the attainment of the first person plural—the capacity of the individual to include himself in a "we," to integrate his free will and individuality within this idea of plurality, and to actually be able to incorporate a range of common affinities. The fashioning of the self as part of a common requires a degree of proximity and sharing that may accommodate multiple venues for each to settle in.

Documented cases of dybbuk possession feature in Jewish sources from the mid-sixteenth century throughout the first decades of the twentieth century.[73] The disappearance of the social phenomenon of the dybbuk during the first half of the twentieth century is attributed to the disintegration of the Jewish traditional communities in Europe due to physical extermination and emigration, and due to modernization. Interestingly, the disappearance of the dybbuk as a social phenomenon correlates with its emergence in the orbit of the Yiddish and Hebrew theater during the 1920s.

Habima's performance continued to stage the sounds of East European communities in its performances of Vakhtangov's production between the years 1922 and 1965. Freddie Rokem underlines the reason for this persistent staging of this play in a cultural understanding of the meaning of the dybbuk: a distressed spirit that speaks through the mouth of a living person. "After the Shoah," Rokem explains, "there were six million potential dybbuks haunting the Jewish people, the state of Israel, as well as all of Europe, and maybe other parts of the world too—constantly speaking through survivors."[74] The vocal Jewish communities that reverberate in the recording could possibly bring forth the common cultural backgrounds of significant hegemonic Ashkenazi Jewish societies that ingathered in Israel by marking their shared fate and common tradition.

Where Do We Meet?
The Making of the Acoustic Theatrical Community

During the more than four decades in which *Habima* performed *The Dybbuk*, the show was staged in various theatrical and social spaces, with the aim of reaching both rural and urban Jewish communities dispersed around the globe. Touring around the country, the troupe performed the play in all kinds of improvised locations—ranging from cinemas to communal dining halls in Kibbutzim—adapting the stage to the venue in which they acted. Wherever *Habima* traveled with *The Dybbuk*, the voices and sounds of the nineteenth-century Brinnitz synagogue journeyed with them. The flexibility of the production became an essential part of the performance, and the accessibility of the public to the theater-surrogate was crucial for the company. Encapsulated in this artistic statement is the idea that the potential of the theatrical performance to become a significant emotional and social event depends upon the degree of communication between actors and spectators and their ability to establish a shared experience, by the agency of the enacted texts and melodies.

What sort of shared experience is formed by listening to a radio production? This query spans beyond the phenomenological or perceptual inquiry. It seeks to underpin the reciprocal conditions for imagining a Jewish community by means of aural production, and entails scrutinizing the significance of the aural dimension in establishing meanings, initially in the public theater-houses, and eventually through the radio waves in the private sphere. Thus, by outlining the discrepancies between the stage manifestations of *The Dybbuk* and its radio adaptation we might, perhaps, trace how the play metamorphosed, how the very listening to the particular sounds emerging from the stage has altered, and how our understanding of the relationship between the individual and the community has changed.

The 1965 radio broadcast of *The Dybbuk* gave voice to the bygone aural world, possibly bringing this sonority into every household.[75] Such an image of an Israeli (Ashkenazi) community listening to its diasporic home-community enhances the historical role played by the radio among Jewish immigrants in Palestine (and also in the United States) during the 1920s. Oren Soffer notes that since most of the Jews in Palestine were immigrants seeking to retain their connections to the worlds they had left behind, they became aware of global radio and went to great lengths to receive it by means of progressive technological developments (such as high frequency waves that enabled remote reception).[76] The fictional community reverberating in *The Dybbuk* recording linked the listeners to a shared theatrical space, a historic time, while also marking their irrevocable separation from this environment. Thus, the radio instantiation of *The Dybbuk*, rendered forty-three years after the Moscow premiere of An-sky's play, no longer reflected the recorded communities, nor did it give voice to the Zionist striving for a cohesive community. With the diminishing of the sonority depicted in the play, this aural tradition was recreated as a rhetorical nostalgic object for lamenting East European Jewry, and for framing the diasporic sonorities that the emerging Israeli culture wished to disengage itself from.[77]

The social function of the dybbuk as a communal vehicle for venting distress—a sort of "theatrical talking cure"—is also apparent in An-sky's play. As Safran writes, the plot of the play resides in the performative recounting of the ethnographic practices. The co-presence of actors and audience, according to Safran, renders the encounter between a loquacious storyteller and his listeners at the center of the performance. In light of this, how can we assess this relationship vis-à-vis the radio production of the play? I would like to suggest that the transformation of *The Dybbuk* production from page to stage and, finally, into an audio recording reflects the evolution in the perception of the vocal communities represented, and in the roles played by these communities in shaping the soundscape during the formative years of the State of Israel.

R. Murray Schafer defines environments in which sound plays a significant role in spatially and temporally outlining the commonalities of their inhabitants by coining the notion of "acoustic community."[78] In an acoustic community, sound plays a crucial role in creating regular intervals, in terms of daily and seasonal cycles, as well as socially and culturally in terms of shared activities, rituals, and other institutions. According to this idea, when a group of strangers gather in a performance space and share the listening experience, they become—for the time they inhabit that space—a community structured by sound and silence. Control over the production of sound, therefore, implies control over the social organization attending to the soundscape. Deprived of the experience of physical togetherness, the radio listeners experience the plot of *Habima*'s performance only through the materiality of the actors' voices in their own individual domestic settings.

How, then, does sound link together members of the community, and how does the aural dimension partake in producing habitual ways of thinking? Barry Truax argues that sounds, and sound organization ingrained in a community, are aural elements that keep the members of the community "in touch" with each other.[79] To follow this train of thought, sounds, voices, or music, for instance, not only enwrap the perceiving subject; they also, in a way, invade his body. Within this body, the sounds of the vocal community transform into a sort of dybbuk that possesses its contemporary listeners. The shared singing of the choruses performing Jewish melodies identified with life in Eastern European Jewish communities, reverberated in Kol Yisrael and transformed the audience into an acoustic community. However, as a late manifestation of a performative instantiation, displaced from its cultural and historical contexts, these sounds transcend the documentation of this diasporic acoustic community, reflecting a nostalgic longing. Thus, *Habima*'s recording articulates a community that is formed by the twin movements of shared sonic associations on the one hand, and, on the other, of their co-presence as listeners. I call them "movements" because neither domain is manifested to be stable, and because they unfold as incomplete processes in the midst of their configuration.

In what way does the community formed in a theater-house differ from the one formed by sharing a listening experience? Jeffrey Sconce explains that radio, from its very inception, has been accounted to foster social alienation, rising from the ability of the medium to separate and isolate even as it enables contact and communication, and thus generate an aural and social "ghostland."[80] The recording of Vakhtangov's production of *The Dybbuk* reached the audience as a virtual listening community. This recording does not form an acoustic community that assembles in a temporally shared space, and therefore it may be perceived in opposition to the vocal communities temporarily woven by *Habima*'s stage performance. The question "Where do we meet?" seems to be crucial here to forge the idea of the audience as enunciating a community, and to carve shared venues for social events that establish, as well as manifest, social commonality.

The audio recording of *The Dybbuk* exemplifies a mechanism of social circulation that does not depend upon the co-presence of its members. Unlike the vocal communities congregating during *Habima*'s stage performance, for the acoustic community proximity is contingent when listening to the audio recording.[81] The community in radio-theater does not materialize in the form of a physical assembly, but through the viral processing of the aural image of the lost vocal communities depicted in the recording. It forms an "imagined community," to borrow Benedict Anderson's coinage, which shares cultural

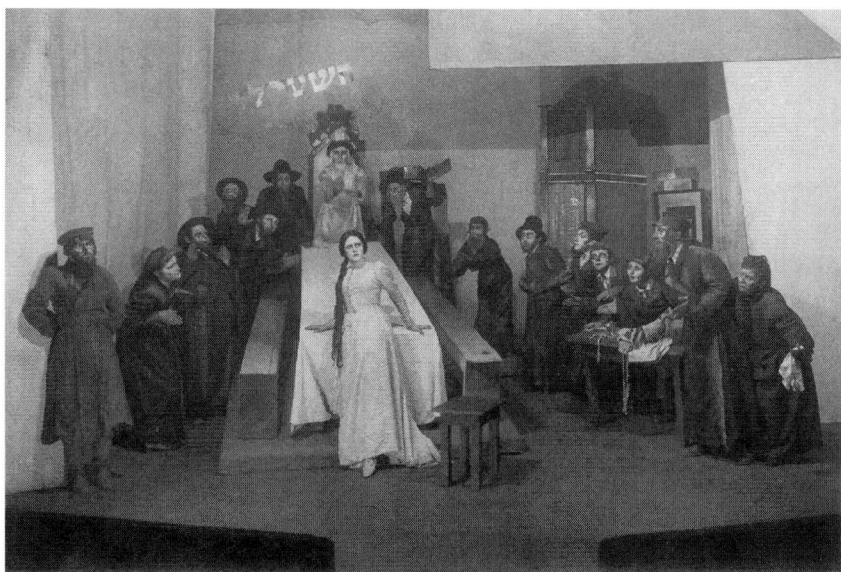

Figure 2.3. The exorcism of the dybbuk, from *Habima*'s 1922 performance. Courtesy of *Habima* National Theater and the Israeli Center for the Documentation of the Performing Arts.

and social codes; this community grows and develops through creation and validation of its individuals qua community, without depending on territorial autonomy.

The sounds of the demised Jewish communities, replayed on the stage and then broadcast on the radio, thus mark a twilight zone between two worlds: the real and the fictitious, the imagined and the actual. In this sense, the broadcast of *The Dybbuk* presented a sonic world shared by significant parts of the Jewish community in Israel, which, presumably, was less familiar to the non-European sectors of this community. But, perhaps, even more prominently, the sonic world encoded in its melodies and speech figures functioned simultaneously as a venue for collective lamentation over a bygone world and tradition; as an object of ridicule depicting the premodern and pre-Zionist Jewish diasporic culture, and as a nostalgic performance of the aspiration of the Zionist *Gemeinschaft*.

Figure 2.4. *The Dybbuk* 1965 Audio Album cover (produced by CBS).

Figure 2.5. Two Batlonim, from *Habima*'s performance of *The Dybbuk* (1922). Courtesy of *Habima* National Theater and the Israeli Center for the Documentation of the Performing Arts.

CHAPTER THREE

"Who Will Save Us?"

Hebrew Specters and the Performativity of Cultural Rupture in *The Golem*

Habima was proclaimed Israel's National Theater—a designation entailing, inter alia, far-reaching financial implications—on the occasion of its fortieth anniversary on October 12, 1958.[1] With three of its towering icons—Hanna Rovina (in 1956), Yehoshua Bertonov (1959), and Aharon Meskin (1960)— receiving the Israel Prize (the most prestigious award granted by the state) the troupe's persistent efforts to gain public and political acknowledgment as a constitutive force in the emerging Israeli national culture proved fruitful.[2] Despite its being rooted in the diasporic Jewish culture of Eastern Europe, and notwithstanding the Modernist Russian training of the theater, *Habima* became the epitome of the artistic energy and creativity yielded by the Zionist project, manifesting the enduring tenacity of the Hebrew culture across continents and throughout national calamities. This "role," however, demanded that *Habima* be garbed in regalia appropriate to the Zionist ideals of the new Israeli Jewish identity. Among other things, this meant that the actors needed to jettison markers of diasporic Ashkenazi culture, and assume attributes of the local contemporary prevailing ideals.

During its first four decades, long after it migrated from its European abode, *Habima* performed its Moscow repertoire in Israel as well as in its tours around the globe, heralding Modernist artistic values, even as late as the mid-1930s whereby regimes of darkness disseminated across Europe, threatening to cover the whole continent. The rupture wedged between *Habima*'s cultural and artistic roots and its Zionist vocation was thus inherent and manifest in its appearances.

The breaking away from diasporic Jewish culture was also evident from the actors' remodeling their Hebrew speech, both on and offstage. In order to accommodate to Israeli Zionist local ideals, the members of the troupe needed to camouflage their East European accents and adjust their speech accent and intonation to the local vocabulary and elocution style. These aural attributes, however, were never completely erased. Thus, the aural shaping of language became an expression of the national and artistic fault line under which the troupe created and acted.[3]

Speech is a common locus in which ambivalence toward displacement hypostatizes, especially through aural residues from the speakers' mother tongues and vernaculars. This was also the case in the immigrant society assembled in the land of Israel during its formative years. The ingathering of Jewish immigrants from various diasporas spurred the need to assimilate the Hebrew language, and to standardize its articulation.[4] The vocation of Zionist ideology to return to the "biblical" homeland and to set the Hebrew language apart from its Jewish diasporic expressions led to the decision to reject the Ashkenazi dialect that was widespread among immigrants due to its considerable proximity—in accent and intonation—to Yiddish, and thus favor the modern Sephardic pronunciation as the official elocutionary style of Israeli Hebrew. Thus, apart from a subtropical climate, and cultural and social hurdles, even those immigrants who were proficient in Hebrew needed to overcome a significant language barrier. This stumbling block, I contend, is metonymic of the dissociative condition that many Jewish newcomers in Palestine, and later in Israel, experienced between their familiar diasporic existence, and their new conditions as immigrants in the national "homeland."

The discrepancy born out of Eastern European Jews' wavering along symbolic and actual spaces in between two worlds during the 1920s marks trajectories of migration constituted by temporal, cultural, and social breaks. This chapter will focus on the aural representation of this catalytic hiatus. The fractured hinge, I argue, is manifested in *Habima*'s performance through an aural expression of "the counter-rhythmic rupture," to draw on Walter Benjamin's terms, as a "caesura, in which, along with harmony, every expression simultaneously comes to a standstill, in order to give free reign to an expressionless power inside all artistic media."[5] This liminal space vacillating in between worlds, I argue, provided a fertile ground for the invocation of latent forces embedded in the performance of the Hebrew language.

In the previous chapter I engaged with the various articulations of the "rise-fall" melodious pattern. In the present chapter, I derail from the melodious line, and focus on the aural materialization of the emptied interval that amalgamates the "rise" with the "fall"—as apparent in a 1961 radio variation of *Habima*'s 1925 performance of *The Golem*.[6] Regarding the creation of the golem as a figuration of "the revival of the Hebrew language," I argue that *Habima*'s theatrical shaping of Hebrew in *The Golem* marks a paradigm shift in their approach to dramatic recitation that reflects transformation processes entailed in the troupe's experiences of immigration and displacement. Furthermore, as I demonstrate in this chapter, when mediated as ethereal voices broadcast on the radio, the aural reproduction of *The Golem* subsumes a nostalgic reflection on the revival of the Hebrew language, this time as one that resuscitates the obliterated European Jewry.

Throughout this chapter I use various derivatives of the term *ghost* not as an empirical conviction, but rather by way of echoing Jacques Derrida, as a theoretical position that

> does not believe in the sharp distinction between the real and the unreal, the actual and the inactual, the living and the non-living, being and non-being ("to be or not to be," in the conventional reading), in the opposition between what is present and what is not, for example in the form of objectivity.[7]

Spectrality is, thus, identified as that which appears in the space between two ontological categories, and traverse temporalities: it appears in the present to conjure the past (*revenant* in Derrida's terms), announces the future and hence associates with the messianic.

~

On the High Holidays of the Jewish New Year of 1961, Kol Yisrael radio station—which until 1968 monopolized Israel's electronic mass communications media—broadcast a modified version of *Habima*'s 1925 production of *The Golem* in the frame of the popular radio drama program "The Screen Rises."[8] *The Golem*, a dramatic poem in eight scenes written by Halpern Leivick (1888–1962) in Yiddish and translated into Hebrew by Benjamin Kaspi, was adapted to the stage by *Habima*'s actors. This performance was directed by Boris Illich Vershilov (1893–1957), with music composed by Moshe Milner, and scenography designed by Ignaty Nivinsky. Since its premiere in Moscow on March 15, 1925, *The Golem* had been staged approximately 340 times in various venues around the globe, becoming one of *Habima*'s most successful productions, second only to *The Dybbuk*.

Leivick's play *The Golem*, as Danusha V. Goska writes, reworks the plot of a 1909 manuscript attributed to Yudl Rosenberg, that narrates the seventeenth-century legend of Rabbi Judah Loew ben Bezalel, also known as the Maharal, a gifted scholar in mystical, magical, and scientific spheres.[9] The Maharal, so the legend goes, created a manmade creature—a golem—in order to protect the Jewish community of Prague from the violence that was expected to be turned against them due to a blood libel scheme—manifested by the presence of bottles filled with the blood extracted, allegedly, from a Christian boy at the local synagogue and used for baking matzos before Passover. Into this fearful atmosphere, Lievick introduces the Messiah, escorted by Eliyahu the prophet (Eliyahu Hanavie), that arrives in Prague in order to redeem the Jewish community. Wishing to realize deliverance through the manmade golem, the Maharal drives off both the Messiah and Eliyahu the prophet (despite recognizing them), and sends the golem to avenge the perpetrators and thus protect the Jews of Prague. However, when the golem returns from his mission, instead of experiencing embracing gratitude, he faces alienation from the Jewish community and from his creator. The golem then turns his aggression toward the Jews, and is subsequently dismantled by the Maharal.

The 1961 broadcast of *The Golem* on the radio devised *Habima*'s 1925 staged performance as disembodied voices severed from their corporeal anchor. Along with the media transformation, several leitmotifs were also transfigured. In the post-Holocaust Jewish culture of 1961, Leivick's theatrical expression of the desperate generational longing for a redemption that failed to find fulfilment assumed a historical reverberation and different meanings than in 1925. In order to understand the perceptual gap between the voices in the two versions of *The Golem*, I begin my investigation by grounding the cultural mobility of the dramatic structure of *The Golem*. When transposed into radio, the figure of the golem, so I argue, appears as a medium channeling a disembodied voice. The adaptation of the creation of the golem to the radio—a medium that surrogates disembodied voices—is then explored through the hypostatization of the Hebrew language "revival." I probe into the theatrical rendering of *The Golem* by looking into the artistic approach undertaken by *Habima* in this production when shaping the Hebrew language. I conclude my discussion by contextualizing the 1961 radio performance of *The Golem*, and the messianic admonitions for redemption expressed within it. Taking into consideration the cultural and temporal cleft between the two performative instantiations, I ask, what sort of body—corporeal or spectral— did the aural dimension of the performance induce in 1925, and how did this body transfigure in its audio adaptation?

The Golem—A Medium

The Golem was the last performance created by *Habima* under the auspices of the Moscow Art Theater—their artistic incubator—before they left Moscow, heading toward five years of roaming. The troupe decided to stage Leivick's drama during the recessive period of 1924–25, following the extraordinary achievement of *The Dybbuk*, after Vakhtangov's death, and during days of increasing personal intrigues between its members. These were turbulent days in which the theater was engaged in fractious deliberations concerning their Jewish artistic identity and organizational future. Leivick's play was purchased for *Habima* by Moshe Halevy during his visit to Berlin in 1924. The play was judged to suit the artistic ideology of *Habima*'s repertoire, due to the Jewish historico-mythical character of the drama. Additionally, the play was based on a legend widely recognized from its many popular literary and cinematic adaptations and could, therefore, captivate both Jewish and non-Jewish audiences.

In *Golem: Modern Wars and Their Monsters*, Maya Barzilai shows the diffusion of "the cult of the golem" in Europe, beyond the Jewish world, during the late nineteenth and early twentieth century. Barzilai explains this cultural phenomenon as a reaction to what were considered the "dehumanizing demands of industrial urban life," which dovetailed with alienation from traditional structures of the tightly knit community (the *Gemeinschaft*, in Tönnis's terms).[10] The spreading of the myth of the golem into the sphere of popular culture transpired, according to Barzilai, during World War I, which for many represented—like the figure of the golem—the pernicious potential entailed in technological progress.[11] Indeed, as Gad Yair and Michaela Soyer demonstrate, the employment of the golem as a nodal point that connects mechanical automatization with impious violence is a recurring discursive strategy adopted by mid-nineteenth and early-twentieth-century German theorists in order to criticize the Enlightenment quest for power and control over nature, the striving of modernity for technological and scientific progress, and the capitalistic conception of productivity.[12]

Leivick wrote *The Golem* in 1921 as a dissident dwelling in New York, after escaping from Siberian prison. From his distant exile, he observed his homeland burning in the flames and bloodshed of the Bolshevist revolutions (1917–20); he witnessed socialist ideals transformed into brutality; emancipatory visions effectively malformed into totalitarianism.[13] His dramatic adaptation of the golem from Prague legend latently interweaves these themes within the archetypical fabric of the lore: the creation of a manmade creature to garner power, the animation of a clay anthropoid that subsequently develops an autonomous will that fatefully turns against its master, leading to personal and social destruction.

Yet Leivick's rendering of the golem deviates from conventional depictions of the legend: Firstly, his golem is not mute; it is programmed with Hebrew speech and throughout the play utters it to express its necessities. Secondly, this golem is represented as a mechanical creature endowed with memory: it can learn language; it remembers its emotions. Thirdly, this golem seems, from the very beginning, to stray from its programmed behavior, to transcend its common depiction as a half-breed creature that possesses no more than nascent primitive emotions. This golem is shown to develop sexual drives; it can feel sorrow and happiness, and can even show compassion and remorse. Highlighting the human traits of this mechanically fabricated redeemer, Leivick's portrayal of the golem emphasizes, above all, the urgent need of the Jewish community to generate a savior that will protect it.

In the post-revolutionary political atmosphere in the Soviet Union of 1925, following Vladimir Lenin's death (on January 21, 1924), after Leon Trotsky was dismissed as the chief executive officer of the Revolutionary Military Council and Joseph Stalin established his sovereignty, the lore of "The Golem" seemed more relevant than ever. These days were specifically dramatic for the Jewish community in the Soviet Union, which faced immediate threats leveled by the Jewish section of the Communist Party that endeavored to close down Jewish institutions. Within this political context, the figure of the golem configured a Jewish position that would no longer passively acquiesce to their historical alignment to victimhood, dramatizing the potential alternative of the revival of a combative spirit. In other words, such social transformation processes undergone by the Jewish communities could, therefore, be associated with and imagined through the lore of "The Golem." The apprehension of social-political phenomena through the prism of folk mythology renders the boundaries between the domain of the fictional and the province of the real as unsettled and fluid. Enfolded within this volatility lies the conception of the mythical and its artistic representation as an integral component in the encoding of the social sphere.

However, these sociohistorical and cultural hermeneutical dimensions of Leivick's mythical play were not accessible to its contemporaries. For *Habima's* members, the entwining of Leivick's drama with their present-day reality was not that intuitive. Although familiar with the popular versions of "The Golem," the troupe was unacquainted with its Jewish roots. The theater initially sought to retrieve the Jewish symbolism of the lore of "The Golem" that would shed light on hidden layers of the play that had remained obscure to them. Raikin

Ben-Ari depicts the challenges that the interpretation of Leivick's play posed for the troupe: "One section of the poem made it appear that the author was arguing for physical strength; later on his argument seemed to be quite the opposite. Then again what was the Golem? A prophet? An invisible presence? Material or spiritual? . . . Who were the phantoms?"[14]

In order to gain a better understanding of the play, Baruch Chemerin-sky, assigned to play the role of the Maharal, resorted to his father's domestic library in order to study the figure of the golem in Jewish exegetic literature. He surveyed the myth and the mystical traditions related to it; however, that did not solve the meaning of the golem for *Habima*. The troupe, therefore, decided to leave open the conundrum of "The Golem." Such a decision entailed a rendering of the golem as a flexible signifier, molded by its varied enactments—a figure of "cultural mobility," in Stephen Greenblatt's terms, that accrues meaning out of the cultural, religious, and political ideas issued from the circumstances and the aesthetic network enmeshed in its depiction.[15]

Approaching *The Golem* as an itinerant model on its own merit is central to understanding the transformation of Leivick's drama into a theater performance, as well as the transposition of *Habima*'s theatrical performance to a radio program. Raikin Ben-Ari provides an intriguing visceral metaphor to describe the process of the transformation of Leivick's play from a dramatic poem into a theatrical script:

> The first thing we had to do was perform a radical operation on the poem . . . since we could not find a suitable individual out-side of our ranks to do the job we had to do it ourselves. And the operation was a delicate one indeed . . . So, like surgeons, we wielded our knives—and cut. Of course, what hurt most was to cut one's own part.[16]

Habima flayed Leivick's drama: they first translated it from Yiddish into Hebrew; together, as a team, they transcribed the verse drama into prose, changed the structure of the narrative, while obliterating complete scenes, and preambled the play with an extensive prologue. Rather than as a textural authority, they related to Leivick's drama as part of an ever-changing oral tradition, and accordingly, worked the script according to their expressive currents. In other words, in order to transform *The Golem* into a living performance and to make room for their own voices, they dismembered the dramatic poetic text.

While they were adapting the staged drama to the radio, transforming it from a corporeal performance into a broadcast aural event, *Habima* further disjoined the textural corpus. The radio production of *The Golem* presents a concise—under an hour—adaptation of the play, including the keynote tune that opened the dramatic hour on Kol Yisrael, and a female narrator voice that directs and positions the listener throughout the performed aural acts. This narrating voice breaks the performance into three distinct dimensions: one, outside the dramatic world, in which the narrator explains the scenes about to be heard; the other, consisting of the fictional world in which fictional characters act; finally, the third dimension refers to the theater performance of the play as a public event.

Inside *The Golem*: Spectral Voices

The disjoining of Leivick's text enabled *Habima* to infuse its own spirit into the drama. For the actors, the play consisted of a kind of instrument—a prolific textual construct that gave vent to their voices through the narrative pattern of *The Golem*. Between 1925 and 1961, *Habima* recorded selections from *The*

Figure 3.1. Aharon Meskin as the golem, from *Habima*'s performance of *The Golem*. Courtesy of *Habima* National Theater and the Israeli Center for the Documentation of the Performing Arts.

Figure 3.2. Tanchum (Raikin Ben-Ari) the lamenting father, from *Habima*'s performance of *The Golem*. Courtesy of *Habima* National Theater and the Israeli Center for the Documentation of the Performing Arts.

Golem as performed on various occasions. For example, during their 1931 tour in London they recorded the "Eliyahu Hanavie" liturgical song on the commercial record (discussed in the first chapter); in 1954, *Habima* registered a fragment from their performance at Théâtre Sarah-Bernhardt, Paris.[17] These recordings present apt figurations of the severed body-voice relations of the golem: a voice projected from a mechanical medium. Such a schism,

Figure 3.3. The Maharal (Baruch Chemerinsky) and the golem (Aharon Meskin), from *Habima*'s performance of *The Golem*. Courtesy of *Habima* National Theater and the Israeli Center for the Documentation of the Performing Arts.

which is essential to the medium of radio, entails, as Allen S. Weiss argues, the *presence-ing* of the division between the corporeal and the incorporeal: "In radio, not only is the voice separated from the body, and not only does it return to the speaker as a disembodied presence—it is, furthermore, thrust into the public arena to mix its sonic destiny with that of other voices."[18] What, then, do we find when we tunnel into the medium of the golem?

Habima's audio recording of *The Golem* opens with an extensive prologue that introduces the listeners to the fictional regime that rules the dramatic world. Divided into three consecutive brief scenes in which three pairs of dramatis personae are presented, the prologue condenses the active forces in the depicted fictional world: Thadeus the priest and his apprentice; The Messiah and Eliyahu the prophet; The Maharal and the golem. All three scenes were performed in the 1925 production on a darkened stage with sharp contrasting shades created by expressionistic lighting effects that generated a hallucinatory atmosphere.

In the first scene, harmonious choral strains that slowly fade into the distance herald Thadeus's entrance. Escorted by his anxious assistant, Thadeus reveals his treachery, and dictates to his apprentice the details of their plot; his assistant repeats his sentences as if he were his echo. At some point in their dialogue, Thadeus roars at him, "Open your mouth wooden dummy," thus referring to him as unwittingly prefiguring the golem.

Then enters the Messiah, a young angelic man, unchaining himself and declaring his intention to come down to earth. The role of the Messiah is performed in the audio recording—according with that of the original stage cast—by Hanna Rovina. Following her notable vocal enactment of the possessed bride and her memorable lamentation as the Messiah's mother, Rovina's performance, as Yair Lipshitz points, was *ghosted*—in Marvin Carlson's terms—by her previous liminal vocal acts of the spirits channeled through her voice and body.[19] This is further enhanced through Eliyahu the prophet's blessing to the Messiah: "Tilt your ears to the humming of the wind." In Hebrew, the word *wind—ruah—*also refers to the conjuring of specters. This apparition transpires in the concluding part of the prologue, whereby the Maharal compels an unbodied voice to imbue the material he has formed.

Assisted by his apprentice (the synagogue's Shammes) Avraham, the Maharal is shown to manipulate and mold the arid clay. With a drift of wind whistling in the backdrop, the Maharal verbalizes his vision:

> Yes, all is done and darkness covers all.
> The hour of wonder comes with the day,
> And as I look upon this great frame
> That has been shaped and kneaded by my hands,
> I can descry his shadow striding here,
> The shadow striding here,
> The shadow of a being breathing life.[20]

Darkness envelops the stage; a distant rustle is suddenly heard, and some shadowy, ghostlike presence, strides across the river. The Maharal calls toward him:

> MAHARAL: Who walks upon the surface of the river?
> Approaches me yet comes no nearer;
> Withdraws from me yet is no further?
> Who are you, dark presence?
> FIGURE: You do not know me?
> MAHARAL: I cannot see your face.
> FIGURE: You do not recognize my voice?
> MAHARAL: Your voice is like cold wind
> That blows in a deep pit
> Without entrance, without exit
> FIGURE: I have a voice that is not yet a voice.
> I have a heart that is not yet a heart.[21]

The Maharal firmly appeals to the ghost to unveil itself before him in a verbal gesture that strikingly echoes the opening scene of *Hamlet* in which the ghost/father makes its mysterious appearance along the outer walls of Kronborg Castle, Elsinore. Like the ghost of Hamlet's father, the golem initially makes its appearance as an articulate phantom who is forced to "descend" from his latency.[22] When this scene was performed on stage, it was structured like a theatrical "screen-scene," in Freddie Rokem's definition. The Maharal stood alone on stage, and talked to a spirit position behind it, outside of the stage.[23] The figure then appeared before the Maharal as a dark presence, and they began to converse:

> MAHARAL: Who are you? Speak. What is your name?
> FIGURE: Not till later will I be known by name.
> I am not yet among mankind.
> I am as yet a shadow's shadow.
> MAHARAL: Whence do you come?
> FIGURE: I have come to warn you: create me not.
> Do not dislodge me from my rest.
> MAHARAL: Vanish. I order you.
> FIGURE: I tell you once again; again I warn:
> Create me not!
> You see: the stars go out, each one.
> So will the light go out
> In every eye that looks on me;
> And where my foot will tread,
> A blight will grow upon that place;
> And what my hand will touch,

To dust and ashes will it crumble.
Do not exchange my darkness and my stillness
For the tumult of the streets and for the noise of men.[24]

Besides the Shakespearean reference, the dialogue between the Maharal and the spirit of the golem also alludes to the Biblical story of King Saul and the witch of Endor (Samuel 1:28). According to the story, on the eve of the fateful war against the Philistines, Saul asked God for advice; however, "the Lord did not answer him by dreams or Urim or prophets" (Samuel 1 28:6). Saul then decided to consult a necromancer, despite the prohibition on activities related to mediums and spiritualists, in order to summon the dead spirit of prophet Samuel. When the spirit of Samuel was roused, his words recall the reaction of the golem: "Why hast thou disquieted me, to bring me up?"[25]

The fashioning of the golem as a spectral voice renders the Maharal as a ventriloquist engaged in a dialogue with a discorporate voice. Such characterization provokes ambivalence toward the performed vocal act: if the Maharal himself produced the spectral voice, then the apparition is nothing but mendacity; conversely, if it is the voice of the golem's spirit, the Maharal's impersonation amounts to—much as Saul's summoning of necromancy—a demonic act of idolatry performed by a Rabbi.[26] This puzzle poses the visceral certainty of sight vis-à-vis the porousness of the faculty of hearing, which cannot always lead its listener to the sources of the sound. In order to speak to the unbodied voice, the Maharal needs to forego positivistic knowledge and adhere to faith; to abandon sensual validation and incline his ears to the obscure voice emerging from the darkness.

Vexed by its awakening, the spirit cautions the Maharal against the possible disastrous outcomes of having stirred it from its burial place and materialized it in the clay. By means of reversal, this scene associates to the exorcism of the dybbuk from within Leah's surrogate body: the Maharal compels the spirit to penetrate the clay mold; conversely, the dybbuk is forced out of a material body. Furthermore, in these two scenes the respective voices of the golem and the dybbuk are shaped alike: much as in the casting out of the dybbuk, the spirit of the golem cries to the Maharal by prolonging the end of its phrases, while rendering them subtly in a melodious recitation. Although the golem, played by Aharon Meskin, possessed a thundering baritone voice—unlike the dybbuk, which was voiced by Hanna Rovina—both uttered the exhausting moment of penetrating and vacating the material matter in a similar fashion: they pronounced the words slowly, emphasizing the diction of the words, lengthening and heightening the last syllables of each sentence to create a vocal resonance that portrayed both the golem and the dybbuk as gargantuan figures in the imagination of the listeners. This vocal effect of reverberation rendered both figures as hollow bodies, in which the voice vibrates much like in the resonance boxes of musical instruments.[27]

The resistance of the golem to penetrating the clay persists, so the dialogue continues as the golem progresses toward its incarnation:

> MAHARAL: O, help me in this heaviest hour, God.
> FIGURE: I know you will not hear my plea.
> Therefore, I come to give you warning—
> And let my warning be a plea.
> The whole night through you kneaded me;
> With coldness and with cruelty you shaped me.
> How good it was to be mere clay,
> To lie, lifeless and calm,
> Among the sands and stones of earth
> Between eternities.
> MAHARAL: Now vanish to your refuge, Figure,
> And take your fear of life,
> Your sorrow, with you to your lair.
> When the hour of wonders comes
> As soon as night retreats before the eastern sun,
> Then, too, will your despair retreat.
> For I was sent by God to knead you,
> Disjoin you from the stony earth
> And with the first ray that lights the sky
> Breathe into you the breath of life.
> FIGURE: I do not want it.
> MAHARAL: Your days and nights and all your deeds
> Have been decreed.
> You are created for more than merely life.
> In silence and concealment, you will do
> Great wonders, but your deeds will be in secret.
> No one will know the hero. You will seem
> A hewer of water, a cutter of wood.
> FIGURE: A Golem, a thing of clay.
> MAHARAL: A people's champion, a man of might.
> FIGURE: A servant—to be ruled, commanded.
> MAHARAL: A living man
> FIGURE: A living man? Why do you stand and wait?
> Where is the soul that will be breathed in me?

Why do you leave my eyes still shut?
Why is a heart not given to me?
Where is the tongue, the teeth, where is the blood
That must be poured to flow in me?
How would you have me? Blind or mute?
Or lame? Or deaf, perhaps?
Or all at once? Speak. The night departs;
The day arrives. O darkness, darkness!
One moment more conceal me in your depth!
One moment more what I have been till now:
A lifeless mound of arid clay.
[*the figure dissolves into the darkness*][28]

The notion of the golem as an embodied revelation of a mystical phenomenon is crystallized in Leivick's textual designation of the spirit as a "figure" (this term was translated from the Yiddish manuscript by Joseph C. Landis; in the Yiddish text, the term Leivick uses is געשטאלט *gestalt,* denoting a shape, form, configuration).[29] Drawing from Erich Auerbach's influential essay "Figura," Stephen Greenblatt explains the concept of *figura* as a master trope for cultural mobility that "allows both for the overarching divine order in which everything that exists is ultimately fulfilled and for the historical specificity of each particular event, phenomenon, and personality."[30] The *figura,* or the golem in our case, incorporates the appropriation of forms and figures while also resisting and distorting them.[31] Furthermore, the aural representation of the golem is a form of speech—in Cicero's terms *figura vocis* ("of the voice"), or *figurae dicendi* ("figures of speech")—that, as Erich Auerbach explains, encompasses the various ways in which normative aural expressions are employed, modified, and garbled by rhetorical postulations in order to embroider narrative, and to draw the affection of the audience.[32]

The incarnation of a spirit in a figure and its animation by means of vocal elocution concurs with the Kabbalistic traditions regarding techniques of creating the golem, defined by Gershom Scholem as a process entailing the articulation of certain letter combinations aloud in a rhythmic replication of sounds, changing combinations, as one of the ecstatic elements entailed in the ceremony.[33] The generative, rousing element in language—articulated by J. L Austin though the statement that "to say something is to do or make something"—is amalgamated in *Habima's* performance with the Kabbalistic technique.[34] The idea of animation through language iteration is already encoded in some versions of the tale of "The Golem," for example, in Chełm and Prague, as well as in Polish tales and versions of Brothers Grimm, in which the figure is inscribed with the Hebrew word *emet* (אמת, "truth" in Hebrew) written on its forehead.[35] When the Rabbi dismantles the golem, he removes the e' (the Hebrew letter א) from its forehead, leaving the word *met* (מת, "dead" in Hebrew) as a performative iteration that signifies the end of its living phase.

Indeed, as in the dialogue quoted above, when the Maharal declares his creation "a living man," the replay of the figure veers toward a lengthy verbalized replica, as though it were assuming life through speech. The animation of the figure of the golem through Hebrew iteration transfigures the language into a living language, part and parcel of the mental and cultural life of speakers, corresponding, concomitantly, to the symbolism of its bygone and its contemporary enunciations. From this point of view, the language performance in *The Golem* does not only represent a mythical narrative of mystical redemption but also enacts the iteration of Hebrew speech—the revival of the Hebrew language—as a significant social ritual, and as a self-referential performance.

How to Revive Spirits with Words

Paraphrasing the eminent title of J. L Austin's lecture "How to Do Things with Words," I will proceed to examine the performative aspects of *Habima*'s staged Hebrew, and the imagination entrenched in the theatrical depiction of the golem as a Hebrew-speaking figure. In the context of *Habima*'s 1925 performance, I regard *The Golem* as a manifestation of the Zionist cultural endeavor to renew and implement modern Hebrew as the main spoken language of the Jewish national enterprise.

The most common metaphor used to describe the emergence of Modern Hebrew during the beginning of the twentieth century was that of "revival" or "resurrection." This metaphor, as Ron Kuzar explains, implies the retrieval of the past—the return of an ancient language in a Modernist social and cultural context.[36] It assumes that the Hebrew language, much like the spirit of the golem, was in a hibernating condition when it was revitalized by the endowment of a voice. From this perspective, an act of revival entails the arousal of latent ghosts by means of enunciation.

In a short paragraph written after his immigration to Palestine, Gershom Scholem parallels the "revival" of the Hebrew language to the making of a golem, derogatorily comparing Eliezer Ben-Yehuda—the pioneer of the Zionist venture to renew and implement Hebrew—to the witch of Endor:

> The "soul" of language has been lost during its wandering from
> the book into life. That, which we praise ourselves with, is by

no means praiseworthy, for we have not revived the Hebrew [language], but only a Golem of it, an Esperanto; that is to say, actually we have achieved something negative. Such language cannot stand the competition with Arabic and English, and it is not true that it should deserve to assert itself therein. The miracle of language is nothing but a successful invocation of a ghost, not that of a language-body, i.e., of a soul. However, to summon ghosts is undeserving. Herein lies the core of deception of the Diaspora through our pretensions: because our ghost is haunting, it claims to be alive. And nobody doubts it. But wherever ghosts speak, the living have to fall silent. Ben Jehuda [sic]—the new witch of Endor.[37]

I found this paragraph in Scholem's archive at the National Library in Jerusalem, among drafts and copies of his famous letter to Franz Rosenzwieg, "*Bekenntnis über unsere Sprache*" ("A Confession about Our Language," 1926). In this letter, Scholem unfolds his anxiety in the face of a potential apocalyptic eruption of the "Zionist undertaking" of the Hebrew, and of the risks entailed in its "actualization" (*Aktualisierung*).[38] Scholem watched with repugnance how, on the one hand, Hebrew was distancing itself from its religious sources by becoming functional, dynamic, and poor, and, on the other, was clinging to its messianic/apocalyptic foundations. In his letter to Rosenzweig, Scholem expresses his concern with the latent ghosts imbued in the Hebrew language, which might be released with its emptying out from sacred sound and content, and its profanation.

In the above-cited paragraph, Scholem uses a much less equivocal language than in the letter to Rosenzweig. He alludes to the golem and the witch of Endor in order to portray what he perceives as the destructive deviation of Hebrew from its biblical and liturgical tradition. Just as the golem does not cease from being "dead" material even when animated, so does Hebrew fail to come to life when it is secularized and used as a modern functional language. Moreover, according to Scholem, if Hebrew is dethroned from its sacred elements, its "soul" will be lost, and the eerie revenant it envelops will be released. Rather than revive Hebrew, the Zionists have resuscitated a golem or an Esperanto, which will have neither the capacity nor the right to compete with English or Arabic. Like a golem, this sort of "dead" Hebrew can grow beyond control and propel its malicious spirit.

Scholem's reference to Ben-Yehuda as a "new witch of Endor" corresponds to the lexicographer's public image of a modern prophet, as well as questions the veracity of his agentive empowerment. The mystical perception hovering above the project of the resuscitation of the Hebrew language was enhanced by Eliezer Ben-Yehuda's persona, also referred to as "the reviver of Hebrew." Immigrating to Palestine as early as 1881, Ben-Yehuda committed himself and his family to speak only Hebrew and became the living example of its "renaissance." Despite the compromises forced by reality that prevented him from fully accomplishing his aspiration,[39] Ben-Yehuda was regarded as a larger-than-life figure who inspired others to follow in his footsteps.[40]

Scholem's pejorative view of Ben-Yehuda depletes the revival of Hebrew from its "miraculous" effects, and likens it to necromancy—communicating with the telluric powers hovering in the purgatory underworld. Thus, when Scholem alerts us to the release of such ghastly forces as those of the golem or the witch of Endor, he refers to the contamination of the high and the low, to the alliance between abnormal elements and supernal entities. The depiction of modern Hebrew as a golem renders it a language detached from its anchor—a spectral voice unleashed from its organic surrogate body.

Habima's aural conception of the creation of the golem as an act of necromancy performed by the Maharal corresponds with Scholem's interpretation of the estrangement entailed in the modern revival of the Hebrew language. Indeed, the secularization of the language is salient in the articulation of Hebrew in *Habima's* audio recording of *The Golem*. As I demonstrate in the following, the aural residues of Yiddish intonation are restrained; the typical dramatization of "Jewish speech" is toned down, and moments of melodious liturgical recitation are rare.

The Paradigm Shift in *Habima's* Dramatic Recitation

The drama in *The Golem* unfolds in three distinctly Jewish sites: The first act takes place in the Maharal's home; the second in the deserted tower where the homeless Jewish beggars dwell; the third and concluding act in the vestibule of the synagogue. In *Habima's* staged production, these sites were designed by Ignaty Nivinsky (1880–1933) in a minimalist setting of geometric shapes, tilted at many angles and slopes, recognizable from other expressionistic theater performances. Unlike the scenery in this performance and, especially, in comparison with its previous productions, a general overview of the speech in this production shows that *Habima* exercised here a different approach to its theatrical manifestation of the Hebrew language.

Overall, the recording reveals a performance fraught with verbal dialogues, often verging on monotonous speech, with but a few musical expressions and moments of melodious speech. This shift in the shaping of language is intriguing and calls for further investigation: Was this sort of aurality also evident in the 1925 performance, or does it attest to the standardization of Hebrew pronunciation norms in the early '60s in the Israeli radio and public sphere? In other words, is this shift in style a sign of the later reification of the performance over the course of time, or does it demonstrate a different artistic approach than that of *Habima*'s earlier performance? In order to provide possible answers to these questions, I combed through the archive boxes in search of theater reviews from the first years in which *The Golem* was staged, in Europe and in Israel, as well as personal memoirs and biographies of *Habima*'s actors in which the rehearsal process of this production is documented.

Journalistic reviews from early productions of *The Golem* assert that *Habima*, indeed, changed its approach to dramatic recitation, shifting from poetic rhythmic recitation to a prosaic naturalistic speech. Menachem Ribalow, a renowned Russian Jewish literary critic, targets *Habima*'s stylistic shift in his review of the show, stating that

> [*Habima*] attempted to be loyal and close to reality, to the simple version of the legend . . . as if withdrawing from the stylized musicality of *The Eternal Jew*. . . . [I]t showed in *The Golem* a well-structured performance and quite understandable, but realistic and limited as such. . . . I recall few paragraphs and poetic phrases, heightened theatrically, because they presented the spirit of moral courage and exalted literary expression—in *Habima*'s performance I heard only few.[41]

A possible rationale for the change in the approach to the modeling of the language might arise from the familiarity of the legend of "The Golem." Presenting a narrative whose basic elements are widely known, this production did not resort to melodious expressions and language intonations in order to communicate the plot to a non-Hebrew-speaking audience.

Delving into the artistic vision of the director Boris Illich Vershilov may further elucidate the aural move of *Habima* in the performance of language in *The Golem*. Vershilov, a self-proclaimed Jew distanced from Jewish life, was a recognized director in the Moscow Art Theater.[42] Although unacquainted with Jewish heritage and culture, as Ben-Ari points out, the fact that Vershilov shared a religious background, an ethnic affiliation, and an ancient language with the troupe was of significance to the actors.[43] The shared cultural/religious orbit meant that key facets of the fictional world needed not be explained or blatantly displayed through stereotypical Jewish imagery.

Vershilov launched his professional directing career as Vakhtangov's apprentice; however, he was considered an admirer of the Stanislavsky method. The different approaches manifested in the respective recitations of *Habima*'s recordings of *The Golem* from *The Dybbuk* or *The Eternal Jew* may thus be ascribed to the dissimilar artistic schemes of the directors that worked with the troupe. Vakhtangov was well aware of the shortcomings of naturalism. Aspiring to find a middle way between Stanislavsky's realism and Meyerhold's symbolism, Vakhtangov articulated his approach to acting as "Fantastic Realism" in order to define the interweaving of realistic forms with abstract and expressionistic qualities.

In *The Golem*, however, *Habima* worked straightforwardly with Stanislavsky's method as advocated by Vershilov.[44] The spoken word was regarded by Stanislavsky as secondary and complementary to the action on stage. When working on *The Golem*, the troupe focused on a rigorous inner investigation of the emotional experience of the actors; they emphasized emotional tensions and motivations by visual and physical means.

Ben-Ari recalls how they worked with the Stanislavsky method of character development in order to shape the tonality of the golem's speech:

> Stanislavsky had taught us—he emphasized the point in his *My Life in Art*—that in order to give an accurate portrayal of an evil person the actor must find those aspects of his life that are not evil; to portray a virtuous man we must discover the evil in him. . . . In the usual theater the method was completely the reverse. There, when an actor portrayed an evil character, he was totally evil, an unrelieved black. . . . He would never speak in a normal voice, but shout—and remain shouting to the end of his acting career.[45]

Thus, the reserved intonations, and toned-down expressiveness in speech could be an outcome of the inherent tensions and emotional dynamics of *Habima*'s acting style.

At this point, the partiality of the aural dimension and the restrictions of sound analysis in performance art once again soars to the surface. In absence of a comprehensive visual "live" documentation, we are left with the restrained intonations of the actors, devoid of the ability to assemble the full picture by adding the necessary balancing—if sometimes also contrasting—elements that render the depth of dramatic characters that Stanislavsky's method was aiming for. Yet, the decision to preserve through recording technology the sounds and voices from the play situates the aural dimension of the performance as a timely sound instantiation in its own right—autonomous voices, apparently severed from their visual counterpart.

In 1961, when the recording of *The Golem* was broadcast, the naturalistic shaping of the Hebrew language seemed as if tailored to the Hebrew spoken on the radio. The radio had a central impact on the aural transmission of spoken Hebrew and on the process of assimilating what Haiim B. Rosén termed "Israeli Hebrew"—Hebrew as articulated in the State of Israel.[46] During those years, Hebrew was the dominant spoken language in Israel; however, it sounded differently when spoken by new immigrants, whether survivors from the war, or refugees from Arab countries. Although the radio was perceived as an important means for learning how to speak and read the language, its effectiveness was limited. The Israeli Hebrew spoken on the radio did not necessarily manifest the benchmark for "correct" pronunciation, but it certainly participated in cultivating the vivid sonic "nonverbal" dialogue between various parts of the Israeli society.

A chronicled meeting between Kol Yisrael representatives and members of the Israeli Hebrew Academy reveals the debates vis-à-vis pronunciation criteria on the radio. The demand to unify the broadcasters' accents, and to set literary standards for public Hebrew speech on the radio, discloses the fact that up until that time (1963) language articulation on the radio did not always reflect the official Hebrew speech and accent. However, the sort of Hebrew articulated on the radio appealed to native-born Israelis for whom Hebrew was their mother tongue—a language imprinted from birth, articulated automatically.[47]

Abba Bendavid, the language consultant for Kol Yisrael between 1959 and 1982, addresses the difference in language articulation on the radio and on the theater stage: "[T]he accent on Kol Yisrael, as appropriate for a state institution, is the 'Literary Standard' of the Hebrew language, that stands in contrast to the many theatrical sub-standards around the country, with no precise fixed definitions, what is obligatory and what is not."[48] The subtle accent, the prosaic intonation and the language in *Habima's* radio recording of *The Golem,* indeed, fits into the articulation of the Israeli (native) Hebrew, while also articulating their wavering experience of displacement, and their lived realities as immigrants in the larger historical perspective.

A Hebrew Actor or a Golem? A Machine Learning Language

For many new Hebrew speakers, both in the Diaspora and in Palestine, the process of acquiring Hebrew speaking skills and adapting to its new phonological spectrum entailed a technical, sometimes artificial internalization of the language. The assimilation of Hebrew among a community of immigrants imposed the use of an external language system. The process of adapting and adjusting to the new Jewish Israeli culture, and the tension it engulfs between the artificial and organic, tapped on a basic displacement experience shared by many new Hebrew speakers in 1925—*Habima*'s among them.

The Zionist agenda introduced a new Jewish subject into almost all facets of life and culture, thus demanding from its adherents a rigorous behavioral revision. Ze'ev Jabotinsky, for example, labored to separate the new Hebrew speech from its diasporic expressivity, consequently to secularize its pronunciation. In his book *The Hebrew Pronunciation* (1930), he assertively advocates:

> Do not sing while you speak. This ugliness is infinitely worse than every other defect I have mentioned and, regrettably, it is taking root in our life. Both the school and the stage are guilty: the first, our sloppiness, the latter, our intention to "revive" for us the ghetto and its whining. The tune of the ghetto is ugly not only because of its weeping tone which stirs unpleasant memories in us: it is also ugly objectively, ugly in the scientific sense—ugly as all superfluous or exaggerated efforts. . . . [T]hat sick frenzy, which we also suffer from in our social life, is also the result of the Diaspora—an abundance of forces with no field and no outlet for the repressed storm except to explode in a bowl of soup—the "singsong" of the ghetto speech is nothing but an echo of this national disease. The exercise that helps against the disease is very simple: exercising monotony—"monotony" in the scientific sense of the word, that is, lack of all vacillation in intonation.[49]

Habima's recorded performance exercises the flat rendering of language as part of the overall behavioral transformation. This is manifested in the first performed scene after the prologue, rendering the Golem's entrance into the Maharal's home, and its learning the basics: how to walk, to stoop, to sit, to respect his own name and to modulate his voice:

MAHARAL: You have a mouth and teeth, a tongue to speak,
Why are you silent
[the golem *is dumb*]
MAHARAL: Speak. I command you, speak.
Yehuda is your name.
GOLEM: [*terrified*].
Yehuda?

MAHARAL: You are a man.

GOLEM: A Man.

MAHARAL: You have a heart to live.

GOLEM: To live.

MAHARAL: You need not be discouraged.
You do recall your name—
[the golem *is silent.*]

MAHARAL: Have you forgotten? Yehuda is your name.
Remember it.

GOLEM: Yehuda.

MAHARAL: and do you know what I am called?

GOLEM: Rabbi [*loudly*]

MAHARAL: What are you doing? Stop. You will awaken everyone.[50]

The first dialogue between the Maharal and his golem is structured as a dramatic reflection of their relationship: beginning with the golem repeating the Maharal's words, and concluding with the golem raising its voice, displeasing its master. Chayim Bloch stated that "some regarded the golem as a 'ghost' of Rabbi Loew," bringing us back to the realm of spectrality, long before Derrida's articulated his ideas of hauntology in *The Specters of Marx*.[51] The fact that *Habima* changed the golem's name from Joseph to Yehuda, like the name of its creator Rabbi Judah Loew, the Maharal of Prague, reinforces Bloch's interpretation. By mirroring the Maharal's unsurfaced, unrealized anger and hatred, the golem unfurls the terrible truth of his master's flaws as contained within its own soul.

Subsumed in this interpretation is the humanizing process the golem undergoes. Beginning his life as an almost-robotic creature, dumbly obeying the orders of the Maharal, the golem gradually becomes more and more human: he gets attached to the Maharal, and after meeting the Maharal's granddaughter, Dvorah'le (originally played by Fanny Lubitsch), he even develops sexual urges. During the course of the play, the golem's speech assumes this dramatic metamorphosis: launching as an acoustic phantom, it gradually grows human. Its baritone dybbuk-like prolonged intonation transmutes into a native dynamic articulation of Israeli Hebrew.

This process of becoming human parallels the embedding of Hebrew as an "inner language" (*inner Sprachform*) or "inner form," a term coined by philosopher Wilhelm von Humboldt (1836). Humboldt regarded "inner language" as the language system construed upon unconscious structures and mental assemblages. It fashions the means for individual expression; it comprises the system into which man weaves himself. In other words, the subject's "inner language" is the organic language of the individual; it is the language that we hear inside our body, the language in which we dream.[52] The golem's speech capabilities problematize the idea of inner language. As a mechanical creation, he acts and speaks automatically; however, as an artificial man-made being, human language is alien to him. In order for the golem to transform from a mechanical creature into a subject, it must internalize language and learn to utilize it for expression. The Humboldtian concept of "inner language" refers to speech as an act through which people actualize their world, and ideas become fixed through expression. Accordingly, for the golem, language articulation is central in the formation of itself as a subject. Its animation through language poses Hebrew as a vital expression of creativity that is iterated through speech.

Following Stanislavsky's method, *Habima*'s actors were required to assimilate Hebrew and articulate it as if it were their medium of spontaneous speech. As Joseph Roach explains, Stanislavsky thought to "objectify the phenomenon of spontaneity" by defining spontaneity in performance as "an activity repeated so often that it becomes automatic and therefore free."[53] According to Stanislavsky, the automatic condition, in which the actor executes his actions in a habitual manner, enables him to perform a dramatic role as "second nature."[54] The figure of the golem expresses this idea: much like the fresh Hebrew acquired by *Habima*—a nascent troupe of nonnative Hebrew speakers—the golem recites a preprogrammed scheme that lacks spontaneity.

The implications of Stanislavsky's approach for *Habima*'s language training were articulated by Prince Volkonsky who argued, in line with Stanislavsky, that the actor's rational analysis should give way to emotional experience: "On stage do not think of these laws and rules, they must sit in you, they will have value only on condition that they turn into something unconscious . . . you should think during the time of preparation and in the time of performance you should feel."[55] Volkonsky understood stage speech as an expressive mechanism that, once internalized, allows room for iteration of "signs of feelings, received by the external organs of hearing and sight."[56]

Accordingly, the emotional experience of the audience is, thus, also an outcome of a fictitious aural performance designed to provoke certain feelings. Emanuel Levy provides an anecdote that sheds light on the audience's reaction to the aural shaping of the drama. The performance of *The Golem*, as evident from the recording, ended with the reverberating admonition of Tanchum, the wailing father that lost his child to the vicious blood libel: "Who will save us?" he weeps loudly outside the synagogue, in the aftermath of the golem's attack on the Jewish community. Tanchum's exclamation is joined by praying voices in the synagogue. During one of the performances that took place in Moscow in

1925, according to Levy's story, Tanchum's cry and the prayer in its background compelled members of the audience to stand, and shout back: "We Will!" and solemnly sing the "International"—the anthem of the communist revolution.[57] Tanchum lamented the Jewish way; they replied with the communist pledge. Did the audiences, as Levy suggests, sense the messianic promise unfolded in *Habima*'s performance? Or does the rupture between the call and its reaction attest to the pressuring demand from Jews to show their absolute fidelity to socialist values, proving their fear of publicly affirming their religious/ethnic identity? Either way, the dissociative reaction to the performed drama adds yet another dimension to the rupture between the internal and the external, voice and body, manifested by the figure of the golem.

In both the stage and the radio performances of *Habima*'s production, the figure of the golem was played by Aharon Meskin (1898–1974). A former officer in the Red Army, Meskin was an actor endowed with a robust theatrical presence, and a basso-profundo booming voice. His casting as the dumb golem underscored the discrepancy between the golem's mighty body and his poor language capabilities. This inconsistency is subsumed in the meaning of the word *Golem* in both modern Hebrew and Yiddish slang, denoting a kind of simpleton or fool. Theater critic Jeanette Wilken refers, in her 1948 review of *The Golem*, to the comic quality of the gap between the golem's folly and its mighty physicality, arguing that there is

> real fun in the first act when the Maharal, played with sustained dignity and intelligence by Shimon Finkel, teaches the robot to walk, to stoop, to sit, to respect his own name and to modulate his voice to less than a frightening bellow. . . . Scenes such as this allow for intrinsic comedy, and are especially good in this case because they helped surmount the language barrier and had even those in the audience unfamiliar with the Hebrew language laughing happily.[58]

These comic elements are missing in the aural dimension of the performance. In the recording, the golem's speech heightens its loneliness and childish dependency on its master. Throughout the performance, the golem appeals to the Maharal with a pleading voice; it reveals its anxiety at the force contained within its body, its passions, and its terror at its undefined future. It expresses absolute naive fidelity to its creator, even when the latter seeks to dismantle it. Only when the Maharal frustrates the golem by refusing to comply to its needs, does the man-made creature violently retaliate against the Jewish community. Interestingly, in the absence of the visual dimension, the sounds and voices in the recording suggest a new understanding of the golem's emotional world, and its violent retribution. The childish intonations, its strong emotional enslavement to the Maharal, and its uncontrollable impulsive reactions, render the golem as a creature in great distress. Shimon Finkel alludes to a review from The *Neue Zürcher Zeitung* (Sept. 5, 1929) relating to Meskin's acting: "This is artistic acting without emphasis on the grotesque. The voice of this monster, its childish laughter—the slow process of becoming human, these highlighted the struggle of the spirit for its own sake."[59]

When *Habima* performed *The Golem* on the stage, the visual and physical elements of the performance coalesced to comprise a complex portrayal of the golem: the comic and sensitive, perilous and mechanical dimensions were depicted as tenuously contained within the figure of golem. In 1961, however, only part of this "whole" was preserved. Once incarnated as a golem, the voice of the golem does not disclose its bestial drives or its ominous power but rather expresses vulnerability and anxiety.

Distorted Voices: Forgetting the Past, Inventing Tradition

According to the legend, catastrophe befell the Jews of Prague when the Maharal forgot to shut down his golem before the beginning of the Shabbat, when the community assembled at the synagogue. Although in Leivick's dramatic version the Shabbat is not mentioned, in *Habima*'s adaptation the Shabbat is present through a number of instantiations in which Shabbat liturgical songs (*piyyutim*) are integrated into the drama. These are not pure melodic moments solely devoted to singing, such as you may find, for example, in musicals. Rather, these are instants in which characters integrate within their dramatic replicas, or in the background of the dialogue, fragments from familiar Shabbat songs. Furthermore, these lyrical performances do not feature in Leivick's dramatic text, nor are they mentioned in any theater reviews of the performance. Only listening to the radio production of *Habima*'s drama could, thus, brings to the fore the songs interspersed within the performance.

The Shabbat chants performed are all familiar traditional songs well known to the audience. However, they are defamiliarized by being performed either in distorted melodies, or by being executed out of their normative tone and conventional rhythm.[60] The first song is introduced in the first act by Dvorah'le—the Maharal's granddaughter—who sings the second verse of the *piyyut* "*Yedid Nefesh*" (lit. "Beloved of the Soul," or "Spirited friend") by Rabbi Elazar Ben Moshe Azikri (1533–1600), a prominent figure among the mystics of sixteenth-century Safed.[61] This *piyyut* is traditionally sung before or after the Mincha service on Shabbat evening, and sometimes also during the third dinner on the Shabbat day. The lyrics of the *piyyut* address, according to the poet himself, "a supplication for union and desire of love."[62] In the context of the play, this union refers to the forbidden alliance of Dvorah'le and the golem. Dvorah'le's soft, feminine voice, is heard in the background of a heated dialogue between the Maharal and the golem, in which the Maharal demands from the golem that it keep away from his granddaughter; the golem, however, expresses its evolving affections toward the young girl.[63] Unlike the traditional Ashkenazi performance of this *piyyut*, Dvorah'le renders the song with an accelerated rhythm, and ornaments it with her high feminine trilling voice, thus emphasizing the very femininity that arouses the golem's passion for her.

The next *piyyut* in the play, sung by the character of Eliyahu the prophet, is *"Amar Adonay le Yaakov"* ("God said to Yaa'kov"), traditionally sung on Saturday evening when bidding farewell to the Shabbat. This *piyyut*, sung throughout the Jewish world, is arranged as an alphabetic acrostic that aims to comfort and elevate the persecuted Jewish nation. In *Habima's* play, Eliyahu performs this *piyyut* when he joins the downtrodden Jewish community dwelling in the tower.[64] Despite the uplifting content of the *piyyut*, the melodious rendering of the song is slow and sorrowful.

Eliyahu the prophet's choral song is yet another example of a traditional Shabbat chant to which *Habima* stages its own interpretation. The wondrous biblical figure of Eliyahu the prophet does not only live in the mythical past, but is also related to future possibilities of redemption through his sporadic appearances in the world. Eliyahu the prophet travels between temporalities, traversing the earthly and heavenly spheres. The choral song about Eliyahu is traditionally sung in the liminal period marking the end of the Shabbat and the beginning of the mundane week. In the context of the Israeli radio, this song gains special meaning as another version of it was regularly played to mark the end of the Shabbat on the radio by cantor and broadcaster Ephraim Di-Zahav. In stark contrast to the rhythmic, festive traditional enactment of this song, which celebrates the harbinger of redemption, in *Habima's* recording this choral song is juxtaposed with Tanchum's wailing, lamenting the loss of his child—the victim of the blood libel.[65] In a mournful intonation, he cries: "Will you not hear? Will you not hear the voice of ruins? They will answer Yokhanan, Yokhanan."[66] Prolonging the last syllable of his son's name, Tanchum's enduring grief coalesces into the choral singing, impressing despair and shattered hope onto the messianic longing expressed in the song.

Like the other Shabbat songs in the recording, "Eliyahu the Prophet" is also reinterpreted by rendering it as a lamentation. As an aural manifestation of a traditional communal practice, this distorted rendering of the

Hebrew Shabbat liturgical poem stages the inability to conserve memory as an embodied practice. Did *Habima*'s actors forget the melodies in the four decades that elapsed between 1925 and 1961? Or did they distort the melody of common liturgies in order to break away from enactments of the diasporic condition, as part of the making of a new tradition? This interrogation taps into the claim for cultural authenticity and thus calls for probing into the discourse of identity construction.

The vocal performance of the Shabbat songs brings to the stage a Jewish legacy performed in the Hebrew language; however, their divergence from the traditional enactment and the alteration of their melodies, underscores the historical mutilation undergone by these communal practices. The distortion of the melodies illuminates both the fictional dimension of the drama and its agency in the resuscitation of the Hebrew language.

The music for *The Golem* was composed by Moshe Milner (1886–1953), a piano player and cantor born and raised in the small village of Rokitno near Kiev (in a region that was part of the Jewish Pale of Settlement). He came from a religious, music-loving family and participated in various synagogue choirs, which granted him a deep acquaintance with both Jewish music tradition and its artistic manipulations. Milner's profound familiarity with Jewish folk and religious music enabled him to skillfully adapt its elements as pliable material, to distort accepted melodic forms and divert from recognizable styles of singing.

The remodeling of melodies fits into the weird atmosphere of the play, which depicts the making of an artificial creature by remolding the traditional Hebrew language.[67] The distorted melodies then become, like the golem, uncanny. The otherworldly, or uncanny, features in the golem as "the other side of nature"—prevailing beyond the veil, in theatrical terms. This idea of the supernatural "other world" conveys the fantasy longing for an external redeemer, the delusion of messianic occurrence. Rendered familiar yet strange, the Shabbat songs contribute to the shaping of an imagined place both related and alien to the audience. This tension also pervades the iteration of the language in the performance: the actors performed the Hebrew language with the (modern) Sephardic dialect that was new and unfamiliar to them and to their audience. They knew Hebrew from the synagogue and from their education; however, enacted in Sephardic dialect, it sounded different to them.

Interlaced throughout the performance, the Shabbat songs act as an aural synecdoche for an inexhaustible capital of experiences and knowledge shared within the community. The insertion of these songs (*piyyutim*) into the dialogic flow of the drama renders them as aural "places of memory," to borrow Pierre Nora's terminology, which refers to literal sites—symbolic, material, or functional—whereby "memory crystallizes and secretes itself."[68] What makes the Shabbat songs a memory site is the interplay between the practice of tradition and its historicizing in the present. They are no longer real environments of memory, but a reflection of this locus. Embedded within the prosaic dialogues of the play, these liturgical songs yield a sense of cultural continuity.

Yet, any observation on the embodiment of memory, or the cultural continuity entailed in this production, must be curtailed by the limited evidence available, especially concerning the discrepancy between the shaping of speech and melodies in the 1925 stage performance and its reproduction as an aural radio show in 1961. We have little knowledge about the salience of the foreign accents in 1925 vis-à-vis the precise melodic rendering of the musical parts of the performance.

Like the golem itself, the aural uncanniness of the melodies depicted in the recording falls under Eric Hobsbawm and Terence O. Ranger's use of the concept of "invention," which designates the duplicity in ostensibly deep-rooted traditions that actually are quite recent in origin.[69] Modern Hebrew was an invented language because it was systematically shaped to fit specific traceable social and cultural needs. The invention of language and its cultural iterations, as Sinfree B. Makoni and Alastair Pennycook point out, is utilized to narrate a nation into being.[70] The invention of Hebrew as a language of mundane speech is, in this respect, part of the national imagination involved in the process of forging a linear historical narrative that points at a geographical and cultural origin, and fabricates the continuity between the ancient past and its revenant ghosts in the present, as one that traverses through generations, landscapes, and social structures.

The distorted melodies of the Shabbat songs underscore the gap between the embedded social habits and their later observation as a sort of "aural souvenir"—to borrow Friedrich Kittler's term[71]—mobilized for triggering memory and a sense of belonging to a tradition. However, with the distorted theatrical rendering of the religious practice, the Shabbat songs become, paradoxically, a reflection of the distance from a social habit. Pierre Nora formulates distance as an enunciation of the gap between memory and history:

> Memory is life, borne by living societies founded in its name. It remains in permanent evolution, open to the dialectic of remembering and forgetting, unconscious of its successive deformations, vulnerable to manipulation and appropriation, susceptible to being long dormant and periodically revived. History, on the other hand, is the reconstruction, always problematic and incomplete, of what

is no longer. Memory is a perpetually actual phenomenon, a bond
tying us to eternal present; history is a representation of the past.
Memory, insofar as it is affective and magical, only accommodates
those facts that suit it; it nourishes recollections that may be out
of focus or telescopic, global or detached, particular or symbolic—
responsive to each avenue of conveyance or phenomenal screen,
to every censorship or projection.[72]

Memory, as Nora points out, originates in the concrete; in familiar spaces, gestures, voices, and social habits. It stages the fragmentary, subjective negotiation of social practices and situations. Entering the world of history, *Habima*'s *Golem* reflects the distance of the troupe from the world represented on stage: their Hebrew speech is standardized to the Israeli pronunciation; its traditional songs, torn from their rooted melodious enactment, become garbled memories. This structural rupture lays out the specific contingencies of nostalgia—the songs mark a cultural reference point that captures a specific time and place. Whether attributed to an individual or to a society, Svetlana Boym explains, performances of nostalgia imply an abyss separating the past and present, the fictional and the actual, and thus generate new notions of place and time.[73] To follow this thread, we might, perhaps, argue that nostalgia splits the listening subject into two epistemological conditions: one situated in the present, the other immersed "in the past." *Habima*'s sound recording plays with this memory, manipulating its performance in order to imaginatively reconstruct a continuity that would heal the abyss of a secularized Hebrew language, in Scholem's terms, and signify a specific cultural fault line in the aftermath of the war-torn twentieth century.

"Who Will Save Us?" Post-Holocaust Vocal Apparitions

"Who will save us?" is the concluding exclamation performed in the play by Tanchum, the father lamenting his son. This admonition reverberates the evolving theme of redemption in Leivick's drama. During the course of this chapter, I have deliberately avoided explicitly tackling the question, Whom does *Habima*'s character of the golem stand for? Who is their redeemer? In order to refrain from reducing the golem's identity into one signifier, and risk overshadowing the import of the aural dimension of the play, I wish to suggest an interpretation that takes into consideration the radio performance of *The Golem* as a dynamic set of signs that change according to the sociopolitical conditions in which the play is read, and the prevailing atmosphere sustained and facilitated by the sensation of an exasperated anticipation for redemption.

Two central Messianic precursors roam the depicted fictional world. The first is the golem that was created in order to save the Jews of Prague by means of physical force. When adapting Leivick's poetic drama for the stage, *Habima* changed the name of the golem from Joseph, as Leivick wrote it, into Judah. The two names of the golem—Joseph in Leivick's text and Judah in *Habima*'s—denote the two references to messianic precursors: one, the redeeming warrior Messiah ben Joseph (from the tribe of Ephraim), who abruptly finds his tragic death in battle before the successful arrival of the second Messiah: the son of David, from king David's pedigrees, who ruled the kingdom of Judah.[74] Another redemptive figure appearing in the play embodies the nomadic, weak, and feminine Messiah that escorted Eliyahu the prophet. Both Eliyahu the prophet and the Messiah are expelled from town by the Maharal. Albeit varied in character and temperament, none of these legendary figures accomplishes their vocation. Tanchum's closing admonition, which verges on social prophecy, puts a lid on the quest for redemption as a pervasive, unfulfilled yearning for relief from ongoing per-secution and suffering.

Throughout the performance, Tanchum, the grieving father, makes several appearances in which he expresses his deep sorrow and frustration over the death of his child in obscure, highly allegorical monologues. His first entrance takes place in the second scene of the play, when he arrives at the Maharal's home looking disheveled and tattered, with one of his lapels deeply rent as a sign of mourning. His bereavement encompasses the whole world; it permeates every aspect of his being. In his second appearance in the play he articulates the impulse to give his sorrow a voice:

> You've heard it?
> Though you heard a thousand times
> You've still not heard.
> How can the deaf hear?
> How can the blind see?
> Do you see my face in the middle of the night?
> Do you hear my voice?
> With arms spread out wide
> And eyes turned inside
> I stretch my throat to the sky;
> Over the roof of the tower,
> Through each of its shattered windows,
> I hurry and scurry and fly
> Five is the number of towers—
> Five.

> One for the east and one for the west,
> One for the north and one for the south.
> The fifth one—for me.
> Who suffers the grief of the towers?
> I do!
> I am the Lord of the ruins.[75]

Tanchum epitomizes ruin; he brings into the staged soundscape the Jewish sounds of sorrow and lamentation. Every time he enters the theatrical aural space, the flow of the drama breaks, opening up for his powerful performance of sorrow. In his mournful verbal expressions and his cryptic, almost prophetic speech, he gives voice to an agony that transcends his own personal anguish.

Raikin Ben-Ari, who was cast in the role of Tanchum, recalls the rehearsal process through which he shaped his performance:

> I began to rehearse the part in my room without the wild gesticulations and exaggerations. I was sure that without these extravagant gestures the portrayal would be meaningless, but at least I would show Vershilov that I could do the part without flailing around. The next day at rehearsal Vershilov liked it better, but he asked me to try it without yelling at the top of my voice, to talk naturally. "Remember," he said, "the sum total of your performance must show that you're mad, but in your speech and movements you are normal. Normal, normal! Remember that." . . . I walked on to the stage quietly and reverently. I began to talk to the Maharal—simple, normal talk—and I could feel an internal warmth welling up in me. I felt the emotions of a careworn man. The dialogue became more spirited and, toward the end, so real that when Tanchum asked the Maharal sarcastically, "Who will save us?" the words seemed torn out of me in a sort of biblical chant, and then I hurried off the stage. . . . Later, analyzing with Vershilov why I had been unable to master the part for so long, the explanation turned out to be simple. From the beginning I had been imitating the idiot boy of my native town, and was simply unable to rid myself of the mental image.[76]

Ben-Ari's memory provides an intriguing example of the temporal and cultural rift between *Habima*'s production and its reproduction; between its staged corporeal manifestation and its transmutation into a disembodied aural instantiation. In 1925, Tanchum's character, according to Ben-Ari, was cast as a native eccentric figure, something between a weird simpleton and a madman, and his expression of grief and rage was shaped accordingly.

How were these admonitions of ruin and redemption perceived when mediated as disembodied voices in post-Holocaust 1961? In the radio version of the performance, Tanchum's lamentations resonate with a shared experience of suffering and loss as the dimensions of the depredations of the Holocaust were gradually exposed. Maya Barzilai argues that with the founding of the Israeli nation (1948), the figure of the golem became associated with its antagonists, metamorphosing into an embodiment of the enemy of the Jews, be they the Arab conglomerate army or the Nazi perpetrators. Thus, the golem no longer stood for the combative Jewish spirit, but came to project the negative evocation of violence. With this understanding of the metaphor, Barzilai explains, Israeli society distanced itself from the diasporic Jewish cultural legacy.[77] Barzilai dedicates a chapter to close readings of *The Golem* in post-Holocaust American comics. She argues that post-Holocaust evocations of the golem have created a protector who can also become a dangerously blind avenger.[78]

At the time *The Golem* was broadcast on Kol Yisrael, a larger drama transpired in another location in Jerusalem—Adolf Eichmann stood for trial at the main auditorium of *Beit Ha'Am* cultural center from April 11 until the verdict sentencing him to death, the first and only death penalty in the state's history, on December 15 for crimes against the Jewish people and crimes against humanity. The trial concluded with the rejection of his appeal on May 29, 1962, culminating in his execution on the night between May 31 and June 1, 1962. This was an unprecedented media event: during its course, Israel's National radio broadcast hours of testimonies by Holocaust survivors who, for the first time, publicly unbound their silence to bear witness to the traumatic experiences that befell "there."[79]

For the prosecution, Shoshana Felman explains, the goal of the trial was to articulate a *monumental narrative* in which the genocide of the Holocaust was "countered, vanquished by an act of historical survival."[80] From silenced traumas it became a collective myth of suffering and redemption. During a conference held in Jerusalem in 1957, Leivick expressed the need of the Jewish nation to let go of their historical identification as victims. In a lecture entitled "The Jew—The Individual," cited in the introduction to the English translation of *The Golem*, Leivick addressed Jewish conceptions of anticipation for redemption, victimhood, and retribution, through their post-Holocaust context:

> [M]ost of all I am pursued by Isaac's lying bound upon the altar, his looking at the raised knife till the angel of God announced

that it was but a trial; . . . it pursues me because I have seen—we all have seen—six million Isaacs lying under knives, under axes, in fires and in gas-chambers; and they were slaughtered. The angel of God did come too late.[81]

In 1961, the radio broadcast of *The Golem*, I argue, took part in metamorphosing the Holocaust into a social narrative of suffering and redemption. The radio's broadcasting the many testimonies transformed the survivors "from bodies without speech into disembodied speech," in Amit Pinchevski and Tamar Liebes's words.[82] The passage from silence to speech, from body to voice, rendered the courtroom as a liminal space, a "threshold event" as Jeffrey Shandler argued, that changed awareness of the atrocities perpetrated during the Holocaust, and the perception of its dimensions, in the public view across the globe.[83] In the following, I will show how *Habima*'s 1961 broadcasting of a performative language that was created in Moscow during the second half of 1920s violated its temporary suspension of disbelief, and participated in transforming mute bodies into disembodied voices.

Felman argues that "while the Eichmann trial can under no circumstances be regarded as a work of art, works of art have come today to imitate, to replicate or mimic, the legal structure of the Eichmann trial."[84] Accordingly, I submit that the broadcasting of *The Golem* during the emotional turbulence provoked by the trial gave new meaning to the disengagement of the performed voices from their corporeality. Tamar Liebes argues that radio in its heyday as the principal arm of mass media in Israel "acted mostly as a medium of 'one thing at a time-ness,' following a packed schedule of serving a variety of societal needs (of surveillance, correlation, acculturation and entertainment) . . . At critical and ceremonial moments in the nation's history," Liebes explains, "the radio exercised its power to turn the psyche and society into a single echo chamber."[85] If we regard the radio as a medium of rupture in which the broadcast voice is severed from the corporeal presence of its speaker, then the 1961 broadcast of *The Golem* tapped into the epistemological, social, cultural, and emotional break from the past experienced by many Jewish immigrants and Holocaust survivors.

The 1961 reproduction of *Habima*'s voices—initiated in Moscow before World War II—generated values and imaginations fostered from the complexities of their return, and reconfigured them in a new temporal and social setting. Examining the diffusion of social reality in the fictional world of the radio drama, I am interested in apprehending how, in *The Golem*, the voices defy the borderlines of the fictional and act on the social sphere; furthermore, how these voices participate in social perception patterns relevant to the circumstances of its broadcasting.

Gideon Hausner, the state prosecutor, opened the trial, declaring: "When I stand before you here, judges of Israel, to lead the Prosecution of Adolf Eichmann, I am not standing alone. With me are six million accusers."[86] The six million haunted the courtroom, populating it with the absent presence of specters. Poet Haim Gouri, who covered the trial, refers to the eerie courtroom atmosphere:

> With an unmatched force, the court has managed to restrain the crushing power of the cry that burst out, now as if for the first time, and to transmit it partially into a language of facts and numbers and dates, while letting the remainder of that cry float over the trial like a ghost.[87]

When Gouri writes of ghosts haunting the trial, he refers to an expression—a cry—that eludes translation into dry "facts." On the radio, however, these absent-present entities were imagined through the disembodied voices of the survivors. In a chapter entitled "A Ghost in the House of Justice," Felman employs the metaphor of the ghost to describe how the survivors' testimonials in the courtroom transformed their bodies into vehicles in order to speak on behalf of the dead: "The speaking body has become a dying body. The dying body testified dramatically and wordlessly beyond the cognitive and the discursive limits of the witness speech."[88] At these moments, Felman writes, the witness—what remains from the calamity—"plunges into the abyss between the different planets and falls as though he were himself a corpse."[89]

How does the physical dimension of these witnesses translate when broadcast? Radiophonic space, as contemporary radio artist and scholar Gregory Whitehead described it, is "a dead nothing" that enables the return of voices from outside of time and thus facilitates an "afterlife."[90] This body-voice split inherent in the structure of radio does not imply that the broadcast voices are disembodied, but rather imply a body that draws on social imagination. The broadcast voices, from this perspective, summon an image, a fantasy, or a memory of their corporeal source; every voice, as Steven Connor argues, summons a speaking body.[91]

The image of Jews as "living ghosts"—disembodied existences hovering in a liminal position between life and death—prevailed in nineteenth and early-twentieth-century European thought, as evident from the writings of Heinrich Heine, Moses Hess, Carl Gutzkow, and others.[92] Susan Shapiro explains that Jews were described as occupying a position on the border between realms of existance; they were envisioned as lacking a national home (*Heimlos*); they were said to be "unwelcome guests and aliens wandering into and within other people's homes, disrupting and haunting them, making them *unheimliche*."[93]

Leo Pinsker (1821–1891), one of the founding members of *Hovevei Zion* movement, wrote in his pamphlet "Auto-Emancipation" (1882) that with the loss of their country,

> [t]he world saw in this people the uncanny form of one of the dead walking among the living. The *ghostlike apparition* of a living corpse, of a people without unity or organization, without land or other bonds of unity, no longer alive, and yet walking among the living—this spectral form without precedence in history, unlike anything that preceded or followed it, could strangely affect the imagination of the nations. And if the fear of ghosts is something inborn, and has a certain justification in the psychic life of mankind, why be surprised at the effect produced by this dead but still living nation?[94]

Pinsker's pamphlet expresses one of Zionism's central claims against the Jewish Diaspora, often denoted as a disembodied existence that would be physically rooted only by substantiating a national life.[95] Indeed, as Yair Lipshitz writes, the corporeal rendering of the character of the golem in *Habima*'s 1925 production partakes in the discursive and performative imagination of the "new Zionist body" as an image of the Zionist redemption.[96] This sort of Zionist male bodily ideal of the "muscle Jew" was articulated by Max Nordau, as a strapping man, an impressively tall and masculine figure who embodied the anti-diaspora-ghostly Jewish aesthetics.[97] However, in *Habima*'s performance these Zionist ideals were problematized. Meskin's rendering of the golem as an ominous yet comic figure, a monster with a childish brain, seem to mock the "muscle Jew."[98] As *Haaretz*'s theater critic stated in his critique of *The Golem*'s Palestinian premiere (on April 1, 1928), *Habima*'s performance did not comply with the depiction of the "new" strong image of the Jew, by summoning to the stage the diasporic Jewish ghosts. The critic writes:

> This is not a fine play. It has cheap moments that are accepted with enthusiasm in the diaspora and amongst the nations of the world, but Israel will not accept them. Such is, for example, the excessive exploitation of the synagogue culture. Israel will not

accept the "ghostliness." Israel has won, or at least is in the process of ridding the ghost. (April 2, 1928)

Haaretz's critic aptly discerned the ghosts that haunted *Habima's* Hebrew performance, and connected them to a diasporic Jewish experience that the Zionist enterprise sought to forgo.

The 1961 broadcast voices of *Habima's* members thus transformed, in the post-Holocaust consciousness, into the disembodied cry—the return of the "people of the air" (*Luftmenschen*) as mediated voices in the radio—by reiterating the 1925 drama.[99] Through the conferring powers of fiction and memory making, *The Golem* enacts the revival of the ghosts embedded in the Hebrew language, the dangers entailed in the attempt to obliterate memory. The voices in *The Golem* thus resuscitate the latent disembodied spirits in the Hebrew language in the form of Holocaust victims and memories conjured to haunt the public sphere in the newly founded state.

CHAPTER FOUR

Yaakov and Rachel

The Experience of Source

In 1922, Chaim Bezalel Panet—my maternal great-grandfather—immigrated to Palestine from Transylvania (the region bordering Hungary and Romania), together with his wife Bina (Dvorah Diamenstein) and his six children. A well-established, engaged member of his community and a pious Jew, he was inspired and led by the biblical divine decree: "Go forth from your country, And from your relatives And from your father's house, To the land which I will show you."[1] Panet would leave behind his mother tongue, his family legacy and culture, as well as most of his material assets, to pursue his dream and establish roots in "the beloved fatherland" (ארץ חמדת אבות), where he would practice agriculture.[2] Rather than drudgery and strenuous life conditions, in his mind's eye he summoned an idealistic vision emanating from his intense biblical readings about the ancient Hebrew patriarchs who dwelled in the Promised Land. In 1920, approximately two years after the Balfour Declaration and just a couple of years prior his immigration, Panet joined a Zionist excursion to Palestine; upon his return to Europe he wrote in his chronicle: "I was there, I saw it all—and I shall go *there*."[3]

Like many Zionist immigrants, C. B Panet longed to embody the biblical ideal of the new Hebrew man.[4] However, for him, as for other Jewish pioneers, the daily conditions of life proved to be extremely challenging, both mentally and physically: with very little running water, no gas or electricity, and poor living conditions, there was hardly any comfort in manual labor in the fields. What gave it all meaning was his profound sense of the emerging national gesture "to be there," sanctioned by the supreme Zionist instauration of the Bible in which it found historical evidence of the enduring connection between the Jews and the Promised Land. Like other Zionists in Palestine at the time, Panet's emotional reality was superseded by the biblical fiction whereby he suffused his world with a spiritual resource from which he gathered the strength to cope with everyday life. Paradoxically, the nearer he drew to living the "authentic" biblical fantasy, the more it revealed itself to be unsettlingly estranged from his native culture, and his day-to-day troubles.

This chapter engages with the aural representation of the Jewish migratory *experience of source*. Probing into the shaping of the Hebrew language that emerges from a 1952 recorded radio fragment of the *Ohel* 1928 theater production of the biblical play *Yaakov and Rachel*, this chapter examines how Jewish immigrants perceived and performed Hebrew in relation to the Zionist diachronic historical narrative of the Jewish "return" to their origins in the Promised Land.

Unlike other theater productions discussed in the previous chapters of this book, this chapter relocates us in the landscape and cultural life that surrounded the Jewish community of Mandatory Palestine (*The Yishuv*) at the end of the long, drawn-out 1920s; it transports us from *Habima*'s diasporic creative environment in Moscow to the *Ohel* (Hebrew for tent)—an amateur theater troupe established in 1925 in Tel Aviv by former *Habima* member Moshe Halevy, under the patronage of the General Organization of Workers in the Land of Israel (*The Histadrut*).[5] The focus on the *Ohel* theater enables us to examine how a geographical place affects the theatrical rendering of the Hebrew language; how imagined Oriental aural sensibilities wittingly access into the artistic performance of the Hebrew language.

In its formative years, the *Ohel* comprised approximately forty amateur actors of Ashkenazi origin, all of them affiliated with the *Histadrut,* most of them immigrants from the third wave of immigration (the Third *Aliyah*). They worked throughout the day at blue-collar labor, and congregated during the evenings to pursue theater rehearsals. The name of the company ("*Ohel*") reflects the diffusion of the biblical fiction into their rough migratory reality: it alludes to the tent camps that housed many of the new immigrants upon their arrival in Palestine, but also to the tents in which the ancient Hebrews dwelled, until their return to Canaan from Egypt, when they became inhabitants of cities (Genesis 4:20), as well as to the mythical meeting-tent (Hebrew for *Ohel Mo'ed*), the tabernacle erected by the Israelites during their wandering through the desert, which housed the Ark of the Covenant (Exodus 33). This multiplicity reflects a pervasive rhetoric employed by many Jewish immigrants in order to imbue their experience of life with the grand national narrative of the historical return to their biblical "homeland."

In the context of the sociopolitical transformations brought about by modernity, the *Ohel*'s theatrical manifestation of "the experience of source," discussed in this chapter, may be interpreted as part of a growing cultural pursuit of "authenticity." As Regina Bendix argues, at the end of the nineteenth century, societies believed to be corrupted by the trapping changes brought by modernization resorted to what they sought as their "authentic" states in order to build a new kind of polity. Within the context of this invocation, expressive oral culture was retraced as the poetic manifestation of authentic being, found in both social and cultural "others," as well as in historical documents. "Pre-Romantic and Romantic philosophers, literary critics, and authors in the eighteenth century," Bendix explains, endeavored to "locate, feel, and ultimately appropriate the expressive culture of the 'folk.' "[6] The Zionist pursuit for the Hebrew source can also be viewed in this historical context.

The *Ohel* theater operated within the Zionist cultural orbit in which the Bible provided the model for the original, and hence "authentic" Jewish nation—the notion of a national homeland and the Zionist narrative frame of homecoming after two thousand years of exile.[7] Above all—as Uzzi Ornan explains—the Bible was perceived as a resource for reimagining Jewish nativity in the land of Palestine:

> The feeling that we live in an era of Hebrew renaissance is shared by very many these days. Every cultural and national revival tends to cherish a certain past. Thus, the people of the European Renaissance went back to the days of ancient Greece, where they found motifs for their new art—in literature, poetry, and visual arts. Similarly, also amongst us there are those who return with a passionate heart to revive the ancient symbols, to a desolate primeval source of new motifs for creativity.[8]

The renewal of the Hebrew language—the language of the Bible—according to Ornan, assumes a central aspect in the Zionist claim that the Jews are the rightful heirs to the Land of Palestine. At the beginning of the twentieth century, prior to the establishment of the State of Israel, Jews had no developed recent history in Palestine. The Hebrew language, Benjamin Harshav explains, furnished the *"first archeology,"* "binding the immigrants to the Bible and to the Land of Israel."[9] Thus, although many Zionist initiatives in the Diaspora actively partook in the renewal of the Hebrew language, Palestine was considered to be the main arena for its revival and the Bible was considered its "primeval source," to apply Ornan's words.

Harshav's reference to Hebrew as archeology underscores the material aspects of the ancient language—namely, its pronunciation and articulation—as central components of its resuscitation. Indeed, the endeavor to renew the biblical language as the main spoken tongue in Palestine became part of a process of fashioning a Jewish national self-identification. Within this perception, the performance of a biblical play in Hebrew, enacted by Jewish immigrants, manifests the enduring connection between language, land, and the diasporic Jewry.

The *Ohel* envisioned linking the biblical "Israelites' history" and the contemporary Zionist migratory movement toward Palestine through the aural rendering and theatrical representation of the Hebrew language. Chaim Shoham explains Halevy's artistic vision, as an artist that

> seeks for inspiration in Jewish sources (the Bible) and in those rudiments of *Eretz Israel* reality that preserved the old and ancient elements, in order to shape through them original and contemporary theatrical norms as well as to establish the relationship between the distant past and present.[10]

The historicization of contemporaneous life in Palestine is a central idea in the *Ohel's* third production, *Yaakov and Rachel*—a three-act biblical play written in Russian by Nikolai Aleksandrovich Krasheninnikov—translated into Hebrew and adapted to the stage (with the addition of a prologue and an epilogue) by Avraham Shlonsky (1900–1973).[11] In this production, which premiered in Tel Aviv in January 1928, Halevy aspired to lay the foundations for an original Hebrew theater.[12] The vocal performance of the Hebrew language in this production is intriguing: despite the fact that all the participants in this performance were Jewish immigrants of Ashkenazi origin, the actors' speech imitates an Oriental accent and intonation. The actors ineffectively attempt to hide their Ashkenazi aural markers; instead, they stage their version of an "authentic" ancient Semitic Hebrew accent, rendered in what they imagined to reflect the deeply rooted biblical Hebrew intonation. By means of vocal execution, the emphasis on the Oriental markers of the language enabled the actors an embodied understanding and a physical reverberation of sounds that, although foreign to them, were largely perceived to be their rooted culture and ethnic source.

Such perception of the performed voices may be read as an experiential representation of the paradigm of "return," articulated in the context of European Jewry by David G. Roskies, as the archetypal modern diasporic plot of the twentieth century.[13] However, in contrast to Roskies thesis, when

Jewish immigrants during the 1920s articulated their desire for a generational symbolic homecoming to their biblical language through its Semitic and Oriental accent and articulation, they, in effect, define a return to a territory they have never bodily been to, in the first place. How can one return to an unfamiliar place?

The Jewish return to the "East," as Amnon Raz-Krakotzkin explains, was directed toward an imagined locus—conceived through cultural images as the proverbial cradle of Western (Judeo-Christian) civilization—fashioned vis-à-vis the real Arab/Muslim world.[14] The ideological need to identify with the ancient Hebrew past through speech, accent, and intonation generated affinities with historical, sensual, linguistic, and cultural elements with other Semitic languages. Thus, notwithstanding the prevailing Zionist imagination of the land of Palestine as an "empty" virgin soil to be redeemed by the Jewish people, there was also a paradoxical calling to incorporate into the Hebrew tongue spoken features from Arab languages in order to resemble the indigenous culture. This chapter focuses on the aural translation of the pictorial imagination of the Hebrew source into the vocal performance of a language iteration that marks the complex relationship with the Palestinian indigenous culture.

In the previous chapters I have discussed theatrical manifestations of sounds familiar to both actors and audiences. I have shown how the staging of Shabbat songs, lamentations, and other known melodies was geared to conjure up cultural and personal memories, through which the listeners could then identify with Jewish national aspirations, reconnect to the reviving Hebrew language, and affiliate themselves with the Zionist imagined community. This chapter, however, presents sounds and rhythms that were new, foreign, unfamiliar to the *Ohel* actors who performed them, and, to a great extent, also to their audience—in 1928, mostly of Ashkenazi origin. Probing into the experience and meaning of performing sounds imported from various Eastern (Arabic) cultures, I wish to capture a "historical sensation," defined by Johan Huizinga as "an understanding that is closely akin to the understanding of music, or, rather of the world by music."[15]

My interrogation in the following is twofold: I begin by asking, How did the shaping of the Hebrew language, and the imagination engrained in its vocalization, historicize the lives of the Jewish (Ashkenazi) newcomers? Subsequently, I examine how speech, intonation, and rhythms enacted on the stage reflect a temporal sense. Analyzing a recorded fragment from *Yaakov and Rachel*'s radio adaptation, I describe the aural gesture of the "return" to the mythical homeland—the experience of source—as one that brings to the stage the migratory experience; namely, a sense of displacement, alienation, and estrangement as central tokens of this movement.

The notion of experience, as Raymond Williams points out, denotes two main senses: (1) knowledge gathered from past events, whether by conscious observation or by consideration and reflection; and, (2) a particular kind of consciousness which may, in some contexts, be distinguished from "reason" or knowledge. "It is evident," Williams explains, "that the grounds for reliance on *experience* past ('lessons') and *experience* present (full and active 'awareness') are radically different, yet there is nevertheless a link between them, in some of the kinds of action and consciousness which they both oppose."[16] I refer to the term *source* in its triple meaning—as origin, evidence, and a fountain of information—in order to question Williams's idea of experience as "the most authentic kind of truth."[17] Accordingly, *the experience of source* is explored throughout this chapter across its various materializations in the *Ohel*'s audio recording: (1) by questioning the ability of the archival recorded source to conjure theatrical performances; (2) through the embodiment of the Hebrew biblical source; (3) in the vocal invocation of the imagery that nurtured the Hebrew performance; (4) through aural dynamics manifesting indigenous dispossession.

Experience of Source: Attending the Archive

Yaakov and Rachel dramatizes the pastoral love story of young Yaakov, a migrant who has recently arrived in Haran, and Rachel, a beautiful young shepherdess and daughter of Laban—the son of Bethuel, who, according to the biblical story, was the maternal uncle of Yaakov and a powerful man in his tribe. Committed to his ancestors' legacy, Laban wishes for his elder daughter Leah—whom no man seems interested in marrying on account of some deformity in her eyes—to wed before his younger daughter. Therefore, he conditions his acceptance of Yaakov and Rachel's matrimony upon Yaakov serving him for a period of seven years. When the seven years are due to end and his firstborn Leah is still a spinster, Laban decides to trick Yaakov into marrying her. He throws a wedding celebration and ceremony for Yaakov and Rachel, and, under cover, replaces Rachel with Leah. The dismayed Yaakov discovers, only at dawn, that he has actually married Leah. When Yaakov angrily protests to his now father-in-law, Laban accounts for his fraudulence by appealing to his unreserved fidelity to his tradition. Laban then conditions his acceptance to Yaakov and Rachel's marriage with Yaakov serving him for an additional period of seven years.

The audio recording of the *Ohel*'s production presents an edited version of the second act of the show. This recording, which can be found in the Sound

Archive of The National Library in Jerusalem,[18] follows the plotline of the dramatic text, though it omits significant portions of the dialogue. It presents the peak theatrical moment of the second act, whereby Laban conspires and executes his scheme to trick Yaakov into marrying his elder daughter, Leah. In this scene, Laban forces Rachel to step back and hide on the night of the wedding while he disguises Leah's face with a veil. At the time of the wedding, Rachel laments the loss of her beloved man. When Yaakov discovers the deception, he cries out to God for having pledged his matrimonial vows to the wrong woman.

This recorded audio fragment is in poor condition. It is marred by various sonic intrusions that constantly disrupt the flow of the recited drama. Metallic noises that break the dramatic sequence, blurred voices, and uneven volume instantiate the very fact that we are listening to a historical recording. Through its rough materiality it performs the allure of the archive, manifesting what Arlette Farge depicts as "a tear in the fabric of time"—a specific moment of the past that draws us into the rabbit hole of a certain time period.[19] Thus, despite its bad quality, as the actors begin reciting the dramatic text, the unique, intense vocal interpretation of this staged performance is, nonetheless, captured, providing a glimpse into a fascinating creative moment in the development of Hebrew culture in Mandatory Palestine.

Let's traverse together the scenes performed in this recording.[20] Laban enters first; in melodious recitation, he states that he will not disavow his family tradition, and, therefore, will not consent to having his younger daughter, Rachel, marry before her elder sister does. His Hebrew enunciation is in the Sephardic style; he underscores the gutturals, as in spoken Arabic languages. The tune in which he performs his statement alludes to the liturgical cantillation of Sephardic Jewish traditions. Through his melodic invocation, he embellishes his recitation by heightening his vocal inflections: prolonging some phrases and, shortening others by way of contrast. Additionally, he fluctuates the tone of his voice: for instance, when he describes his nefarious plan to deceive Yaakov, his voice becomes quieter and lower; when he unfolds his loyalty to his dynasty, he prolongs the names of his patriarchs.

The next vocal performance presents Laban and Rachel's controversy over the planned treachery. She speaks in a high-pitched voice; her Hebrew accent reveals clear aural residues of her foreign, Eastern European homeland. Thus, although she is Laban's daughter, her vocal performance associates her with a different place and culture. Rachel's voice is characterized by a gentle, feminine, trembling inflection; it stands in clear opposition to her father's oriental tone, rhythm, and synagogal-like cantillation. Rachel reacts to her father's plot to replace the bride under the wedding canopy with a loud, pure vocal interjection, a scream of horror—which immediately transforms into a lingering cry over her miserable fate and her desire to die. Upon completing her emotional outlet she, nevertheless, succumbs to her father's aggression and acquiesces to his plan; the scene then fades out with orchestral music.

The dramatic dialogue continues with Laban praying to his gods. His prayer leads the cantillation-like singing, further enhanced by his sons, who join in as a chorus in melodic recitation. The choral singing infuses the staged soundscape with the celebratory atmosphere of the forthcoming wedding. In their singing, the choir alludes to Yemenite songs; they sing in quivering voices that create an aural image of the bleating of sheep, ironically referring to Rachel's vocation as a shepherdess. "Come, my bride," they sing, according to the wedding liturgical poem derived from the *Song of Songs'* biblical phrase.[21]

These celebratory sounds contrast with the sequencing vocal moment of Rachel lamenting over her lost love. In a romantic, melodramatic scene, Rachel grieves in a high-pitched, clear voice over her broken heart. The orchestrated melody responds to each recited phrase with the appropriate musical phrases to redouble the expression of her sorrow. The repetition of sorrowing sounds forms a musical reciprocity of echoes that string together Rachel's voice with the instrumental music.[22] Through this dialogue the drama shifts from the kinfolk intrigue to a presentation of Rachel's internal reverberating pain.

Rachel's pain, expressed through lamentation, resonates her posthumous intervention: a mother weeping for her children, as she views them striding into their Babylonian exile. It is her cry that engenders the Lord's promise, "and sons shall return to their borders," as mentioned in the book of Jeremiah (31:15–22). In this case, the dramatization of Rachel's lamentation in *Yaakov and Rachel's* audio recording associates to her literary typology as the national matriarch (*Em HaUma*, in Hebrew), following her children through times and generations, reminding them the prophesy of return.[23]

The last scene depicted in this recording is that of Yaakov protesting angrily about having been beguiled by his father-in-law. His speech, much like Rachel's, is characterized by East European residues. Neither Yaakov's nor Rachel's respective pronunciation of the Hebrew emphasizes the gutturals in the same heightened manner as Laban's Oriental pronunciation. We could, therefore, deduce that Yaakov's and Rachel's speech portrays them as immigrants; they do speak in the Hebrew language; however, they are not proficient in the native articulation nuances.

Unlike the irreclaimable world of unrecorded sound, this audio recording evokes the experiential dimension of voices of the past. However, despite the availability of the audio recording of *Yaakov and Rachel*, it poses intricacies that overall challenge my hermeneutical attempt to listen to theater, to sense the source, to reconstruct the sounds emerging from the stage, and to extract cultural insights from the shaping of the Hebrew language. The first problem I have encountered is technical, deriving from the poor conservation procedures of radio programs aired until mid-1950s on the Israeli radio. Up until the mid-1950s, broadcast items were considered ephemeral materials, and were usually discarded after airing—without being either preserved or archived. The artifacts that, somehow, survived were stored in Kol Yisrael archives in unsuitable conditions and with disregard for temperature control, a fact that damaged the sound quality. The recording of *Yaakov and Rachel* is such an example: it was transferred from the radio station storage room into the National Sound Archive at the National Library, where it was then digitized and refined to improve its sound quality.

Furthermore, this recording poses several questions stemming from missing metadata: The conditions under which the *Ohel* Theater recorded this play, as well as the concrete context of its radio broadcast, remain unknown to me; most significantly, I cannot tell how reliable this recording is in capturing the live event it supposedly documented. The inscription on the label of the record indicates that this recording was made by the *Ohel* theater troupe on January 31, 1952, and is one of two records that documented the performance. On this label appears another serial number of a record that features the beginning of the performance, which, I assume, registers the soundtrack of the prologue and first act of the play. Unfortunately, I could not find this record. The radio fragment that is the subject of my study is a residue from a reproduction of the theater production. It demonstrates the elusive experience of recording as an "authentic" source, as articulated by Walter Benjamin in his analysis of art in the age of mechanical reproduction: "Precisely because authenticity is not reproducible, the intensive penetration of certain technological processes of reproduction was instrumental in differentiating and gradating authenticity."[24] With reproduction, according to Benjamin, the aura "falls back to a last entrenchment: the human countenance. . . . In the cult of remembrance . . . the cult value of the image finds its last refuge." The separation from the origin thus generates a quest for a verifiable linkage to a sense of source and essence—authenticity. Within this quest, as Benjamin writes, the aura is "the unique appearance or semblance of distance, no matter how close the object may be."[25] In other words, it is the appearance of the authentic that looms from the separation from its origin.

In my attempt to recapture the "forever lost voices" of the *Ohel* actors, I visited the Yehuda Gabay Theater Archive (situated in the Tel Aviv municipal library Beit Ariela), in which I traced correspondences and photographs from the production, as well as the Yisrael Gur Archive and Museum of Theater at the Hebrew University of Jerusalem.

The archive, as Greg Dening argues, performs its own kind of theater, which can be defined as a juxtaposition of two modes of being:

> The one is our sense of "being there." The other is our performance consciousness. "Being there" is that feeling for the past that can only be matched by the hours, the days, the weeks, the months, the years I sit at the tables in the archives. It is an assurance that my extravagance with time here is rewarded with a sensitivity that comes in no other way. It is an overlaying of images one on the other. It is a realization that knowledge of the past is cumulative and kaleidoscopic, extravagantly wasteful of my energy.[26]

"Being" in the archive—digging into the dusty boxes and leafing through old diaries, directing books, and theater manuals—was crucial in this study. During my many visits to theater archives I discovered various materials related to the performance: programs, interviews, reviews, and other publications. Browsing through the illustrated material, I uncovered sketches and paintings of the scenography and costumes, along with photos from the staged production. I also found the dramatic text used in the rehearsals, as well as a parody of this play written by Avigdor Hameiri and staged in 1929. These materials were complemented by an unpublished academic article written by Freddie Rokem and Yael Admoni that presents a comparative study of the *Ohel's* play and its parody.[27] Additionally, I found Moshe Halevy's personal director's diary, featuring notes about the acting method and the characterization of the figures in the play; the administrative diary of the theater indicating the rehearsal schedule, including a list of tours and lectures by speech trainers, acting coaches, voice lessons, who formed part of the actors' training process; several administrative correspondences between Halevy and figures from the cultural scene of the time; as well as numerous reviews and articles on the performance that were published in local papers. As I read and observed the various documents, I began to wonder if these circumstantial archival objects could really be considered to be "the bones and flesh"—to borrow Rebecca Schneider's terminology—relics from the performance?[28] To what extent do these materials provide an experience of their source—the theater performance? Or, alternatively, do they only account for an experience of the archival source as such?

The archive boxes contain materials that have already been handled, sifted, and sorted by an archivist who arrogated to him or herself the right to decide which records are deemed to be preserved as "historical artifacts" and which are doomed to oblivion. The *Ohel* archive boxes that I ventured to explore whetted my appetite, yet they left much to be desired: I could not decipher from the documents the mystery of Halevy's rehearsals, the outline of the actors' language pronunciation tutorials, or the content of the lectures the actors attended as part of their training. Furthermore, the hierarchy of documents presented in the archive can be very confusing: the number of copies from each document, its classification, and categorization entail prioritization and denote importance. Does the fact that only part of the production has been recorded disclose anything about the vocal quality of the rest of the performance? And, perhaps these lacunae only provide an indication of the archiving culture of the theater in which the performance was produced. These are not merely technical questions, but rather crucial historiographical issues that shed light on the way historical narratives tend to blur the conditions and the reliability of their formation. As Dening argues,

> A claim of "being there" is blind arrogance if it is not accompa-
> nied by performance consciousness. There is a double quality in
> performance. Performance is always *to* somebody, an audience, a
> reader, self. In the loneliness of research and writing that some-
> body else might only be oneself. But when there are others, it is
> always *also* to oneself. In performance, we research and write in
> stereo consciousness.[29]

Dening's perspective entails focusing on the embodied experience of the archival work, from which the historian extrapolates and phrases so-called historical truths. In archival research, "[t]he historian," according to Carolyn Steedman, inhales "the dust of the workers who made the papers and parchments, the dust of the animals who provided the skins for their leather bindings, the by-product of all the filthy trades that have, by circuitous routes, deposited their end products in the archives."[30] The materiality of the archive, Steed-man contends, enters the historian in every lungful taken, embellishing the historical narrative with embodied experience.

The sound recordings I study expand on this idea; they generate an embodied knowledge foregrounded on the faculty of listening. As an analyti-cal historical method, listening is premised on the inextricable reciprocity of subject and object; sound recording positions the historian's physical sensibili-ties as central to affectively understanding the performance. In listening, as Deborah Kapchan writes, the scholar's body becomes a vehicle, enabling the resonance of his aural substance.[31] Listening positions me simultaneously as being with the performed sounds and distant from them.

The "double quality" of the "being there" archival gesture mentioned by Dening in the above citation unfolds a basic feature of digital audio media. Recording technologies offer the ability to resuscitate performative fragments from a vanished present; consequently, "they generate the feeling of not being coterminous with our time," as Diana Taylor writes.[32] Digital technologies enable us to record and reproduce past aural moments in many ways that overcome the fundamental ephemerality of the vocal dimension in performance. Having said that, we should always bear in mind the phenomenological discrepancies between the live instantiation and its technological recurrence. The tense dynamics between the fleeting moment and its technological reenactment expands the temporal array to be considered in the framework of theater historiography to encompass three instants: the moment of production, the moment of the recording, and the replayed performance are all interlocutors in this setting.

Digital preservation technologies, namely, present an archive that combines materials associated with the repertoire, to draw once again on Taylor's dichotomous observation.[33] Thus, the ability to "rescue" some gestures from the repertoire also underscores the disappearance of others. The audio recording of *Yaakov and Rachel* provides an indication of the vocalities of the second act of the performance; however, it also draws attention to the loss of the other two acts, the prologue and epilogue. Mostly, the remaining fragment uncovers an all-embracing, yet invisible quality that hovers in the abyss between the archival source, its related social fictions, and cultural narratives. The recorded source of *Yaakov and Rachel*, I argue, defines a cultural atmosphere—sensed but not grasped—involved in and influenced by the enveloping material world.

This cultural mood—or *Stimmung*, to use the German substantive term—expresses nostalgia for a place and time never visited; summoned, however, by fictional aural images. It is an iteration of voices devoid of bodily memory that seek to conjure up the biblical past they had never experienced.[34] In order to explore the cultural climate prevalent during both the 1928 production and the 1952 broadcast of *Yaakov and Rachel* and understand their imagined performed vocalities, I shall construe a web—a network of sources and evidence—consulting photos, biographies, and theatrical reviews of the time, in search for reports about the sort of speech and sound performed on the stage that would complement and contextualize this audio recording.

I seek to understand the artistic rationale behind this archival audio source, and the various hidden expressions stratified by the tessellation of artisans and social agents who took part in the stylization of the language in this performance—the director, the translator, the diction teacher, and the composer, who fashioned the melodious speech of the actors. F. R Ankersmit explains our knowledge of reality as comprised like a mosaic of which each

Figure 4.1. The stage in the *Ohel*'s 1928 performance *Yaakov and Rachel.* Courtesy of the Yehuda Gabay Theater Archive.

Figure 4.2. Yaakov (Ze'ev Barban) in the *Ohel*'s performance *Yaakov and Rachel* (1928). Courtesy of the Yehuda Gabay Theater Archive.

Figure 4.3. Laban (Simcha Tzehoval) in the *Ohel*'s performance *Yaakov and Rachel* (1928). Courtesy of the Yehuda Gabay Theater Archive.

individual piece of marble corresponds to a certain profession, artistic skills, and so on.[35] Probing into the logic behind the mosaic of professionals, and the various influences emerging from different sources, I examine the sonority in the performance and its significance both in its staged and broadcast contexts. I, thus, situate the different sources of the archive as part of a larger web vis-à-vis their relevant cultural and ideological contexts in order to show how the social context bestows its meaning upon sonority, and how the transformation of a post-Romantic ephemeral performance of authenticity is encoded into reproducible commodity.

Modernizing the Biblical Drama: Embodying Myth

Yevgeny Vakhtangov introduced Krasheninnikov's play, under its original title *Rachel's Lament* (first published in 1910), to Moshe Halevy during his affiliation with *Habima*. In the early 1920s, diasporic Judaism seemed to be detached from biblical images. Halevy was fascinated by the dynamic biblical narrative, yet felt dispassionate about what he perceived to be a Christian depiction of the biblical world.[36] Crossing over from the gentile appeal to the other side, the translation and adaptation from European biblical drama into Hebrew was perceived by Zionist authors to portray the desired return to the source; it endowed the "secular" Jewish creation with cultural significance and rendered biblical Hebrew the fountainhead for the new literary language.[37] Accordingly, Halevy aspired to imbue the drama with the spirit of the Hebrew national renaissance. He changed the name of the play to *Yaakov and Rachel* and adapted it to correspond with the Zionist image of the Hebrew forefathers and the ancient Promised Land. Halevy presented to *Habima's* members the play, explaining his artistic concept:

> We collided with the accepted approach to the Bible: long clothes with wide sleeves, earrings, turrets, long birds, rods and wicks— artificial ornaments. Not a living person, with flesh and soul, but a decorated icon. That is the Christian approach that has diffused into the Hebrew art and influenced it. We must find the original Hebrew style and clean it from any foreign influences. For us, the bible is not an ancient scroll mummified in holy shrouds, but a living book, that appeals to the heart of the Israeli person.[38]

Habima rejected Halevy's idea and decided to shelve the play. Halevy, however, did not give up; after immigrating to Palestine, upon the establishment of the *Ohel* theater, he continued to work on the play. In Palestine, his work was especially aimed toward yielding a theatrical embodiment of the annals of the Hebrew culture, and the renewal of the antique Jewish settlement in the "Promised Land":

> Along with the national revival, the Hebrew art aspires to cleave to the origin. The origin is in the material terrain and in the spiritual domain—it is the ancient literature, especially the bible. . . . *Yaakov and Rachel* initiated our search for an original biblical theater. Indeed, we drew from two sources—the bible

and our land. From the bible we took fantasy, innocence and
simplicity, and from the land—the folklore and the succulence,
the temperament and expression.[39]

Under the auspices of the cultural committee of the *Histadrut,* the *Ohel*
was compelled to negotiate its artistic aspirations to conform with Zionist
proletarian ideals. The Labor movement in Palestine underscored socialist
interpretations and humanist values in biblical stories.[40] Within this approach,
the biblical idea of a Jewish "exemplary society" was imagined as a concept
that should be fulfilled in the Land of Israel by Jews grounding their various
social institutions upon socialist values.[41] *Yaakov and Rachel* seemed to be a
dramatic choice that engaged with "the two crucial problems of humankind
in our times: the problem of capital and labor in society and the problem
of war and peace among the nations," in David Ben-Gurion's definition.[42]
However, in order to infuse the biblical play with these values, which advo-
cate Socialist Zionist ideals, it needed to be translated and adapted to fit the
new Hebrew spirit.[43]

   Poet, translator, and publicist Avraham Shlonsky, a central figure in the
Hebrew cultural scene of Mandatory Palestine, was assigned to work on the
Hebrew translation and the dramatic adaptation of Krasheninnikov's play.
Shlonsky anachronistically imposed biblical language onto the Hebrew translation of the Russian play, thus strengthening the connection between the play
and its biblical source. He inlaid verses from the Bible into his translation
and worked the dialogue, idioms, and grammar of the text to a language as
close as possible to that of the Bible.

   The appeal to biblical Hebrew as a lingual resource reverberates in
debates, which arose during the first two decades of the twentieth century,
centering on the Bible vis-à-vis the rabbinical exegetic literature, as sources
and resources for modern Hebrew grammar. This controversy over the primary
cradles of the Hebrew language bore far-reaching ideological ramifications,
as it implied the prioritization of some religious texts over others, rendering them more accessible to the general public (in terms of their available
translations and the ability of Hebrew speakers to understand them). To put
it schematically, this debate manifested two definite stances: the secular one,
which drew on the *Haskala* movement, reached for the Bible, and renounced
everything that was considered related to diasporic Jewish traditions. The
antithetical standpoint, however, favored rabbinical texts that were widely
studied in religious institutions.[44] By translating Krasheninnikov's Russian
biblical play into a language as close as possible to that of the Bible, and by
interlacing it with biblical verses, Shlonsky, in effect, presented the Russian

play as a Jewish drama, and transformed this pseudo-biblical Hebrew text into a language embodied by Jewish immigrants.

The language of the play was highly criticized, as is attested by newspaper reviews of the time. Criticism centered on two main claims: the first argued that the use of biblical idioms and manners of speech did not contribute to the innovation of the Hebrew language. The second reservation contended that the language staged many lingual anachronisms, mixing and matching verbs and phrases from different biblical periods.[45] Shlonsky's rejoinder to these critiques was that his rendering of the biblical language did not aspire to be historically accurate. In his Hebrew translation of the play, Shlonsky clarified, he sought to represent, through the shaping of language, a folk dirge, transmitted through generations by lamenters.[46]

By allegedly retaining biblical vocabulary, phonology, morphology, and syntax, the Hebrew in this play thus manifests Jewish continuity. This claim is premised upon the binding of disconnected historical instants through one diachronic enduring thread, while ignoring other "diasporic" phases of spoken Hebrew, on the one hand, and emphasizing lingual elements that enhance it, on the other.[47] This pursuit for Jewish continuity risks overlooking the plurality of traditions, multiplicity of expressions, and varied experiences of the source. The focus on a single source is intentional: the adoption of the biblical Hebrew as a paradigm of the Jewish homecoming to their mythical land advocates the "negation of exile" cultural stance. Thus, within the Zionist consciousness there arose a need to narrow down multiplicity, and focus on biblical expressions of Jewish sovereignty over the Land of Palestine, as a token of the fulfillment of Jewish history unfolded in its generational aspiration.[48]

The theatrical embodiment of *Yaakov and Rachel* in the Hebrew language transfigures the ancient biblical narrative into a plot presenting the supreme model of the new Hebrew Jew—engaged in physical work and connected to the soil of the land—as a realized, albeit fictional, presence. Throughout the enacted staged spectacle, the Bible transforms into a prefiguring frame for Zionist ideals: the prologue stages Yaakov's dream, depicting the profound connection of Yaakov with the "Promised Land" and with God; the epilogue presents the struggle between Yaakov and the angel, concluding with the command from Genesis 32:28: "Your name shall no longer be Jacob, but Israel; for you have striven with God and with men and have prevailed." The three acts of the play are structured according to the European genre of pastoral symbolism, which venerates the rural life of the native shepherds as "a totemic badge for the Hebrew nation" in David L. Jeffrey's words, "including sheep, tents, wandering, flocks needing care and guidance, nourishing pastures and refreshing waters."[49] The European pastoral symbolism is diffused in *Yaakov and Rachel* in order to depict the new Hebrew archetype, articulated by David Ben-Gurion as deriving from the biblical forefathers: "Our character [דמות] was not shaped during our wanderings. Here in our native land the Hebrew nation was born, grew and cohered, and here it created its eternal possession . . . the Book of Books."[50] By employing the term *character,* in the sense of a persona, to picture the authentic cultural origin of Judaism, Ben-Gurion emphasizes the authored nature of the new Hebrew society. Throughout the Zionist political spectrum, the essence of the new Hebrew person was described vis-à-vis the biblical predecessors, characterized by attributes such as authenticity and vitality; a person with a direct link to his organic landscape, embodying the national and political ethos in his personality.[51]

Yaakov and Rachel represent the profound connection to the land through their respective lamentation. Rachel bewails her aborted wedding:[52]

> Oya, Oya, Oya!
> Is there pain as mine?
> Stars of the sky!
> Desert mountains!
> Wind of the night!
> Look and see
> Is there pain as mine?

Rachel cries out to nature: she apostrophizes her recitation to both heavenly and earthly entities, creating an expression that metamorphoses lamentation, traditionally directed toward God, into a dirge that pleads to the cosmic forces of nature. Yaakov, for his part, during his moments of despair, cries out to the Angel of God:

> You did this to me!
> You came to try me!
> You challenged Abraham at mount Moriah
> Yitzhak, my father, in the binding!
> You wish to challenge me!
> I do not want this!
> I do not want this!
> Ahh! damned will be the night
> Damned!
> Damned!
> Damned!
> [*he falls down*]

In these instances, the voices of the characters, and the musical score that accompanies them, are shaped in affinity to Occidental melodies. Yaakov and Rachel, as they sound in the recording, have not forgotten their diasporic European heritage; at moments of grief, distress, and sorrow, they resort to familiar modes of vocal expressions. Halevy's dramatic aural approach, thus, aims to find a middle ground between the demand to establish novel representational paradigms for the new Hebrew man, and the impulse to draw expressive means from the European artistic sources and Modernist modes of representation. What, then, accounts for the authentic source of the Hebrew language and culture? Historical narrative and ancient Jewish myth, or everyday immersion in diasporic culture? Is it the embodied, experiential "being" in the time period, or the reflexive consciousness of history?

The search for the authentic Hebrew expression through Oriental representational modes is inspired by Johann Gottfried von Herder's attribution of authenticity to the pastoral way of life in the land. In the *Ohel* production, however, this approach assumes an intriguing twist: played by immigrants for an audience mostly comprised of immigrants, the characters of Yaakov and Rachel are rendered, through speech, movement, and costumes, culturally distinct from the indigenous people represented by Laban and his sons. By choosing the biblical episode of *Yaakov and Rachel*—a patriarchal narrative unfolding in the premonarchical Israelite tribal society, reflecting the family clan—the *Ohel* represents immigration as the foundational grounding condition of Jewish nationality, thus realizing Clifford Geertz's reflection, "It is the copying that originates."[53]

The European ties of the fictional world are especially salient in the stage and costume design. Both Yaakov and Rachel work the land, and belong to it; yet, their Oriental characteristics are significantly toned down, although still apparent. In other words, the portrayal of Yaakov and Rachel, according to the model of the new Hebrew person does not divorce from its European ties.[54] The scenery, designed by Halevy, with the collaboration of Boris Poliakov and David Shendor, presented an open stage onto which constructivist geometric shapes were painted as symbolic markers of the biblical landscape. The actors were accoutered to resemble living statues. Wearing a heavy cubistic makeup, their heads seemed as if sculpted in stone or wood. Furthermore, the movement of each character was designed according to the stereotypical movements of specific animals: Yaakov as a deer and Rachel as a doe; Leah as a calf; Laban as a goat; and so on.[55] Nathan Bistritzky, a dominant figure in the cultural life of the Jewish *Yishuv*, emphasized, in his review of the performance, the deviation of the *Ohel* from their ancient landscape. "The *Ohel*," he points out, presented Yaakov and Rachel as ethnographic pictures that evoke our curiosity, and not the racial complexity that provokes sentiments of communion, and the shared spiritual world. . . . We believe it is our duty to expose the world to the Orient not through exotic images as it has been perceived by humanity for centuries . . . but as the humanness, tragic nature of (humanity's) homeland. *The Ohel* however depicts the festivity of the Orient, as perceived by the European tourist.[56]

The depiction of the biblical story as an Oriental spectacle could be contextualized as part of the Zionist call for a Jewish return to "the East." The designation of "Oriental" was, thus, not only about Muslim or Eastern societies, but also about the Jews. The Jews, as Arieh B. Saposnik explains, took part in the conceptualization of both the Orient and of Europe's own Orient at home. In the mid-nineteenth century, the Eastern European Jews who began to flow into Western European cities were identified as "Eastern"—*Ostjuden*—precisely because of their Eastern "tribal" marker origins and Oriental nature.[57] Saposnik addresses the fact that those engaged in the Zionist project of fashioning a new national culture rooted in the "Oriental" soil of Palestine were, by and large, immigrants from *Eastern* Europe. The very concepts of "Eastern Europe" and the "Orient" were of contemporaneous origin, articulated in direct relation to one another around the late eighteenth century as the twin counterpoints to the idea of a Western, or European civilization. The conceptualization of the *Ostjuden* could, thus, also be discerned in *Yaakov and Rachel*, through their depiction as immigrants bearing subtle "Oriental" traits. The visual elements on stage and the choreography of the actors portrayed a highly stylized plastic world, meticulously executed. In tandem, the speech and vocal performance in this production, as well as the scenery, manifested a cultural *mélange,* paradigmatic to migrant imaginaries to the extent that it simultaneously expresses multiple cultural affinities.

This East-West mixture manifests a conflicting dichotomy, experienced by many Jewish immigrants, between a nostalgic longing for the culture they had left behind and the ideological aspiration to partake in the creation of a new Jewish national culture. The shaping of speech, be it on the stage or in other social arenas, was a crucial element in the Zionist reclaiming of the public sphere in Palestine by enhancing the dominance of Hebrew. The poet and columnist Yehuda Karni encouraged a profound aural transformation:

You must keep quiet for a while, and in your silence try to free yourself of all impressions and sounds in which you had been

engulfed in the Diaspora. . . . The wild cry which one hears in this
country at an Arab wedding is more significant for the Hebrew
art of the future than the formal European tune, and the dances
of our road construction workers are more important than the
most modern foreign dances. We must learn from the Sephardi
and from the Yemenites.[58]

Karni expresses a regnant Zionist rhetoric during the 1920s, when he identifies Sephardi, Yemenite, and Arabic iterations as prototypical embodiments
of the renewing Hebrew culture. The *Ohel's* theatrical manifestations of the
Hebrew language, however, unwittingly epitomized the difficulties entailed in
erasing residues of European-diasporic aural remnants, even when attempting
to adopt such aural attributes. In this sense, the *Ohel* did not only participate
in implementing Hebrew in the collective sphere, but also expressed the
problematical aspects of language assimilation.

Yaakov and Rachel manifests the quest for a native "authentic" Hebrew
culture, while concomitantly downplaying the European personal badges of
the actors. The endowment of the biblical characters' speech with Arabic
aural traces, thus, seeks to stage an apparent connection between the Hebrew
language and the habitat in the Land of Palestine. However, because Arabic
was considered a token of authenticity, Jews could run afoul in two ways,
either by overemphasizing the Arabic characteristics in their pronunciation or
by not being Arabic enough.[59] In a 1925 article published in *El Jazeera*, the
writer claims that the Jews' inability to pronounce gutturals is proof of their
non-Semitic origin. The conclusion from this hypothesis was that the Jews
did not belong in Palestine.[60] Speech, accent, and intonation surface as markers of geographic, ethnic, and cultural origin, and thus bestow autochthony.
The Sephardi Hebrew dialect spoken by Jewish immigrants epitomizes their
itinerant path, as one that can be traced back to Europe.

Yaakov and Rachel in this respect stages the Jewish forefathers—the
cradle of Hebrew culture—as immigrants. The constructivist mise-en-scène
does not imply the "silencing" of European culture, as Karni suggests in the
above-mentioned quotation, but rather the apparent influence of Russian
orientalist images—an artistic materialization of the experience of source as
multicultural. These elements are also made manifest in the aural dimension
of the performance, especially during Rachel's lamentation: her sadness infused
with orchestrated melodramatic music. Despite the attempt to situate the
scene within the ancient biblical world, the Ashkenazi vocal residues within
the Sephardic speech of both Yaakov and Rachel reflect the specific language
reality that European immigrants faced in Palestine.

In the effort to generate a modern spoken Hebrew that would correspond to the new Zionist culture emerging in Palestine, the fathers of Modern
Hebrew, nearly all European in origin, advocated that an authentic speech,
stripped of "exilic" influences, would exist in a language endowed with a
distinctly Hebrew timbre. Although the Sephardic inflection was sought in
order to be closer to the "original" modulation of biblical Hebrew, that which
ultimately emerged as Israeli Hebrew was a Sephardic-influenced enunciation
that maintained certain traits of the Ashkenazi pronunciation, embodying, as
Benjamin Harshav argues, "the lowest common denominator" between the
two main dialects. Sephardic and Ashkenazi dialects, East and West, fused
together in the *Yishuv*'s speech.[61] Thus, whereas the delineation of boundaries
determined inclusion into the new nation, it also served to set the nation apart
from what was gradually emerging as its principal "other"—Palestinian Arabs.

The Jewish people's journey back to its "authentic" source cast the "East"
not only as an image of an "other," an echo of a lost origin, but also was
driven by the aspiration to recreate the lost world in the reality of the Land
of Palestine, entrenching its position as the new homeland. Reflecting this
dual quest, *Yaakov and Rachel* succeeds in having it both ways: it depicts the
Oriental, indigenous Jew while preserving its migratory, diasporic character.

"Being There": Cross-Cultural Vocal Gestures

Alongside the national Zionist aspiration to renew the Jewish roots in the
land, while implementing socialist models (according to the biblical narrative),
the indigenous Arab society was perceived to "hold the mirror up to nature,"
reflecting a previous form of national life. Like many Jewish immigrants to
Palestine of his generation, Halevy sensed that the local rural Arab tribes
preserved the lifestyle of the ancient Hebrew shepherds, dating back thousands
of years. Halevy and his peers perceived the mythical past as almost tangible,
and therewith, also as an inexorable object of investigation. As part of the
Ohel's rehearsal process, Halevy decided to take the actors on an excursion to
a Bedouin village in southern Palestine—the Negev—in order to observe the
habits and customs of the local Arab shepherds.[62] The practiced traditions of
the Bedouins were, thus, experienced by the *Ohel* theater troupe as historical/
anthropological knowledge.

Halevy's anachronistic ethnographic approach tallies with Shlonsky's biblical translation of the play. In the range spanning from rooted authenticity to
touristic orientalism, Halevy's venture was premised upon the palpable ability
to physically return to the Hebrew past by visiting the nomadic indigenous

Arab tribes. This approach, crystallized in the ethnographic excursion to the Negev, was inspired by S. An-sky's ethnographic expedition to the Pale of Settlement (1912–14), which would become the cornerstone for *The Dybbuk*. Much like An-sky, Halevy, who took part in *Habima*'s 1922 performance of *The Dybbuk*, understood the vitality of actually engaging with folkways he considered to amount to authentic residues of the past.[63]

The imposition of biblical drama upon the Bedouins; the gesture of "being there"—which resonates with Dening's archival theatrical presence—subsumes the ability to conjure the past from present ethnographic performances. Herder defined the deeply rooted aural expressions of ethnic societies, especially the underrepresented and suppressed groups, as "archive of the folk."[64] This experience of source could, accordingly, parallel listening to the archival audio recording from the *Ohel*'s 1928 performance: it enables us to "be there" in an immediate mode; to experience the voices, and to imagine the proximity between the fictional dramatic sounds and the cultural realm of Palestine. Compelled by the quest to summon a lost biblical past in an other's timeless present, the *Ohel* actors drove southward, to the deserts surrounding the capital of the Negev, the town of Beersheba, whereby—according to the biblical story—Yaakov used to dwell.[65]

Upon arriving at the Bedouin tribe, the actors enjoyed traditional warm hospitality. The Sheikh of the tribe invited them into the tent, offered them fresh brewed coffee, and encouraged an engaging conversation, while the women from the troupe assembled with their counterparts outside the tent. As the day came to its end and twilight hours elapsed, the troupe was compelled to stay for the night and fraternize in a more intimate manner with the Bedouin tribe. Although the warm welcoming hospitality continued, as the Sheikh ordered the slaughter of a sheep and feast for the actors, the troupe increasingly began to feel the awkwardness of the intimate situation. This sense reached its peak when, after the meal, the Sheikh organized his boys to play in front of the troupe. Halevy describes the scene:

> The wide square between the tents was lit with the headlights of our car, and "Al-Shabab"[66] began to play. On the stage two actors-dancers appeared with unique costumes and makeup: one of them, an agile negro,[67] wore a woman's dress and powdered his face with white flour; the other tied to his chin a hairy sheep tail, that made him look like the satyrs painted on Greek vases. The rest of the youngsters stood in a half-circle and began singing while rhythmically clapping their hands, cheering the lead actors. Against the backdrop of these sounds, the two actors pursued an

erotic rhythmic dance, the like of which I have never seen even
on the best Variety stages in Europe and Asia. The "male" was
masterly seducing the "female," and "she" was avoiding his arms in
incredibly virtuous and erotically stimulating movements . . . the
clapping and singing intensified, until they transformed into an
ecstatic savage dance like the Dervish dances, and that itself aroused
the "couple." Shocked and appalled we watched this spectacle of
passionately mad temperament. The Bedouins crowded around
us, as our guide, Vilnai, whispered to us that we better watch our
women. "Al-Shabab" continued to sing enthusiastically, accompanying their singing with snoring and wild rhythmic clapping while
swaying their bodies back and forth.[68]

The *Ohel* company spent two days with the Bedouins, eating and sleeping
together. During that time, the Bedouins presented their habits and costumes
before the actors, who all of a sudden became an audience in this ethnographic
theater. The symbolic crossing over of the actors, who unawares became
spectators, underscores their liminal position during this excursion and the
vast ethnic differences between them and their hosts. Although the nomadic
Arabs dwelling in the Negev were widely perceived to resemble the ancient
Hebrew forefathers, the *Ohel* members did not experience their cultural source
during this visit. When the actors visited the Bedouins, they mirrored their
otherness to the natives. Apprehension, suspicion, and Oriental fascination
dominate Halevy's description of their experience among the Bedouin.

The *Ohel* arrived at the Bedouin tribe in order to learn about the
ancient Jewish past, through the lifestyle of the shepherds. However, they
found themselves perplexed by the different culture they encountered, and,
as Halevy accounts, were relieved to return home from the desert. This visit
was later used as a resource for his theatrical rendering of Laban as a Bedouin
Sheikh, patriarchal and cunning. The dance performed by Laban's sons in the
wedding depicted in the second act of the play, he admits, is modeled after
the "Al-Shabab" Bedouin dance. These dimensions of the performance do not
come through in the audio recording. However, echoes of Halevy's ethnographic approach surface in the shaping of the melodious speech of Laban and
his sons. Using the phonetics of the Semitic language as a model, the *Ohel*
sought to transform the oral expression or "natural poetry" (*Naturpoesie*)—in
Herder's terms—into an artificial artistic expression (*Kunstpoesie*).[69] Through
such transfiguration, the troupe members allegedly affiliated themselves with
the indigenous "authentic" spirit.

קיקי לב אבא (מישאל) בלבונינו (מיצעע) אפקית ל יי

Figures 4.4 and 4.4a. The *Ohel*'s ethnographic expedition to the Bedouin tribe in the Negev. Courtesy of the Yehuda Gabay Theater Archive.

The sonic encounter between the Jewish East European immigrants and the native people from the land of Palestine is represented in the play as hierarchical: Rachel and Yaakov are depicted as belonging to a European cultural order, whereas native Laban and his family are portrayed as unrestrainedly savage. This order reproduces ethnic preconceptions, reflecting the Ashkenazi hegemony in Palestine. The rendering of Laban and his sons as inferior to Rachel and Yaakov can be read in the context of the intra-Jewish, Eurocentric, dominant perception of social and cultural hierarchies, according to which the Ashkenazi Jews are superior to the "Mizrahi" (literally meaning *eastern* in Hebrew).[70] The aural depiction of shepherds and fieldworkers as Arabs from all kinds of origins reverberates with earlier Zionist racial preconceptions of Arab Jews, considered, like the Arabs, to be "natural" manual laborers—more suitable for husbandry and blue-collar labors, well suited, therefore, to substitute the Arab workers, and contribute to the national renaissance of Jewish agriculture in the Promised Land.[71]

Rendering the dramatic text with affiliation to Arab attributes of accent and intonation, the actors—all immigrants from Eastern Europe—evoke the world they lost with the emergence of the new social and political dispersion of the 1920s. When Rachel laments the loss of her love in a high-pitched, trembling voice, or when Yaakov expresses his pain and misery in an enduring cry to God, not only do they iterate their reaction within the dramatic world, but also give vent to their actual experience of migratory dispossession. In this sense, we can regard this performance not as a manifestation of the link between the Promised Land and the Hebrew forefathers, but rather as a presentation measuring the abyss between past and present.

Enacting the Sources of the Hebrew Language

The Hebrew theater was perceived as a critical channel for propagating the new Sephardic Hebrew accent. The theatrical shaping of the Hebrew language by the *Ohel* theater members necessitated extensive language training and pronunciation lessons. These actors were, in 1928, but amateur theater practitioners engaged in an oral transference of knowledge, which relied on personal communication, a dynamic exchange of ideas in the rehearsal room, and shared aural associations. Halevy elaborates on the vocal approach in *Yaakov and Rachel*:

I wished the language to present an original Israeli phonology; not just by staging the correct accent and the Eastern style of pronunciation of the gutturals, but in terms of the musicality of the language. In *Yaakov and Rachel*, I wanted to find and embody this melody. . . . we learned the correct and original Hebrew accent from our Oriental ethnic groups, the Yemenites and the Sephardim, and their synagogue cantillation. For example, in Laban's command to his daughter Rachel—"Hurry to the tent, my child, I need three sacks of flour to make cakes"—I used the melodious cantillation of the weekdays, as the command bears practical nature. In Yaakov's invitation to his bride Rachel to enter his tent, an invitation that bears the nature of a festive ritual, I used the melodious cantillation of Shavu'ot.[72]

As indicated from the quote above, the sonic reference to the Hebrew language, as heard in the recording, is not limited to spoken Arabic. It manifests a broad understanding of what an Arab accent is, encompassing liturgical rhythms of Hebrew recited by Sephardic and Yemenite Jewry. Some of the various sonic references that Halevy considered for the staging of the speech are listed in his personal diary, in which he mentions Arab, Yemenite, Shomeronite, and Sephardic liturgies. Halevy drew on these ethnic sonic associations, which he perceived to mark indigenousness, as both aural images and signs for Jewish cultural rootedness. The theatrical manifestation of language in this production, as I demonstrate in the following, reflects a linguistic crux vis-à-vis the socio-ideological function of the performance of Hebrew in the land of Palestine. It taps into the ability of language iteration to claim the public social space, capturing the exuberant search for sounds that reflect "the soul of the people," in Herder's term.[73]

Halevy invited Yitzhak Epstein (1862–1943), a Russian-born Zionist pioneer and pedagogue, to work with the actors on their accent and elocution, as well as on the Sephardic pronunciation and diction of the dramatic text, during 1927. Epstein arrived in Palestine during 1886, at the age of twenty-four, as part of a delegation that would study agricultural techniques and instruct newcomers. Although Epstein had learned Hebrew in Odessa, he insisted on adopting the Sephardic pronunciation and proper accent. He thought the Sephardic pronunciation style contained profound emotional and ideological elements; namely, the idea of the revival of Hebrew by returning to its ancient sources and land.

During his work in the fields, he would follow the Arab fieldworkers (*Fellahin*), listen to their speech, and study their pronunciation style.[74] He had a clear image of ancient Jewish life as interlaced with Arabic language and culture. These cross-cultural connections with the Arab fieldworkers were part of a wider worldview Epstein articulated in his essay "The Hidden Question" (1907), based on a lecture he gave at the seventh Zionist Congress in Basel (1905), stating that coexistence between Jews and Arabs in Palestine was a prerequisite for Zionist revival in the Promised Land.

Epstein saw in the theater an artistic laboratory for Hebrew oral expression that would contribute to the development of the Hebrew spoken accent in Palestine. For this reason, he was keen on training actors to deliver the Hebrew language on stage. He also coached the *Eretz Israel Theater* (TAI) in 1924, when the company arrived back from Berlin. Among his other educational activities, Epstein worked in Kol Yerushalayim (The Voice of Jerusalem, part of the Palestine Broadcasting Service) during the 1930s, where he trained broadcasters to pronounce Hebrew and also answered linguistic questions on the air during *The Hebrew Lesson* daily program.[75]

Epstein articulated his ideological perceptions of the Hebrew accent in the theater in a series of articles published in *Bama* (1933), a journal devoted to theater theory and criticism in Mandatory Palestine.[76] In these articles, Epstein unfolds his opinion on the performative articulation of the Hebrew language. He writes that in the deep layers of the national sensation resides a mysterious attraction to the Ishmaelite people that resemble our ancient forefathers: nomadic, tent-dwelling shepherds.[77] Arabs and Jews, according to Epstein, share many religious beliefs, customs, and habits. These cultural similarities are salient primarily in their ancient languages, and, in particular, in the Arabic accent, which he perceived as living evidence of the Hebrew ancient inflection and pronunciation style.[78] The practical implication of this approach was the adoption of the Semitic accent by modern Hebrew.

An alternative to Epstein's approach to and vision of the Hebrew language can be traced in Ze'ev (Vladimir) Jabotinsky's writings. In *The Hebrew Accent* (1930), Jabotinsky argued that the accent enacted on the theater stage is wrong, as it has absorbed too many features from Russian, German, and Yiddish.[79] Hebrew, according to Jabotinsky, is a Mediterranean language and its sounds are closer to Italian and Spanish than to the languages of the Orient. Jabotinsky rejected the phonetic and grammatical similarities and affinities between Hebrew and Arabic, despite the fact that they are both categorized as Semitic languages. He argued that the Arabic language has developed under a different cultural climate than the Hebrew, which had arguably been practiced mostly in European environments. The Hebrew accent should, therefore, be stylized to fit European harmonic, musical and aesthetic standards. Jabotinsky, thus, opposed the integration of Arabic elements into Hebrew pronunciation, claiming that our ancestors were not influenced by an Arabic accent either.[80] He argued that the Hebrew was formed as a Mediterranean man, in whose blood and soul several aspirations and several flavors of the nations of the North and the West were blended. . . . To set the rules for the pronunciation of the renewed Hebrew, if we must seek pints of support in other languages, let us look for them not in Arabic but in Western languages, especially in those which were born or developed on the shores of the Mediterranean.[81]

The dispute over the resources of the new Israeli Hebrew was not only theoretical. For many Jewish European immigrants, articulating Hebrew in a Sephardic style was an almost impossible task. As Israeli linguist Haiim B. Rosén argues:

> One might of course ask: would it not be desirable to bring us back to the real state of the scriptures in Biblical times, at least as far as the sounds of language are concerned? Perhaps this would be desirable, but it is impracticable, not only because we cannot force a whole community into a pronunciation that is not theirs, but also for the simple reason that we have no clue about the phonetic nature of the Biblical language in Biblical times.[82]

Epstein did not eschew the difficulties that Jews of Ashkenazi origin faced in articulating Hebrew in the "correct" Sephardic way. He coached the actors to accentuate the guttural sounds, in the traditional Sephardic style, stressing the melody in oxytones; the heightening of the light T; the pronunciation of the heightened Hebrew vowel *Kamatz* (aaa) as *Patach* (light aa); the pronunciation of the vowel *Holam* (O) as *Kamatz* and the vowel *Zere* (E) as *Segol* (light E).[83] The actors, however, could not pronounce the gutturals (ח-ע-ק) according to the Semitic accent.[84] Epstein explains:

> In this country, it is widely known that when the gutturals are articulated in an oriental fashion they can harm the delicate tissues in the throat and that their friction might cause inflammation and hoarse voice. This fact is known through experiment: anyone attempting to pronounce the gutturals in a Semitic fashion might suffer from this chafing that may lead to medical treatment . . . as it turns, the Semitic accent, when acquired in early childhood needs no effort and does not harm the vocal organs. In accent, as in style, the origin of damage is in the organic normal carrying

of the language, and the way he trembles his pronunciation vocal organs as one natural mechanism.[85]

In 1925, Epstein published a programmatic article entitled "Aesthetic Hebrew" in the first issue of *Theater and Art* (*Te'atron ve-Omanut*), a journal for the performing arts. In this article, he argued that an altogether aesthetically pleasing speech was a value of the modern enlightened world; contemporary spoken Hebrew was rendered as defective due to the European accents of its new speakers.[86] Not only did they mispronounce the Semitic gutturals but also imported the phonemes of their native languages into Hebrew. In order to solve this problem, Epstein proposed replacing diasporic guttural sounds with properly articulated Semitic or Sephardic sounds.[87] Extrapolating from Halevy's attempt to create a new Hebrew theater that would reverberate with various cultural sources, Epstein worked toward the creation of a new original Israeli accent and mode of pronunciation of the Hebrew language that would correspond to the migratory culture in Palestine during the 1920s, on the one hand, and to the national Zionist ethos of the Bible as the historical proof of the Jewish origins in Palestine, on the other.

Earnestly concerned with the proper treatment of voice, Epstein was the first writer to elaborate on the harmful effects of the Sephardic accent, advocated by the Hebrew Language Council, on Ashkenazi speakers.[88] He argued, nevertheless, that contemporary spoken Hebrew was rendered un-aesthetical due to the difficulty of Ashkenazi immigrants to pronounce it correctly. He especially referred to the mispronunciation of the gutturals, and to imported phonemes of their native language into Hebrew. This language, Epstein maintained, should be purified from all foreign influences and reconnected to its biblical sources. Since the return to biblical Hebrew could not have been carried out, Israeli Hebrew should iterate a symbolic return to this model of language. In practical terms, the Israeli Hebrew accent, according to Epstein, reflected the easiness of the articulated language—that is, its articulation with minimum effort. Some isolated features, such as two guttural sounds—*ayin* and *het*—pronounced by most Mizrahi Jews, were preserved as symbols of correct spoken Hebrew.[89] Yet, European immigrants found even these gutturals difficult to articulate. For this reason, by the beginning of the 1930s it was recommended to relax this effort, as it yielded unpleasant sounds whose utterance could be harmful to the throat.[90]

In the audio recording of *Yaakov and Rachel*, only Laban unconvincingly pronounces the *ayin* and *het,* in an unnatural and inconsistent manner. His conspicuous phonetic imitation coincides with his duplicity as a character in the performed drama. Yaakov and Rachel, however, do not emphasize the gutturals at all. A more salient Oriental feature in the enacted voices surfaces in the melodies and the rhythmic recitation they resort to in order to heighten their dramatic declamation. They endow language intonation and melo-declamation, a European concept as such, familiar to the actors both from Yiddish rhythmic speech, synagogue liturgies, and from the Modernist European tradition—with an Oriental tinge.

Salomon Rosowsky (1878–1962), a founding member of the Society for Jewish Folk Music in Saint Petersburg, was invited by Halevy to work with the *Ohel* actors on the musicality of their recitation. Rosowsky referred to his work with the *Ohel* theater in the local newspaper *Art and Theater*, stating that the Bible and its stories are the foundation for the creation of the new Jewish music. This music, he contends, should concomitantly reverberate with ancient Jewish poetry as well as serve as a repository of Jewish sonority.[91] In *Yaakov and Rachel*, Rosowsky explains, he based the relationship between music and speech upon the idea of a "dramatic musical conversation," in which the music shapes the temperament of the action. However, the musical conversation arising out of the recorded fragment seems more as an enveloping Occidental sound rather than a dynamic, leveled cultural dialogue.

Rosowsky was considered a loyal follower of Yoel Engel's doctrine, which held that the survival and renewal of Jewish culture depended upon the invention of a new style of Jewish art music based upon the ethnography of folk songs and dances.[92] On his part, Rosowsky professed that the new pillars of the musical drama should be established upon the Hebrew Bible cantillation. The Bible, he points out, is not only our poetry treasure house, but also a memory book of the Jewish sonority.[93] The aural texture that Rosowsky sought to create in this performance was formed from the interlacing of various melodious sonorities: one melodic line leads the scenes involving Yaakov and Rachel (the prologue, Jacob's dream, Jacob's grievance to God, and Rachel's cry), and another holds sway in the scenes of Laban and his children (the wedding music and the convoy singing in the epilogue). Jehoash Hirshberg describes the texture of the music of this performance as implying a Dorian mode and a syncopated dance rhythm, both associated with the orientalist style rather than to Eastern or Middle Eastern music.[94] As surfacing from the recording, the two lines are in constant interaction, forming, once again, an eclectic musical fabric. However, these different sonorities do not point at multiple cultural origins, but rather to their reproduction, materialized through an Oriental echo. The replication of sonic references generates the source as a migratory elusive reverberation that highlights dispersion and a conspicuous absence of roots. The intangible experience of origin is further enhanced in the radio recording of *Yaakov and Rachel*, whereby the migration of the body from the voice is structurally manifested.

From Possession to Dispossession: 1928/1952

The ostensible goal of reproducing an Oriental accent in the performance of a play based upon a biblical story is imbued by ideology. The emphasis on the diachronic historical narrative—namely, that the origins of Hebrew life and language may be found among the Bedouins and in the liturgical practices of Mizrahi Jews—generates the adoption of a synchronic dimension as well, which then becomes entangled with social power dynamics among the various ethnic Jewish communities, as well as between Jews and Arabs. The attempt to create a multicultural soundscape, in which European aural traditions and representational modes are interlaced with Oriental markers, exposes cultural discrepancies. We could thus say that this recording presents a *potential* source of experience. That is, rather than providing an authentic evidence, or a trace that conjures past events, it presents us with a speculative, contingent, fragmentary experience materialized though its disembodied reproduction.

Underneath the ostensible "East-West" vocal mosaic, which underscores a common origin among the interlocutors as it emerges from the audio recording, a dramatic plot of deception and fraudulence is revealed. Laban, shaped like the Bedouin Sheikh the troupe visited during their excursion to the Negev, beguiles Yaakov, the Hebrew immigrant, into an undesired marriage. The emotional spectrum wavering between suspicion and trepidation was highly relevant in the simmering atmosphere of 1928, even when coexistence between Jewish newcomers and local Arab populations seemed a realizable concept among significant sectors of the Jewish community. *Yaakov and Rachel* is a performance that depicts the last moments of this hope. The summer of 1929, however, manifested a political deterioration that culminated, at the end of August, in the exponential eruption of violent attacks by Arabs on Jewish communities all over Palestine.[95] Thereafter, things would change between Palestinians and Jews.

As in other case studies discussed in this book, the transformation of the theater performance from a live social engagement into a disembodied aural instantiation problematizes the immediacy of interaction between agents and the way it is articulated by means of proximity, accountability, and empathy. In other words, the recording of the theater performance altered the individual perception of the aural images represented in it. How, then, does the separation of the voices from their corporeal anchors affect their presence in the social soundscapes?

Israeli radio was characterized by a clear Ashkenazi hegemony.[96] In a world in which the radio was literally always an inseparable companion, due to a prevailing and widespread sense of emergency, this meant the silencing of the aural markers of Mizrahi Jews as well as of Arabs. The ten-minute radio recording of *Yaakov and Rachel* offers a wide array of sonorities that stage an aural encounter between Jewish and Arab sounds. These recorded voices, thus, become a unique example of an attempt to ventriloquize other voices through a mediated cultural representation.

The date inscribed on the radio recording of the performance is January 31, 1952. The context of the 1952 broadcast may insinuate the cultural resonance of the radio performance of the play. What was the context that produced this recording? Who was in charge of it? With no historical source to account for the specific recording or broadcasting date of this record, I am but left with hints encoded in Moshe Halevy's personal diary. Among the correspondence, I found a letter, written in 1950, from radio broadcaster Ephraim Di-Zahav (Goldstein), in which he mentions a radio program conducted by him, devoted to the musicality in the *Ohel*'s performances. Di-Zahav, a synagogue cantor himself, was in charge of broadcasting Jewish liturgy from different traditions. If he, indeed, played fragments from *Yaakov and Rachel* in his program, his choice could stem from their imitation of Yemenite and Sephardic cantillation. In such a Jewish-oriented context, the Arabic Jewish dialogue, the art of conversation, I argue, is apparently overshadowed in the broadcast recording of the performance.

The political context of 1952 affirms this proposition, as it entails momentous events: four years after the declaration of the Independence of the State of Israel that ignited a bloody war, in whose aftermath many Palestinian refugees fled from their homes (Al-Nakba); three years after "Operation Magic Carpet," which brought a massive number of Yemenite Jews to the new State of Israel. The resonance of the 1928 voices changed within the 1950s cultural realpolitik, and the way people listened to them had radically altered. From this perspective, authenticity and the ability to experience source from a vocal performance seems more elusive than ever.

The radio performance of *Yaakov and Rachel* could be contained within Renato Rosaldo's notion of "imperialist nostalgia," that is, the colonizer's mourning over the demise of the indigenous culture he had contributed to transforming or deporting.[97] Thus, the archival impulse to preserve an ephemeral oral culture partakes in the transformation of practiced traditions into commodified theatrical performances, passing for historical sources.

The recoded fragment offers a decontextualized experience, drawn from a decontextualized object.[98] The story of the fragment, in this sense, may also be understood in terms of the story of immigration as the source of experience.

Our story began with *Habima*'s recording at the final stages of their wandering; it ends with the Palestinian refugee crisis of 1948. After 1948, Israel, like other modern nation-states in Europe, was aspiring for national homogeneity through the deportation and dispossession of its minority Arab society.[99] The creation of the homogenous nation-state is based upon an idea of self-definition: a state territory is determined by ethnic, national, and allegedly religious borders in which the state represents one people. Homogeneity in this model was premised upon the idea that in order to thrive as a unified nation, it must minimize the presence of minorities. The radio recording from *Yaakov and Rachel* provides an experience of such homogeneity: broadcast in the context of the Jewish "melting pot" of the different diasporic traditions gathered in the State of Israel, the Oriental sound marks diversity within the Jewish soundscape. The distortion of Oriental pronunciation and the residues of the Ashkenazi accent heard in the recording attest to the power relationship in this performance, in which the *experience of source* is imbued with migratory aural dispossession.

Epilogue

Against Ephemerality

The Dead Sing

THE DEAD: But there is mercy in the world
And we laid to rest.
Thus the dead lie patiently,
With silence are we blessed.
Grass grows on our flesh,
The scream dies in our breast;
But there is mercy in the world
And we are laid to rest.

—*The Torments of Job*/ Hanoch Levin[1]

If gravestones stood as symbols at the beginning of culture itself, our media technology can retrieve all gods. The old written laments about ephemerality, which measured no more than distance between writing and sensuality, suddenly fall silent. In our mediascape, immortals have come to exist again."

—Friedrich A. Kittler, *Gramophone, Film, Typewriter*[2]

Our aural journey arrives at its final destination with the chorus of the dead singing in the concluding scene of Hanoch Levin's 1981 play *The Torments of Job*. Buried underneath the ground, these dead sing of their silence, yet they utter their lucid voices on the stage. Levin's dead present a contradiction that persists throughout the subject matter of this book: like the voices documented in the audio recordings, they perform a mode of being that consists in the decisive exclusion of human presence. The buried condition

157

of the dead renders a physical barrier between the living human realm on the surface and the buried sphere underground. Levin's dead bodies show signs of petrification; their voices, however, resonate on stage long after they have severed from their declining bodies, and they haunt the realm of the living. The corporeality of these voices, as Levin writes, can be traced to their dusty repository, their entombment underneath the ground. And yet, they sing—resounding a familiar intoning of pain and mercy that resonates from their eternal echo chamber—from their graves. Although the realm of the dead and that of the living are depicted as permeable, an effective line of division separating the nonburied from the buried endures. This division harbors different modes of being, by which the speaking voice—the performance—is infused with its past.

Hanoch Levin was born in Tel Aviv in 1943 into the migrant Ashkenazi culture of Tel Aviv in Mandatory Palestine. The singing dead he depicts, a dramatic figuration of *possessed voices,* are in search of a vocalizing vehicle—a medium—that would ventriloquize them by granting them breath, rhythm, inflection, and volume. The singing dead are in need of a channel through which they can conjure as disembodied voices. The singing voices of the dead are not ghosts but actual resonances within the depicted fiction.

Possessed voices is the performative paradigm that looms large from this study. The Modernist Hebrew theater staged such infatuated voices through mythical figures such as the voice of the dybbuk emanating from Leah's body, the spirit incarnated in the golem, the generic sorrow expressed in the Messiah's mother lamentation, or the imagination of source voiced in *Yaakov and Rachel.* Such voices stage a profound rupture between the speaking body and the produced dramatic recitations. The possessed Leah, the lamenting Messiah's mother, the disembodied ghost entrapped inside the golem, or the Oriental image of "source" enacted in the speech played in *Yaakov and Rachel* present the acting body as a sonic repository by which the decisive historical and discursive caesura in East European Jewry at the outset of the twentieth century and recording media converge.

In the confluence between historical circumstances and cultural reproduction, the enactment of language assumes a crucial position. At the beginning of the twentieth century, as Friedrich Kittler writes, with the emergence of technological media and psychoanalysis, the recording, storing, and repeating of experiences, in sounds and images, texts and traces, embodied or imagined, manifest as physical symptoms or as phantom sensations.[3] As Kittler argues, along with Sigmund Freud's "talking cure" and Edison's phonograph, the mandate for cultural memory and information processing that used to be the monopoly of literature has shifted from the written text to the speaking body.

The reproduced voices discussed in this study—all mediated through sound technologies—are traces rooted in acting bodies that dramatize their storage capacities: the dybbuk, the golem, and the mother's lamentation all iterate a voice other than their own, however surrogated by and infused within their identity. Although these figures present the body as a repository, the voices they resound have long since severed from their corporal anchor. Through recitation, vocal rendering, and musical speech these figures (in) spirit the Hebrew language, while animating a profound mythical sensation, ventriloquizing voices summoned from the premodern occult.

Gershom Scholem addresses the dangers subsumed in summoning each new, secularized form of Hebrew voices in his famous letter "On Our Language: A Confession" to Franz Rosenzweig.[4] Scholem writes: "We live within that language above an abyss." As if walking on top of a hollow ground from which "no sound rises," Hebrew, according to Scholem, is "heavy with impending catastrophe." Plagued by telluric powers, it is "a vestigial, ghostly language." These powers, lurking under the evincing energies of renewal and regeneration proclaimed by Zionism, also herald the dangers awaiting the misuse of these creative powers. Either way, the Hebrew language surfaces on top of specters.

The abyss exposed when opening the vocalic bodies—be it the golem, or Leah's body—is loaded with sounds that beckon apparitions tracing back to the diasporic sonorities originating in Eastern European Jewry. These ghosts, as I have attempted to show in this study, associated with the Jewish diasporic past, haunt the Israeli soundscape. When these voices were performed in the diaspora, they were entrenched within the corporeality of the theater. However, when they severed from their bodily anchor, they rematerialized as disembodied voices, mediated through the airwaves of the radio. These voices "haunt" Jewish culture before and after the establishment of the State of Israel. Their transmission through recording technology severed them from their corporeal anchor and transcribed them as disembodied voices, played and replayed on the radio, penetrating households and permeating public arenas.

The story of the Modernist Hebrew theater cannot be reduced to the narrative of a subject, an artist of a theater troupe, nor to the specific chronology of a concept or a case study of the lived past; rather, it seeks to trace the linkage of technology, bodies, Jewish nationality and religion that has furnished and orchestrated *Habima*'s and the *Ohel*'s voices as a staged performance and as disembodied broadcast aural instantiations. This idea is premised on the generalization of the concept of "medium" as encompassing both living bodies and technological mechanical apparatuses of sound recording and transmission.

The sounds stowed within *Habima*'s vocal performances, later inscribed in the audio recordings, transcend their semantic interpretation, manifesting the language through its phonetic properties and musical performance. Approaching theater as media entails thinking of the modes it processes, stores, and conveys signifiers, and the ways its content is reshaped according to the historical circumstances and its technological transmission. The differences between the staged performance and the recorded instantiations provide the epistemological pivot for its assessment. Since we can only be privy to the voices reverberating in theatrical performances through their recordings, we are constantly compelled to shift between the theatrical discourse and its relevant cultural network, and evaluate the transformations that took place in Modernist interwar aesthetics when rendered through recording technologies. Conspicuously, the circumstances of the performance and the medium of its transmission affect its interpretation and social signification. The theatrical stage enactment and the disembodied vocal performance are, thus, observed not only as genealogical media, but also contrasted as two knowledge systems—the scopic and the auricular.

The case study of Hebrew and its unique historical circumstances enables us to trace the transformation of kinesthetic substrata by its mediating frameworks: from the written word onto the live stage, and as disembodied voices played through recording technologies. Listening to *Habima*'s theater enables a hermeneutics that moves beyond and beneath the written text and centers on voice as a mnemonic sign. When mediated through sound technologies, these voices surpass both the fictional drama and the theatrical performance. Sound is unselective in the aural information it records, capturing indiscriminately the intentional and unintentional elements of recitation, orchestrated sounds, and noises.

The dramatic meanings are conveyed in the texts together with the accents, rhythms, intonations, vocal inflictions, and sonic associations. Thus, *Habima*'s voices stage rhythms, intonations, accents, and aural imagery that evoke nostalgia to the perished European Jewish culture. Through their lingering presence in the Israeli public sphere they perform, each time anew, the discrepancy—the rupture—between their staged performance and their ongoing, repeating, and altering presence as mediated unbodied aural manifestations.

At the center of this book resides a recurring rhythmic pattern: abyss and volcano, rise and fall, redemption through calamity. Rhythm, as Jean-Luc Nancy argues in his influential book *Listening*, "is the time of time."[5] From this point of view, the rhythmic pattern reduces a melodious idiom into a cultural code that depicts the curves of history in the shape of the unbounded model of the rise and the fall. Rhythm, thus, points at its effect of immediacy as a

discursive network by performing its aural materiality, style, and signification. In this study, I have listened to several rhythmic occurrences: (1) the
rhythms of language recitations employed in the theatrical manifestation of
the Hebrew language; (2) the circular repetitive rhythm of the performance—
both live and recorded—whereby the archive transforms into an ongoing
replaying; (3) the rhythm of history and its rupture—the flow and the ebbs
of speech—as a reflection of modern technology. The rhythmic patterns
enacted in the language performance of the Modernist Hebrew theater staged
the historical Zionist narrative of the twentieth century: national revival that
passes through catastrophe.

The sound recordings of the Modernist Hebrew theater demonstrate the
volatile, deflected temporality of the theatrical event. These voices render the
archive as an ongoing, repetitive performance in which binary distinctions
between the live and the recorded, the corporeal and the absent, the enduring
and the ephemeral are undermined. These aural remains enable us to listen
to the voices of the past as recurring aural instantiations, and to experience
them as vestiges. The disembodied voices reiterated in the recordings summon diasporic specters by evoking both their rupture from their theatrical
corporeality and the circumstances of their demise. They are the possessed
voices that continue to haunt our soundscapes.

Notes

Preface

1. "Das Tier in der Synagoge," translation from Franz Kafka, "The Animal in the Synagogue," in *Parables and Paradoxes*, ed. Nahum N. Glatzer, trans. Ernst Kaiser and Eithne Wilkins (New York: Schocken, 1961 [1946]), 49–59.

2. Ibid., 57.

3. Ibid., 49.

4. Ibid., 55.

5. Ibid.

6. Michel Chion, *Audio-Vision: Sound on Screen*, trans. and ed. Claudia Gorbman (New York: Columbia University Press, 1994), 25–34.

7. Franz Kafka, "The Animal in the Synagogue," 57.

8. Ibid., 51.

9. Ibid., 49.

10. Jonathan Boyarin, "The Other Within and the Other Without," in *The Other in Jewish Thought and History*, eds. Laurence J. Silberstein and Robert L. Cohn (New York: New York University Press, 1994), 445.

11. Ibid.

Introduction

1. Visit https://www.ruthieabeliovich.com/possessed-voices to listen to the audio recordings.

2. The precise date of *Habima*'s establishing is debatable. The official inauguration of the theater was the occasion of their theatrical debut on October 1918 with the staging of *Neshef Bereshit* (literally, "Genesis Gala"). Yet other dates are also sought to signify the constitution of the theater: The first meeting of its founding members—Zemach, Rovina, and Gnessin—during the spring of 1917; the listing of "The Jewish dramatic association *Habima*" in the Moscow municipal registrations in October 1916; or, the first Hebrew performance by a young acting group in Bialistock,

led by Nachum Zemach, on June 1909. See Vladislav Ivanov, *Russkiye Sezony Teatra "Gabima"* (Moscow: Artist. Rezhissyor Teatre, 1999), 10–16.

3. The story of *Habima* has furnished numerous historical studies, among them: Emanuel Levy, *The Habima, Israel's National Theater, 1917–1977: A Study of Cultural Nationalism* (New York: Columbia University Press, 1979); Raikin Ben-Ari, *Habima*, trans. A. H Gross and I. Soref (New York: T. Yoseloff, 1957); Freddie Rokem, "Hebrew Theater from 1889 to 1948," in *Theater in Israel*, ed., Linda Ben Zvi (Ann Arbor: The University of Michigan Press, 1996), 51–84; Shelly Zer-Zion, *Habima in Berlin: The Institutionalization of a Zionist Theater* (Jerusalem: Magnes Press, 2015); Elena Tartakovsky, *Habima: The Russian Heritage* (Tel Aviv: Safra, 2013).

4. Gad Kaynar, "National Theater as Colonized Theater: The Paradox of Habima," *Theater Journal* 50, no. 1 (March 1998): 1.

5. The Modernist Hebrew theater is not a stand-alone tradition and did not develop in isolation to the Modernist Yiddish theater. For an elaborate discussion on the profound stylistic and thematic connections and influences of the Modernist Yiddish Theater on *Habima*, see Shelly Zer-Zion, "The Birth of Habima and the Yiddish Art Theater Movement," in *Jewish Theater: Tradition in Transition and Intercultural Vistas*, ed. Ahuva Belkin (Tel Aviv: Assaph, Tel Aviv University, 2008), 73–88.

6. On the Yiddish dramatic repertoire in the Hebrew theater that developed in Mandatory Palestine, and the Yiddish theater as an artistic foundation for the Israeli theater stage, see Dorit Yerushalmi, "The Inter-relationship between Hebrew Theater and Yiddish Theater through the Work of Mandatory Palestine Directors," *Criticism and Interpretation* 41 (Bar-Ilan University Publishers) (Winter 2009): 7–39.

7. Sergei Glagolin, quoted in Yehoshua A. Gilboa, *A Language Silenced: The Suppression of Hebrew literature and Culture in the Soviet Union* (Rutherford, NJ: Fairleigh Dickinson Press, 1982), 131. On the new sounds of *Habima* see Shelly Zer-Zion, "The Creation of New Sounds: Hebrew as a New Spoken Language on the Israeli Stage of the 1920's," in *Théâtre: Espace Visual*, ed. Christine Hamon-Sirejols and Anne Surgers (Lyon: Presses Universitaires de Lyon, 2003), 359–63.

8. The term *Ashkenaz* broadly refers to the distinctive generational Jewish tradition, liturgy, synagogue rituals, and culture, originating in the diasporic communities dwelling in the Rhineland Valley and northern France during the Middle Ages, and later, after the Crusades (eleventh to thirteenth century), in the Slavic lands and Europe at large.

9. On the genealogy of the proto-Israeli accent as it functioned in the burgeoning Hebrew literature, see Miryam Segal, *A New Sound in Hebrew Poetry: Poetics, Politics, Accent* (Bloomington: Indiana University Press, 2010).

10. On early Soviet theater and culture, see René Fülöp-Miller and Joseph Gregor, *The Russian Theater: Its Character and History with Especial Reference to the Revolutionary Period* (New York: B. Blom, 1968; originally published by George G. Harrap, London, 1930). See also, Fülöp-Miller, *The Mind and Face of Bolshevism: An Examination of Cultural Life in Soviet Russia* (New York: A. A. Knopf, 1928) especially the chapter entitled "Theatricalized Life"; Lars Kleberg's book *Theater as Action: Soviet Russian Avant-garde Aesthetics*, trans. Charles Rougle (Houndsmills, Basingstoke, Hampshire: Macmillan Press, 1993) examines the avant-garde involvement in the Soviet theater.

11. For an elaborate discussion of *Habima*'s voice and language classes with Prince Sergei Volkonsky, see Elena Tartakovsky, *Habima: The Russian Heritage* (Tel Aviv: Safra, 2013), 125–35.

12. Carrie J. Preston, *Modernism's Mythical Pose: Gender, Genre, Solo Performance* (New York: Oxford University Press, 2011), 92.

13. For further reading on Delsarte and Delsartism in Modernist theater, see Carrie J. Preston, "Posing Modernism: Delsartism in Modern Dance and Silent Film," *Theater Journal* 61, no. 2 (2009): 213–33; E. T Kirby, "The Delsarte Method: 3 Frontiers of Actor Training," *The Drama Review: TDR* 16, no. 1 (1972): 55–69; George Taylor, "François Delsarte: A Codification of Nineteenth-Century Acting," *Theater Research International* 24 (1999): 71–82.

14. On the centrality of myth to Modernist literature, see Shanyn Fiske, "From Ritual to the Archaic in Modernism: Frazer, Harrison, Freud, and the Persistence of Myth," in *A Handbook for Modernism Studies,* ed. Jean-Michel Rabaté (Chichester, West Sussex, UK: John Wiley and Sons, 2013), 173–91; Michael Bell, *Literature, Modernism and Myth: Belief and Responsibility in the Twentieth Century* (Cambridge: Cambridge University Press, 1997).

15. Carrie J. Preston, *Modernism's Mythical Pose: Gender, Genre, Solo Performance* (New York: Oxford University Press, 2011), 5–9.

16. Delsarte himself was once a vocalist who turned to teaching only after his own prospects for an operatic career were ruined by the early misuse of his voice.

17. Julia A. Walker, "Voice: Oratory Expression and the Text/Performance Split," in *Expressionism and Modernism in the American Theater* (Cambridge: Cambridge University Press, 2005), 58–83.

18. Julia A. Walker explains that in the Delsarte method each expression or gesture was granted specific meaning. It, was, according to Walker "like the neoclassical system of rhetorical gesture in its codification of bodily movement." Walker clarifies that "Unlike the neoclassical decorum, however, it held that its signification was discovered in nature rather than produced by convention." See Walker, *Expressionism and Modernism in the American Theater*, 43.

19. Today the Delsarte movement is best known on account of its satirical treatment in the 1957 Broadway musical *The Music Man*. Nonetheless, the Delsarte poses, like music, were, for a time, popular additions to a recitation. For further reading, see Marian Wilson Kimber, "In a Woman's Voice: Musical Recitation and the Feminization of American Melodrama," in *Melodramatic Voices: Understanding Music Drama,* ed. Sarah Hibberd (Aldershot: Ashgate, 2011), 61–82.

20. Julia A. Walker, *Expressionism and Modernism in the American Theater*, 62.

21. Ibid.

22. Archibald MacLeish's poem "Ars Poetica" includes the line: "a poem should not mean but be." This poem first appeared in *Poetry: A Magazine of Verse* edited by Harriet Monroe in June 1926, and was later published in Archibald Macleish, *Collected Poems 1917–1982* (Boston: Houghton Mifflin Harcourt, 1985). I thank Talia Trainin for pointing out this reference to me.

23. Elena Tartakovsky, *Habima: The Russian Heritage* (Tel Aviv: Safra, 2013), 124–25.

24. Ibid., 131–33.

25. "Just as myths already entail enlightenment, with every step enlightenment entangles itself more deeply in mythology." See Theodor Adorno and Max Horkheimer, *Dialectic of Enlightenment: Philosophical Fragments* (Stanford: Stanford University Press, 2002), 8.

26. Lynda Jessup, ed., *Anti-Modernism and Artistic Experience: Policing the Boundaries of Modernity* (Toronto: University of Toronto Press, 2001), 3.

27. The term "scopic regime" was coined in 1975 by the film theorist Christian Metz in his book *The Imaginary Signifier* in relation to the distinction between cinema and theater. Martin Jay expounded this term in relation to modernity. See Martin Jay, "Scopic Regimes of Modernity," in *Vision and Visuality: Discussions in Contemporary Culture* No. 2, ed. Hal Foster (Seattle, Washington: Bay Press, 1988), 3–27.

28. On the shift to corporeality in Jewish studies, see Barbara Kirshenblatt-Gimblett, "The Corporeal Turn," *JQR* 95, no. 3 (Summer 2005): 447–61.

29. The station, then named Kol Yerushalayim, opened with a ceremony in which Hanna Rovina, the first lady of the *Habima* theater, recited Chaim Nachman Bialik's prose poem "Megilat Ha-esh" ("Scroll of Fire"). Her Hebrew words resonated throughout the country with a heavy Russian accent. "Megilat Ha-esh" was initially published in 1905. See *Songs from Bialik: Selected Poems of Hayim Nahman Bialik* [*sic*], ed. and trans. Atari Hadari (Syracuse: Syracuse University Press, 2000).

30. Tamar Liebes, "Acoustic Space: The Role of Radio in Israeli Collective History," *Jewish History* 20 (2006): 69–90.

31. Itamar Ben-Avi expressed his exhilaration regarding the inaugural ceremony of the Hebrew radio:

> This is a great day for our national language, perhaps the greatest day in all of its generations, from the time that the Hebrews created one of the most concise, precise, and melodious languages on earth. For on this day, Monday, the Canaanite dialect—"the language of Canaan" in the words of our noble prophet—will soar into the air. It will reverberate from the heights of Judea and Benjamin, in their united borders, not only to all corners of our national home in its third resurrection, but also to all ends of the globe.

In Tamar Liebes and Zohar Kampf, "Hello! This Is Jerusalem Calling": The Revival of Spoken Hebrew on the Mandatory Radio (1936–1948)," *Journal of Israeli History* 29, no. 2 (2010): 143.

32. Derek Jonathan Penslar, "Transmitting Jewish Culture: Radio in Israel," *Jewish Social Studies* 10, no. 1 (Fall 2003): 1–29; Derek Jonathan Penslar, "Radio and the Shaping of Modern Israel 1936–1973," *Zionism, Ethnicity, and National Mobilization*, ed. Michael Berkowitz (Leiden: Brill, 2004), 60–82.

33. Ruth HaCohen's *The Music Libel against the Jews* (New Haven: Yale University Press, 2011) further develops the idea of social and cultural idioms as rendered within fictional music from the Medieval period until Nazi Germany. HaCohen reveals symbolic configurations of noises and voices within imaginary worlds created in different artistic media, depicting the sonic representation of Jews and their relations to Christians. Especially relevant to the current context is her development of the idea of "performed vocalities" as defying fictionality and expressing the ethnographic and historical dimension of the "real." See HaCohen, *The Music Libel Against the Jews*, 11–16.

34. Hans Ulrich Gumbrecht, *Our Broad Present: Time and Contemporary Culture* (New York: Columbia University Press, 2016), xiv.

35. Svetlana Boym, *The Future of Nostalgia* (New York: Basic Books, 2001), 41–43.

36. On the incorporation of diasporic voices in Israeli popular music, examined through the prism of the concept of nostalgia, see Edwin Seroussi, "Nostalgic Zionist Soundscapes: The Future of the Israeli Nation's Sonic Past," *Israel Studies* 19, no. 2 (2014): 35–50.

37. Friedrich A. Kittler, *Gramophone, Film, Typewriter*, trans. G. Winthrop-Young and M. Wutz (Stanford: Stanford University Press, 1999), 16. The term *sound souvenirs* is also at the core of Karin Bijestfield and José van Dijck, eds., *Sound Souvenirs: Audio Technologies, Memory, and Cultural Practices* (Amsterdam: Amsterdam University Press, 2009).

38. Jonathan Sterne, ed., *The Sound Studies Reader* (New York: Routledge 2012), 5–6.

39. Theodor W. Adorno and Thomas Y. Levin, trans., "The Curves of the Needle." *October* 55 (1990): 50.

40. Peggy Phelan, *Unmarked: The Politics of Performance* (New York and London: Routledge, 1993), 146.

41. Rebecca Schneider, *Performing Remains: Art and War in Times of Theatrical Reenactment* (New York and London: Routledge, 2011).

42. On the distinction between the ephemeral and the archival in theater and performance historiography, see Peggy Phelan, *Unmarked: The Politics of Performance* (New York and London: Routledge, 1993), 146; Rebecca Schneider, *Performing Remains: Art and War in Times of Theatrical Reenactment* (New York and London: Routledge, 2011), 87–110; Diana Taylor, *The Archive and the Repertoire: Performing Cultural Memory in the Americas* (Durham and London: Duke University Press, 2003), 18–26.

43. Bruce R. Smith's pioneering book *The Acoustic World of Early Modern England: Attending to the O-Factor* (Chicago: University of Chicago Press, 1999) addresses the sonic experience of Shakespeare's contemporaries, by focusing on sixteenth-century manuscripts and print culture. Gina Bloom's *Voice in Motion: Staging Gender, Shaping Sound in Early Modern England* (Philadelphia: University of Pennsylvania Press, 2007) aims to reclaim sixteenth-century aural artifacts by targeting the conditions involved in the communication of voice, in an effort to theorize the relation between voice and agency. Despite their emphasis on the materiality of the voice, both Smith and Bloom relay on literary, theoretical, and historical textual evidence that, through

recording sound and voice, remain silent. Peter Holland's "Hearing the Dead: The Sound of David Garrick" (2007) and Judith Pascoe's *The Sarah Siddons Audio Files: Romanticism and the Lost Voice* (Ann Arbor: University of Michigan Press, 2011) are further examples of such theoretical modes of inquiry. In the dearth of available audio recordings, both Holland and Pascoe draw on textual and visual sources that describe the theatrical phenomenology of the voice; these, however, lack the reflective experience of listening to Garrick's or Siddons's voices.

44. Jonathan Sterne, *The Audible Past: Cultural Origins of Sound Reproduction* (London and Durham: Duke Univeristy Press, 2003), 23.

45. Michael Bull and Les Back, eds., *The Auditory Culture Reader* (Oxford: Berg, 2013); Trevor Pinch and Karin Bijsterveld, eds., *The Oxford Handbook for Sound Studies* (New York: Oxford University Press, 2012).

46. Jonathan Sterne, ed., *The Sound Studies Reader* (New York: Routledge 2012), 4.

47. Regina Bendix, "The Pleasure of the Ear: Toward an Ethnography of Listening," *Cultural Analysis* 1 (2000): 33–50.

48. Deborah A. Kapchan, ed., *Theorizing Sound Writing* (Middletown, CT: Wesleyan University Press, 2017), 4.

49. Freddie Rokem, "Has This Thing Appeared Again Tonight? Deus ex Machina and Other Interventions of the Supernatural," in *Things: Religion and the Question of Materiality,* ed. Dick Houtman and Brigit Meyer (New York: Fordham University Press, 2012), 136.

50. Amit Pinchevski and Tamar Liebes, "Severed Voices: Radio and the Mediation of Trauma in the Eichmann Trial," *Public Culture* 22, no. 2 (2010): 265–91.

Chapter One. The Messiah's Mother Lamentation

1. Shelly Zer-Zion's book *Habima in Berlin: The Institutionalization of a Zionist Theater* (Jerusalem: Magnes Press, 2015) tells the story of *Habima* during its itinerant years (1926–1931), outlining the interconnection between the troupe and the German Jewish elite.

2. At that time *Habima's* repertoire included biblical and mythical plays, among which were *The Eternal Jew, The Dybbuk, The Golem, Jacob's Dream, Uriel Acosta*, and also their less familiar performances, such as *David's Crown* (*Los Cabellos de Absalón*) by Calderón de la Barca and *Amkha*, a Hebrew translation of Shalom Aleichem's Yiddish play.

3. On *Habima's* reception in Berlin, see Shelly Zer-Zion, *Habima in Berlin: The Institutionalization of a Zionist Theater* (Jerusalem: Magnes Press, 2016), 29–43.

4. The most significant anti-Semitic reaction against the troupe was the Nazi demonstration at the city theater in the German town Würzberg, on November 19, 1930. National Socialists protested outside of the venue in which *Habima* performed *The Dybbuk*, calling out to stop what they perceived as a "cultural disgrace." For a report on the Würzberg scandal, see Hans Steidle, "Der Habima-Skandal in Würzburg 1930/31," *Mainfränkisches Jahrbuch*, Jg. 35, 1983, S. 152 bis 210, Zitat: S.161.

5. Cited from "The *Habima* Players: Season at the Phoenix," *The Era* newspaper, January 1, 1931.

6. Eliyahu the prophet is addressed here in the Yiddish pronunciation as "Hanovvi," as indicated on the record's label. In future references to his name I will use the Hebrew pronunciation—Eliyahu Hanavie.

7. Visit https://www.ruthieabeliovich.com/possessed-voices to listen to the audio recording.

8. I thank Michael Aylward of *Der Yidisher Gramophone* website (http://www.yidisher-gramofon.org) for providing me this important information, and musicologist Edwin Seroussi of the Hebrew University for introducing us.

9. The legend of the birth of the Messiah on the day the Temple in Jerusalem was destroyed, and the never-ending quest to find him after his mysterious disappearance, appears in many Jewish sources, among which are: *Genesis Rabbah*, ch. 42; *Ruth Rabbah*, 1; *Esther Rabbah*, Proem, 11; *Sifre d'Aggadata*, on Esther, *Midrash Panim Aerot*, Buber (ed.), Vilna 1886, version B ch. 6 p, 39b. For an elaborate discussion of the legend as it appears in various sources, see Haviva Pedaya, "The Wandering Messiah and the Wandering Jew: Judaism and Christianity as a Two-Headed Structure and the Myth of His Feet and Shoes," in *Religion und Politik,* ed. Gesine Palmer und Thomas Brose (Tübingen: Mohr Siebeck, 2013), 73–103.

10. The story of Eliyahu's departure from earth is narrated in the Book of Kings 2, Chapter 2:1: "When the Lord was about to take Eliyahu up to heaven in a whirlwind, Eliyahu and Elisha were on their way from Gilgal."

11. Despite similarities between the Wandering Jew and Eliyahu the prophet, scholars refuse the identification of the two characters as one. For further discussion on the connections between Eliyahu the prophet and the legend of the Wandering Jew, see Harold Fisch, "Elijah and the Wandering Jew," in *Joseph Lookstein Memorial Volume, ed. Leo Landman* (New York: Klav, 1980), 125–35; Galit Hasan-Rokem, *Web of Life: Folklore and Midrash in Rabbinic Literature* (Stanford: Stanford University Press, 2000), 160.

12. The Biblical book of *Lamentations Rabbah* is attributed to a poet or poets in Judah reflecting on the destruction of Jerusalem in 586 BCE.

13. For a detailed description of *Habima's* rehearsal process with V. L. Mchedelov see Raikin Ben-Ari, *Habima*, 96–105.

14. Galit Hasan-Rokem discusses how body-voice performances of mothers' lamentation go beyond the individual expression and contribute to the processing of social conflicts and crises. See "Bodies Performing in Ruins: The Lamenting Mother in Ancient Hebrew Texts," in *Laments in Jewish Thought: Philosophical, Theological, and Literary Perspectives*, eds. Ilit Ferber and Paula Schwebel (Berlin: De Gruyter, 2014), 33–63.

15. Visit https://www.ruthieabeliovich.com/possessed-voices to listen to Rovina's recording of the discussed lamentation.

16. The translation of Rovina's monologue is comprised from David Pinski's English translation of "The Stranger," in *Six Plays of the Yiddish Theater: Second Series* (Boston: John W. Luce, 1918), 59–60.

17. I thank musicologist Ruth HaCohen for pointing out to me the various liturgical modes present in Rovina's performance.

18. Galit Hasan-Rokem, "Bodies Performing in Ruins: The Lamenting Mother in Ancient Hebrew Texts," in *Laments in Jewish Thought: Philosophical, Theological, and Literary Perspectives*, eds., Ilit Ferber and Paula Schwebel (Berlin: De Gruyter 2014), 42; Nicole Loraux, *The Mourning Voice: An Essay on Greek Tragedy*, trans. Elizabeth Trapnell Rawlings (Ithaca: Cornell University Press, 2002), 39.

19. Shimon Finkel, *Hanna Rovina: A Memory Monograph* (Tel Aviv: Akad Press, 1978), 42.

20. Shimon Finkel writes in his biography of Hanna Rovina:

> Her father's prayers, in Leibowitz Hasidic style, while striding across the room, in beautiful voice and cantillation; her mother's reading of these prayers, while echoing his sounds, intertwined with the clatter of her sewing machine; Her mother's recitation of Ninth of Av *Kinot* to the neighborhood women that used to gather in their house—Rovina absorbed all these sounds into her soul, and these sonorities were later poured into her singing-lamenting of the future actress.

In: Shimon Finkel, *Hanna Rovina*, 26.

21. Bloody assaults, riots, and violence against Jews in Ukraine were especially brutal after World War I, casting terror on the cohesion of the basic social units and its more vulnerable parts—women and children. In her role as the Messiah's mother, Rovina's lamentation resonates these atrocities. Gur Alroey discusses the pogroms against Jewish communities in Ukraine from a gender perspective. See Gur Alroey, "Sexual violence, Rape, and Pogroms, 1903–1920," *Jewish Culture and History* 18, no. 3 (2017): 313–30.

22. This was Rovina's first visit to Rosenzweig's residence in Frankfurt. The second visit took place a few weeks before Rosenzweig's death, during December 1929. In her second visit, Rovina recited to him from *Keter David* (David's Crown) based on Pedro Calderón de la Barca's play *The Crown of Absalom*. Upon her departure, Rosenzweig gave her a copy of the book of Samuel and wrote her a poem that is his last creative piece of writing. More on this encounter in Paul Mendes-Flohr, "Hebrew as Holy Tongue: Franz Rosenzweig and the Renewal of Hebrew," in *Hebrew in Ashkenaz: A Language in Exile*, ed. Lewis Glinert (Oxford: Oxford University Press, 1993), 222–41.

23. At the time of the meeting, Rosenzweig's paralysis deprived him of the ability to speak and even to smile. Paul Mendes-Flohr explains that despite his severe illness, Rosenzweig "communicated his emotions through his powerfully expressive eyes, and with one finger that has not utterly atrophied he laboriously and ever so painfully communicated his thought on a specially constructed typewriter." In Mendes-Flohr, "Hebrew as Holy Tongue," 222.

24. Cited in the letter by Eugen Mayer to his wife Hebe from 28.01.1928. Franz Rosenzweig holdings Universitätbibliothel Kassel- Landes- und Murhardsche Bibliothek des Strat. Shelfmark 2° Ms. philos. 39 part A [6,1 (Nr. 009) and G [14,4 (Nr. 681). I thank Ms. Sabine Wagener from the Universitätsbibliothek Kassel for assisting me in

attaining these archival documents, and Dr. Laura Jockusch for her kind assistance in translating them.

25. Rafael Rosenzweig writing to Hanna Rovina, June 6, 1972. Franz Rosenzweig holdings Universitätbibliothek Kassel- Landes- und Murhardsche Bibliothek des Strat. Shelfmark 2° Ms. philos. 39 part A [6,1 (Nr. 009).

26. The musicologist and composer Abraham Zvi Idelsohn narrated a strikingly parallel incident between himself and the philosopher Hermann Cohen. In their meeting in the winter of 1913–14 in Berlin, Idelsohn sang to him several tunes from the Days of Awe prayer which deeply moved the aged Cohen, consequently causing him to pass out. When he recovered he muttered: "The Hebrew melody it is, that has shaken my heart." This episode is quoted in Abraham Zvi Idelsohn, "He-hayah ve-Hehove. Zikhronot 'al Herman Kohen," *Shay shel sifrut (Literary Supplement to the Palestine News)* 10, no. 7 (Aug. 23, 1918): 8–10; Hartwig Wiedebach, " 'Hebräisches Fühlen': Hermann Cohens Deutung des *Schma' Jisrael/ 'Höre Israel,' " *Kalonymos. Beiträge zur Deutsch-Jüdischen Geschichte aus dem Salomon Ludwig Steinheim-Institut* 6, no. 2 (2003): 1–4; and, Ruth HaCohen, *The Musical Libel Against the Jews* (New Haven: Yale University Press, 2011), 473, fn. 27. James Loeffler's analysis of the meeting between Idelsohn and Cohen appears in his article "When Hermann Cohen Cried: Zionism, Culture, Emotions," in *Zionism as a Cultural Movement,* ed. Israel Bartal and Rachel Rojansky (Boston and Leiden: Brill, n.d.).

27. Paul Mendes-Flohr, "Hebrew as Holy Tongue," 227.

28. Jean-Jacques Rousseau, *Œuvres complètes*, V, 417, 380.

29. Julia Simon, "Singing Democracy: Music and Politics in Jean-Jacques Rousseau's Thought," *Journal of History of Ideas* 65 (July 2004): 437.

30. Jean-Jacques Rousseau, *Œuvres complètes*, V, 417. Translation appears in Julia Simon's article "Singing Democracy: Music and Politics in Jean-Jacques Rousseau's Thought," 438.

31. Paul Mendes-Flohr discusses Rosenzweig's deep love of the Hebrew language as closely related to Jewish religious culture. See "Hebrew as Holy Tongue," 222–41.

32. Eugen Rosenstock-Huessy, "Prologue/Epilogue to the Letters—Fifty Years Later," in *Judaism Despite Christianity: The "Letters on Christianity and Judaism" Between Eugen Rosenstock-Huessy and Franz Rosenzweig,* ed. Eugen Rosenstock-Huessy (New York: Schocken, 1971), 74.

33. Paul Mendes-Flohr, "Franz Rosenzweig and the German Philosophical Tradition," in *The Philosophy of Franz Rosenzweig* (London: University Press of New England for Brandeis University Press, 1988), 6.

34. The story of Rosenzweig's 1913 experience during the Yom Kippur synagogue service has been told and retold by almost every Rosenzweig scholar. It originates in Nahum N. Glatzer's essay "Franz Rosenzweig: The Story of a Conversion" (1952), reprinted as the introduction to Nahum N. Glatzer, *Franz Rosenzweig: Life and Thought* (New York: Schocken, 1953). A recent study by Benjamin Pollock, *Franz Rosenzweig's Conversions: World Denial and World Redemption* (Bloomington: Indiana University Press, 2014) re-examines the influence of the synagogue experience upon

Rosenzweig's decision to recommit to Judaism, and proposes to view this event as part of a thoughtful process that Rosenzweig had been going through, culminating in his concluding insight to return to Judaism. For further elaboration, see Benjamin Pollok, *Franz Rosenzweig's Conversions: World Denial and World Redemption*, 97–127.

35. Franz Rosenzweig, The *Star of Redemption*, trans. Barbara E. Galli (Madison: University of Wisconsin Press, 2005), 365.

36. Ruth HaCohen elaborates on the idea of "togetherness" in the liturgical setting in Rosenzweig's thought. See Ruth HaCohen, "Vocal Communities in the Twilight: Real and Imagined Sonic Spaces in Central European Jewry at the Opening and Closing of the Gate," in *The Interpretive Imagination*, eds. Richard I. Cohen, Ruth HaCohen, Galit Hasan-Rokem, Ilana Pardes (Jerusalem: Magnes Press, 2016).

37. Paul Mendes-Flohr, "Hebrew as Holy Tongue," 223–24.

38. Franz Rosenzweig, "Classical and Modern Hebrew: A Review of a Translation into the Hebrew of Spinoza's Ethics," in *Franz Rosenzweig: His Life and Thought*, ed. Nahum N. Glatzer (New York: Schocken, 1953), 263–71.

39. Galili Shahar, "The Sacred and the Unfamiliar: Gershom Scholem and the Anxieties of the New Hebrew," *The Germanic Review: Literature, Culture, Theory* 83, no. 4 (Fall 2008): 304.

40. Franz Rosenzweig, "It Is Time: Concerning the Study of Judaism (1917)," in *Franz Rosenzweig: On Jewish Learning*, ed. Nahum N. Glatzer (Madison: University of Wisconsin Press, 2002), 27–54.

41. Franz Rosenzweig, "The Jewish People," in *Franz Rosenzweig: His Life and Thought*, 296–97.

42. Steven Connor, *Dumbstruck: A Cultural History of Ventriloquism* (Oxford: Oxford University Press, 2000), 36.

43. Translated by Gad Kaynar. Cited in David Vardi, *On My Path* (Tel-Aviv: Massada, 1950), 126. Quoted in Gad Kaynar, "National Theater as Colonized Theater: The Paradox of *Habima*," *Theater Journal* 50, no. 1 (March 1998): 6.

44. Gad Kaynar, "National Theater as Colonized Theater: The Paradox of *Habima*," *Theater Journal* 50, no. 1 (March 1998): 5. The passages are quoted from "Book of Isaiah," in *The Holy Scriptures According to the Masoretic Text* (Philadelphia: The Jewish Publication Society of America), 2:2–4, 34.

45. For an elaborate discussion of the space in Classical Greek theater, see David Wiles, *Tragedy in Athens: Performance Space and Theatrical Meaning* (Cambridge: Cambridge University Press, 1997). For a discussion of the relationship between the theater audience and the Athenian topography, see Nicole Loraux, *Mourning Voice: An Essay on Greek Tragedy*, trans. Elizabeth Trapnell Rawlings (Ithaca: Cornell University Press, 2002).

46. See, for example, *The Wandering Jew: Essays in the Interpretation of a Christian Legend*, ed. Galit Hasan-Rokem and Alan Dundes (Bloomington: Indiana University Press, 1986).

47. Moshe Halevy, *My Way on the Stage* (Tel Aviv: Masada, 1954), 42–43. Quoted in Kaynar, "National Theater as Colonized Theater," 11.

48. Kaynar, "National Theater as Colonized Theater," 10.

49. Moshe Halevy, *My Way on the Stage*, 62. Quoted in Kaynar, "National Theater as Colonized Theater," 11.

50. Carmit Guy writes in Rovina's biography that *Habima*'s members, who worked on the play, expressed anger toward Mchedelov's underconsideration of the national symbolism in the play. See Carmit Guy, *The Queen Took the Bus* (Tel Aviv: Am Oved, 1995), 54.

51. Kaynar, "National Theater as Colonized Theater," 11.

52. Carmit Guy, *The Queen Took the Bus*, 55; my translation (RA).

53. Emanuel Levy, *The Habima, Israel's National Theater, 1917–1977: A Study of Cultural Nationalism* (New York: Columbia University Press, 1979), 31.

54. Ruth HaCohen, *The Musical Libel Against the Jews*, 21.

55. Maxim Gorky, cited in Emanuel Levy, *The Habima—Israel's National Theater 1917–1977: A Study of Cultural Nationalism*, 29–30.

56. The local publicity of *The Eternal Jew* performance in the early 1940s states: "Tonight at *Mugraby* theater house *The Eternal Jew* by *Habima*, according to its annual tradition in the week of Ninth of Av" (*Hamashkif*, July 20, 1942); further evidence of this tradition appears in Israel Gur's memoirs:

> I recall, that distant Ninth of Av evening, in which my friends and I—all from the Working and Studying Youth movement—had seen her on the stage of "The People's House" in Tel Aviv. It was a night of heat wave in which. . . . we listened to the saturated voice of the lamenting mother. (Israel Gur, *Playing the Pauper and the King: Masses on the Hebrew Actors* [Jerusalem: Theater Press, 1959], 31–32)

57. Victor Turner, "Liminality and Communitas," *The Ritual Process: Structure and Anti-Structure* (Ithaca: Cornell University Press, 1991), 96.

58. On the relation of Ninth of Av to religious traditions of Holocaust commemoration, see James E. Young, "When a Day Remembers: A Performative History of 'Yom Ha-Shoah,'" *History and Memory* 2, no. 2 (1990): 54–75.

59. Gershom Scholem, "On Lament and Lamentation," trans. Paula Schwebel and Lina Barouch, *Jewish Studies Quarterly* 21, no. 1 (2014): 6.

60. Ibid.

61. Ilit Ferber, "A Language of the Border: On Scholem's Theory of Lament," *Journal of Jewish Thought and Philosophy* 21 (2013): 167.

62. Galit Hasan-Rokem, "Bodies Performing in Ruins: The Lamenting Mother in Ancient Hebrew Texts," in *Laments in Jewish Thought: Philosophical, Theological, and Literary Perspectives*, eds. Ilit Ferber and Paula Schwebel (Berlin: De Gruyter 2014), 37.

63. Mikhail Gnessin, "*Habima* and Musical Opportunities Regarding Its Performances," in *The Birth of Habima: Nachum Zemach*, ed. Yitzhak Norman (Jerusalem: Zionist Library Press, 1966); my translation (RA).

64. Claude V. Palisca, *Musica and Ideas in the Sixteenth and Seventeenth Centuries* (Urbana: University of Illinois Press, 2006), 107–29.

65. Jacopo Peri, *L'Erudice*, "Preface." Quoted in ibid., 111.

66. Galit Hasan-Rokem, "Bodies Performing in Ruins: The Lamenting Mother in Ancient Hebrew Texts," in *Laments in Jewish Thought: Philosophical, Theological, and Literary Perspectives*, eds. Ilit Ferber and Paula Schwebel (Berlin: De Gruyter, 2014), 47.

67. I thank Edwin Seroussi for pointing out the various aspects of gender construction in Rovina's liturgical rendering.

68. Galit Hasan-Rokem, "Bodies Performing in Ruins: The Lamenting Mother in Ancient Hebrew Texts," in *Laments in Jewish Thought: Philosophical, Theological, and Literary Perspectives*, ed. Ilit Ferber and Paula Schwebel (Berlin: De Gruyter 2014), 36.

69. I thank Moshe Blidstein for pointing these aspects in the Ninth of Av ritual in the synagogue.

70. Nicole Loraux, *The Mourning Voice: An Essay on Greek Tragedy*, trans. Elizabeth Trapnell Rawlings (Ithaca: Cornell University Press, 2002), 82.

Chapter Two. The Rise and Fall

1. For an elaborate discussion of *The Vilna Troupe*'s production of An-sky's play, see Michael Steinlauf, "'Fardibekt!' An-sky's Polish Legacy," in *The World of S. An-sky: A Russian Jewish Intellectual at the Turn of the Century*, eds. Gabriella Safran and Steven J. Zipperstein (Stanford: Stanford University Press, 2006), 232–51; Debra Caplan, *Yiddish Empire: The Vilna Troupe, Jewish Theater, and the Art of Itinerancy* (Ann Arbor: Michigan University Press, 2018); Jolanta Mickutė, "The Vilner Troupe, 1916–30: A Transformation of Shund Theater—For the Sake of National Politics or High Art?" *Jewish Social Studies* 22, no. 3 (2017): 98–135.

2. Debra Caplan, "Nomadic Chutzpah: The Vilna Troupe's Transnational Yiddish Theater Paradigm, 1915–1935." *Theater Survey* 55, no. 3 (2014), pp. 304–5. For further discussion on *The Vilna Troupe* see Debra Caplan's book *Yiddish Empire: The Vilna Troupe, Jewish Theater, and The Art of Itinerancy* (Ann-Arbor: University of Michigan Press, 2018).

3. On the stylistic connections between *The Vilna Troupe*'s Yiddish production of *The Dybbuk* and *Habima*'s production, see Shelly Zer-Zion, "'The Vilna Troupe': Prologue to the History of *Habima*," *Bikoret ve-Parshanut* (Criticism and Interpretation) 41 (2009): 65–92; Shelly Zer-Zion, "*The Dybbuk* Reconsidered: The Emergence of a Modern Jewish Symbol Between East and West," *Leipziger Beiträge zur Jüdischen Geschichte und Kultur* 3 (2005): 175–97.

4. Visit https://www.ruthieabeliovich.com/possessed-voices to listen to *The Dybbuk*'s audio recording. This audio recording features some of the cast of *Habima*'s iconic production featuring, among others, the voices of Hanna Rovina, Aharon Meskin, Yehoshua Bertonov, Refael Klatchkin, Shimon Finkel, Zvi Friedland, and Tamar Robins. The directing of the voices for this recording was made by Michael

Ohad, a prominent figure in the dramatic department of Kol Yisrael, who guided the actors according to Vakhtangov's original instructions.

5. Since I deal here with the Hebrew recording of An-sky's play, I refer to the Hebrew transcription Hanan, and not the Yiddish Khonen.

6. Alicia Schmidt Camacho, *Migrant Imaginaries: Latino Cultural Politics in the U.S.-Mexico Borderland*s (New York: New York University Press, 2008), 5. I thank Talia Trainin for pointing me to this reference.

7. Raymond Williams, *Marxism and Literature* (Oxford: Oxford University Press, 1977), 128–35.

8. The entire play unfolds in three venues: it opens in an old synagogue in the town of Brinnitz, continues in Sender's (the bride's father) courtyard, in which the customary feast for the poor takes place. As the plot evolves, the public locations change to depict Reb Azriel's house in Miropol in which the exorcism ritual is performed.

9. Connor, *Dumbstruck*, 21.

10. Ibid., 402.

11. The Pale of Settlement refers to the territories of Czarist Russia in which Jews were permitted to permanently dwell. This restriction confined Jews to the western regions of the Russian Empire, including much of today's Latvia, Lithuania, Belarus, Ukraine, Moldova, and Poland. These territorial restrictions on Jews endured from 1791 to 1835, and were abolished by after Bolshevist revolution of February 1917 by the provisional government.

12. For further reading on An-sky's ethnographic expedition see Benyamin Lukin, "'An Academy Where Folklore Will Be Studied': An-sky and the Jewish Museum," in *Words of S. An-sky: A Russian Jewish Intellectual at the Turn of the Century,* eds. Gabriella Safran and Steven J. Zipperstein (Stanford: Stanford Universtiy Press, 2006), 281–306; Liudmila Uritskaya, "Ashkenazi Jewish Collections of the State Ethnographic Museum in St. Petersburg," in *Tracing An-sky: Jewish Collections from the State Ethnographic Museum in St. Petersburg; Catalog of the Exhibition in Joods Historish Museum,* eds. Mariëlla Beukers and Renée Waale (Zwolle, Netherlands: Waanders Uitgevers, 1992), 24–57.

13. Gabriella Safran, *Wandering Soul: The Dybbuk's Creator, S. An-sky* (Cambridge: Harvard University Press, 2010), 187.

14. Ibid., 221.

15. Pearl Fishman points out that the theme of the dybbuk is thought to be a theatrical adaption derived from the many dybbuk legends that An-sky's team collected. In the town of Miropol, An-sky came across the story of the great Tzaddik who had exorcised a dybbuk. During the second season of the ethnographic expedition, the delegation worked in the central Hasidic town of Sataniv in the Podolia region of Ukraine, in which they came across a legend about a Jewish couple that was assassinated immediately after their wedding ceremony and buried in close vicinity to the synagogue. In Pearl Fishman, "Vakhtangov's *The Dybbuk*," *The Drama Review* 24, no. 3 (1980): 43–58.

16. Chaim Nachman Bialik, "Darkei hateatron haivri," *Dvarim Shebeal Peh* (Tel Aviv, 1935), 112–13.

17. For further examples of the retrieval of Jewish traditions in Modernist contexts, see Jack Wertheimer, ed., *The Uses of Tradition: Jewish Continuity in The Modern Era* (Cambridge: Harvard University Press, 1992).

18. Safran, *Wandering Soul*, 213.

19. The German sociologist Ferdinand Tönnies developed the theoretical distinction between two social paradigms: the *Gemeinschaft*—a traditional community formed around individual relationships and sentiments of organic belonging—and the *Geselleshcaft*—the instrumental civil large-scale society. See Ferdinand Tönnies (1893), *Society and Community* (New Brunswick, NJ: Transaction Books, 1957).

20. In the Modernist context of the early twentieth century, the shift from individual to social experience originates, according to Erika Fischer-Lichte, a deep yearning for communal experience. See Erika Fischer-Lichte, *Theater, Sacrifice, Ritual: Exploring Forms of Political Theater* (New York: Routledge Chapman and Hall, 2005), 90.

21. Ruth HaCohen, "The Birth and Demise of Vocal Communities," *AJS Perspectives: The Magazine for the Association for Jewish Studies. The Sound Issue* (Spring/Summer 2016) http://perspectives.ajsnet.org/sound-issue/the-birth-and-demise-of-vocal-communities; Ruth HaCohen, "Vocal Communities in the Twilight: Real and Imagined Sonic Spaces in Central European Jewry at the Opening and Closing of the Gate," in *The Interpretive Imagination*, eds. Richard I. Cohen, Ruth HaCohen, Galit Hasan-Rokem, Ilana Pardes (Jerusalem: Magnes Press, 2016).

22. Naomi Seidman, "The Ghosts of Queer Loves Past: An-sky's 'Dybbuk' and the Sexual Transformation of Ashkenaz," in *Queer Theory and the Jewish Question*, eds. Daniel Boyarin, Daniel Itzkovitz, and Ann Pellegrini (New York: Columbia University Press, 2003), 232. On the issue of time within An-sky's writings, see Sylvie-Anne Goldberg, "Paradigmatic Times: An-sky's Two Worlds," in *The Worlds of S. An-sky: A Russian Jewish Intellectual at the Turn of the Century*, eds. Gabriella Safran and Steve J. Zipperstein (Stanford: Stanford University Press, 2006), 51–52; On the theatrical manifestation of the body in *The Dybbuk* in relation to its temporal problematics, see Yair Lipshitz, "The Dybbuk's Body: Traditions, Revolutions, Crises," in *"Do Not Chase Me Away": New Studies on The Dybbuk*, eds. Shimon Levy and Dorit Yerushalmi (Tel-Aviv: Tel-Aviv University Press, 2009), 137–62.

23. Rachel Elior, *Dybbuks and Jewish Women in Social History, Mysticism and Folklore*, trans. Joel Linsider (Jerusalem: Urim Publication, 2011).

24. Elena Tartakovsky traces the preservation and canonization of *The Dybbuk*. After Vaktangov's death David Vardi was appointed to be in charge of keeping the performance according to the specificities of the director; after the troupe left Moscow and for almost forty years of the running performance Zvi Friedland was in charge of preserving *The Dybbuk*. See Elena Tartakovsky, "Vakhtangov's *The Dybbuk*: Paradox of Preservation and Canonization," in *"Do Not Chase Me Away": New Studies on the Dybbuk*, eds. Shimon Levy and Dorit Yerushalmi (Tel Aviv: Tel Aviv University Press, 2009), 168–73.

25. See reviews in *Bama* (April 1938).

26. Elena Tartakovsky, "Vakhtangov's *The Dybbuk*: Paradox of Preservation and Canonization," 175.

27. Elena Tartakovsky, *Habima: The Russian Heritage* (Tel Aviv: Safra, 2013), 234–37.

28. Rovina continued to play Lea in all the important performances of the play until it was removed from the stage in the mid-sixties, even though she was more than seventy years old. See Dorit Yerushalmi, "In Hanna Rovina's Shadow," *Zmanim a Historical Quarterly* 99 (2007): 26–38.

29. Freddie Rokem, "*The Dybbuk* in Israel: Theater, Criticism, and the Establishment of Hebrew Culture," in *"Do Not Chase Me Away": New Studies on the Dybbuk*, eds. Shimon Levy and Dorit Yerushalmi (Tel Aviv: Tel Aviv University Press, 2009), 195.

30. Barbara-Kirshenblatt Gimblett, "Sounds of Sensibility," *Judaism: A Quarterly Journal of Jewish Life and Thought* 185: 47, no. 1 (Winter 1998): 56.

31. B. C. Forbes, "Edison Working on How to Communicate with the Next World," *American Magazine*, XC (October 1920): 10.

32. Jeffrey Sconce, *Haunted Media: Electronic Presence from Telegraphy to Television* (Durham: Duke University Press, 2000), 83–84.

33. Plato, *The Symposium*, trans. Robin Waterfield (Oxford: Oxford University Press, 1952). I thank Talia Trainin for this insight and for pointing me to this reference.

34. Yoram Bilu, "Dybbuk and Maggid: Two Cultural Patterns of Altered Consciousness in Judaism," *AJS Review* 21, no. 2 (1996): 341–66.

35. Seth L. Wolitz, "Inscribing An-sky's Dybbuk in Russian and Jewish Letters," in *The Worlds of S. An-sky: A Russian Jewish Intellectual at the Turn of the Century*, eds. Gabriella Safran and Steve J. Zipperstein (Stanford: Stanford University Press, 2006), 193.

36. "By Consorting with Fellow Students," in *The Mishnah*, trans. Herbert Danby, D. D. (Oxford: Oxford University Press, 1933), 460. Chapter 6 in *Pirkei Avot*.

37. For an elaborated discussion of "Mipnei Ma," see Seth L. Wolitz, "Inscribing An-sky's Dybbuk in Russian and Jewish Letters," in *The Worlds of S. An-sky: A Russian Jewish Intellectual at the Turn of the Century*, eds. Gabriella Safran and Steve J. Zipperstein (Stanford: Stanford University Press, 2006), 190–94.

38. The original version of the song was sung in Hebrew in Ashkenazic pronunciation. The inscription brought here was made by Seth L. Wolitz, "Inscribing An-sky's Dybbuk in Russian and Jewish Letters," 190.

39. The expedition amassed more than 1,500 folk songs and plays, 500 wax cylinders of folk music that were created for use with a phonograph, and 1,000 melodies of songs and Hasidic tunes (*nigun*). See Izaly Zemtsovsky, "The Musical Strands of An-sky's Texts and Contexts," in *The Worlds of S. An-sky: A Russian Jewish Intellectual at the Turn of the Century*, eds. Gabriella Safran and Steve J. Zipperstein (Stanford: Stanford University Press, 2006), 207.

40. Wolitz, "Inscribing An-sky's Dybbuk," 190.

41. Albert Weisser, *The Modern Renaissance of Jewish Music* (New York: Bloch, 1954), 222.

42. Menachem Gnessin, *My Way with the Hebrew Theater* (Tel Aviv: Kibbutz Me-Uchad Press, 1946), 119. This anecdote also appears in Vladislav Ivanov's article "An-sky, Evgeny Vakhtangov, and *The Dybbuk*" [*sic*], trans. Anne Eakin Moss, in *The Worlds of S. An-sky: A Russian Jewish Intellectual at the Turn of the Century*, ed. Gabriella Safran and Steve J. Zipperstein (Stanford: Stanford University Press, 2006), 253.

43. Ruth HaCohen, "Between Noise and Harmony: The Oratorical Moment in the Musical Entanglements of Jews and Christians," *Critical Inquiry* 32, no. 2 (Winter 2006): 256.

44. Erika Fischer-Lichte, *Theater, Sacrifice, Ritual: Exploring Forms of Political Theater* (London and New York: Routledge, 2005), 23.

45. For more on the history of the term *Kahal* and the Kehilla premodern autonomous community governing system in Eastern European Jewish communities, see Eli Lederhendler, *The Road to Modern Jewish Politics: Political Tradition and Political Reconstruction in the Jewish Community of Tsarist Russia* (New York: Oxford University Press, 1989).

46. Anke Hilbrenner, "Simon Dubnov's Master Narrative and the Construction of a Jewish Collective Memory in the Russian Empire" [*sic*], *Ab Imperio* 4 (2003): 157–59.

47. Dubnow's study of the cultural history of Hasidism was initially written as articles in the Journal *Voskhod* (1888–1893), and only in 1930 published in book form. For more on the nationalist view on Hasidism, see Moshe Rosman, "Hasidism as a Modern Phenomenon—The Paradox of Modernization without Secularization," in *Simon-Dubnow-Institute 2007 Yearbook IV: Early Modern Culture and Haskala—Reconsidering the Borderlines of Modern History*, eds. David B. Ruderman and Shmuel Feiner (Leipzig: Vandenhoeck and Ruprecht, 2007), 215–27.

48. Erika Fischer-Lichte focuses on the emergence of the chorus in Modernist theater as a perceptual pattern that reflects European political changes. See Fischer-Lichte, *Theater, Sacrifice, Ritual*, 44–45.

49. On An-sky's approach to the community as an active participant in performing and conducting ethnography of traditional Jewish practices, see Nathaniel Deutsch, "Thrice Born; or, Between Two Worlds: Reflexivity and Performance in An-sky's Jewish Ethnographic Expedition and Beyond," in *Going to The People: Jews and The Ethnographic Impulse*, ed. Jeffrey Veidlinger (Bloomington and Indianapolis: Indiana University Press, 2016), 27–44.

50. Gad Kaynar elaborates on the expressionistic distortion of Jewish images and rituals in the performance. See Kaynar, "National Theater as Colonized Theater," 14–16.

51. Alexander Kugel is quoted in Emanuel Levy, *Habima*, 35–36. Quoted in Kaynar, "National Theater as Colonized Theater," 16.

52. https://www.merriam-webster.com/dictionary/batlan.

53. In contrast to Ruth HaCohen's term "Vocal Community," Dell Hymes' notion of "speech community" refers to a collective that shares linguistic norms regarding when and how to speak. Dell Hymes, *Speech and Language on Inequality: Towards an Understanding of Voice* (London, UK, and Bristol, PA: Taylor and Francis, 1996), 33.

54. S. An-sky, "*The* Dybbuk, or Between Two Worlds: A Dramatic Legend," in *The Dybbuk and Other Writings*, ed. David G. Roskies, trans. Golda Werman (London and New Haven: Yale University Press, 2002), 6.

55. Ken Friedman, "Innovation by Translation: Yiddish and Hasidic Hebrew in Literary History," in *Arguing the Modern Jewish Canon: Essays on Literature and Culture in Honor of Ruth R. Wisse*, eds. Justin Daniel Cammy, Dara Horn, Alyssa Quint, and Rachel Rubinstein (Cambridge, MA: Centre for Jewish Studies and Harvard University Press, 2008), 417.

56. For an elaborate discussion of the figure of the Jewish "Badkhn," including its historical evolution and theatrical poetics, see Ariela Krasney, *The Badkhn* (Ramat Gan: Bar-Ilan University Press, 1998).

57. Sergei Volkonsky, "On *The Dybbuk*," *The Birth of Habima—Nachum Zemach in Vision and Deed,* ed., Yitzhak Norman (Jerusalem: The Zionist Library, 1966), 279. (Quotes are my translation, RA.)

58. Zelda Kahan-Newman, "Yiddish Haunts: The Yiddish Underpinnings of Appelfeld's Laylah ve'od Laylah," *Mikan* 5 (2005): 88.

59. Benjamin Harshav, *Language in Time of Revolution* (Stanford: Stanford University Press, 1993), 18.

60. Volkonsky, "On *The Dybbuk*," 279.

61. See Ruth HaCohen, *The Music Libel Against the Jews* (New Haven: Yale University Press, 2011); Gabriella Safran, "Some Russian Jewish Writers in Switzerland and the Valorization of Jewish Argument Style," in *East European Jewish in Switzerland: New Perspectives on Modern Jewish History*, eds. Tamar Lewinsky and Sandrine Mayoraz (Berlin: De Gruyter, 2013), 77–96.

62. Volkonsky, "On *The Dybbuk*," 279.

63. Naomi Seidman, "The Ghosts of Queer Loves Past: An-sky's 'Dybbuk' and the Sexual Transformation of Ashkenaz," in *Queer Theory and the Jewish Question*, eds., Daniel Boyarin, Daniel Itzkovitz, and Ann Pellegrini (New York: Columbia University Press, 2003), 232–33.

64. Volkonsky, "On *The Dybbuk*," 279.

65. Yair Lipshitz, "Embodied Redemption: Past, Future and Acting in Habima's '*The Golem*,'" *Reshit* 1 (2009): 279–304.

66. Chayale Grober (Feb. 16, 1898–Dec. 10, 1978) was an actress and a Jewish folk singer. See Berl Kagan, comp., *Leksikon fun Yidish-Shraybers* [*Biographical Dictionary of Yiddish Writers*] (New York: R. Ilman-Kohen, 1986), col. 168.

67. This experience from the rehearsal process was delivered to Yossi Yzraely by Chayale Grober in an interview. See *Vakhtangov Directing the Dybbuk* (Unpublished PhD dissertation, Carnegie Mellon University, 1970), 131; Elena Tartakovsky, *Habima: The Russian Heritage* (Tel Aviv: Safra, 2013), 83.

68. Galit Hasan-Rokem, "Bodies Performing in Ruins: The Lamenting Mother in Ancient Hebrew Texts." in *Laments in Jewish Thought: Philosophical, Theological, and Literary Perspectives*, eds. Ilit Ferber and Paula Schwebel (Berlin: De Gruyter, 2014), 48.

69. For additional analysis of the Dybbuk as a Jewish dissociative phenomenon see Yoram Bilu, and Benjamin Beit-Hallahmi, "Dybbuk Possession as a Hysterical

Symptom: Psychodynamic and Socio-cultural Factors," *Israel Journal of Psychiatry* 26, no. 3 (1989): 138–49.

70. Yoram Bilu, "The Taming of the Deviants and Beyond: An Analysis of Dybbuk Possession and Exorcism in Judaism," in *Spirit Possession in Judaism: Cases and Contexts from the Middle Ages to the Present*, ed. Matt Goldish (Detroit: Wayne State University Press, 2003), 41–72.

71. Steven Connor, *Dumbstruck: A Cultural History of Ventriloquism* (Oxford: Oxford University Press, 2000), 35.

72. Ibid., 36.

73. On "Dybbuk tales" as a literary genre in Jewish culture, see Gedaliah Nigal, *Dybbuk Tales in Jewish Literature* (Jerusalem: Reuben Mass, 1983).

74. Freddie Rokem, "Has This Thing Appeared Again Tonight? Deus ex Machina and Other Interventions of the Supernatural," in *Things: Religion and the Question of Materiality*, ed. Dick Houtman and Brigit Meyer (New York: Fordham University Press, 2012), 136.

75. Derek J. Penslar explains that in 1948 there was one receiver for every four Israelis, a higher percentage than in most industrialized countries at the time. See Derek J. Penslar, "Broadcasted Orientalism: Representations of Mizrahi Jewry in Israeli Radio 1948–1967," 183.

76. Oren Soffer, *Mass Communication in Israel: Nationalism, Globalization, and Segmentation*, trans. Judith Yalon (Oxford: Beghahn Books, 2015), 80–81.

77. The social function of the text of *The Dybbuk* as a medium for communal lamentation emerges in the circumstances of the staging of An-sky's play during 1922 by an amateur theater group of Hebrew Pioneers, devised by Yhuda Yaari, a prominent figure in the Jewish cultural life of the time. During 1922, a few months after *Habima*'s premier of *The Dybbuk* in Moscow, a group of Hebrew Pioneers staged Bialik's Hebrew translation of An-sky's play, at the intersection of the road construction between the town of Haifa and the Arab village *Jeida* (today named Ramat Ishay) in which this group worked. Members of this group, all part of the Zionist Left youth movement "HaShomer HaTzair," originated in Galicia, Ukraine, and Poland, and many of them came from Hasidic homes. During the days, this group was occupied in a highly demanding physical labor, and during the nights they would gather and converse in a confessional mode of speech about their emotional struggles, and ventilate their pressures. Life under these circumstances proved to be challenging. Freddie Rokem notes in his article about this performance that a few days before Bialik's translation to An-sky's dramatic text appeared in the local journal "Hatkufa," one of the members of the group who is described as a sensitive and romantic person, committed suicide. After his death, his girlfriend would wander around in a hallucinatory manner. The staging of An-sky's play, Rokem explains, provided a framework for the group to express their distress regarding these events and perhaps lament the deceased member of the group. See Freddie Rokem, "The Dybbuk on Haifa-Jeida Road: The First Performance of *The Dybbuk* in Israel," *Cathedra* 26 (1983): 103; *Kehilatenu*, 1922 collection, with commentary by Muki Zur (Jerusalem: Ben-Zvi Institute, 1988), 129.

78. R. Murray Schafer, *Our Sonic Environment and the Soundscape: The Tuning of the World* (Rochester, VT: Destiny Books, 1994), 215.

79. Barry Truax, *Acoustic Communication* (Norwood, NJ: Ablex Publishing, 1984), 57–59.

80. Jeffrey Sconce, *Haunted Media: Electronic Presence from Telegraphy to Television* (Durham: Duke University Press, 2000), 67.

81. One of the most famous radio events that transformed into a physical social assembly in which people congregated in order to listen together to a broadcast was the United Nations General Assembly's vote to recommend the termination of the British Mandate in Palestine, and the adoption and implementation of the plan for the partition of Palestine, as recommended by the majority of the UN Special Committee on Palestine (UNSCOP). Thirty-three states voted in favor of the resolution and thirteen against. Ten states abstained.

Chapter Three. "Who Will Save Us?"

1. The idea of *Habima* as a national theater was part of the troupe's initial manifesto, written more than a year before the premiere of their first staged performance (1918). Only in 1958 did the theater gain official state authorization.

2. On *Habima*'s effort and branding as a national theater, see Diti Ronen, "On *Habima*'s recognition as a National Theater: Circumstances, Meanings, and Implications"; and, Gad Kaynar "On *Habima*'s Branding as a National Theater (1931–1958)," both in *Habima: New Studies on National Theater*, ed. Gad Kaynar, Dorit Yerushalmi, and Shelly Zer-Zion (Tel Aviv: Resling, 2017).

3. As a marker of modern Jewish identity, the Hebrew language was perceived to be a central identity signifier. This entailed the elimination of Yiddish from the public sphere. The regulation and standardization of Hebrew pronunciation were considered core elements for the new Israeli culture. On the cultural complexity of language in Israel, see Diego Rotman, *The Stage as a Temporary Home: The Theater of Dzigen and Schumacher (1927–1980)*, (Jerusalem: Magnes Press, 2018), 157–208; William Safran, "Language, Ideology, and State Building: A Comparison of Policies in France, Israel, and the Soviet Union," *International Political Science Review* 13 (1992): 397–414.

4. On the politics and ideologies behind the pronunciation of Hebrew during the formative years of the Zionist movement and especially in poetry, see Miryam Segal, *A New Sound in Hebrew Poetry: Poetics, Politics, Accent* (Bloomington: Indiana University Press, 2010), 1–19.

5. Walter Benjamin, "Goethe's Elective Affinities," in *Walter Benjamin: Selected Writings, vol. 1: 1913–1926*, eds. Marcus Bullock and Michael W. Jennings (Cambridge: Harvard University Press, 1996), 341.

6. Visit https://www.ruthieabeliovich.com/possessed-voices to listen to *Habima*'s recording of *The Golem*.

7. Jacques Derrida, *Specters of Marx*, 12. On theoretical approaches to "the spectral turn" and approaches to the ghost as actuality, metaphor, and concept, see

María Del Pilar Blanco and Esther Peeren eds., The *Spectralities Reader: Ghosts and Haunting in Contemporary Cultural Theory* (London: Bloomsbury, 2013).

8. "The Screen Rises" was edited by Michael Ohad, who also directed *Habima's* album of *The Dybbuk*, discussed in the previous chapter. This popular radio program featured radio plays, from both the canon of Western world drama and local playwrights.

9. Danusha V. Goska, "Golem as Gentile, Golem as Sabra: An Analysis of the Manipulation of Stereotypes of Self and Other in Literary Treatments of a Legendary Jewish Figure," *New York Folklore* 23, no. 1–4 (1997): 39.

10. "The Golem" was first introduced into the cinematic tradition by German expressionist filmmaker Paul Wegener in 1915. This original silent film has been lost, but in 1920 he reworked the tale and created *The Golem: How He Came into the World* (*Der Golem, wie er in die Welt Kam*), which became a German cinematic classic and cemented Wegener's place in German expressionistic cinematic history.

11. Maya Barzilai, *Golem: Modern Wars and Their Monsters* (New York: New York University Press, 2016), 3–4.

12. Gad Yair and Michaela Soyer, *The Golem in German Social Theory* (Lanham, MD: Lexington Books, 2008).

13. This play is the second in Leivick's Yiddish trilogy *Redemption Spectacles*, which includes: *The Golem, The Golem's Dream*, and *Chains of Messiah*.

14. Raikin Ben-Ari discusses *Habima's* rehearsal process on the play in length. See Ben-Ari, *Habima*, 116.

15. Stephen Greenblatt, "Cultural Mobility: An Introduction," in *Cultural Mobility: A Manifesto*, eds. Stephen Greenblatt, Ines G. Županov, Reinhard Meyer-Kalkus, Heike Paul, Pál Nyíri, and Friederike Pannewick (Cambridge: Cambridge University Press, 2010), 1–20.

16. Raikin Ben-Ari, *Habima*, 117.

17. Visit https://www.ruthieabeliovich.com/possessed-voices to listen to *Habima's* 1954 recording.

18. Allen S. Weiss, *Phantasmic Radio* (Durham and London: Duke University Press, 1995), 79.

19. Yair Lipshitz quotes Marvin Carlson's term in relation to the various resonances embedded in an enacted role. See Yair Lipshitz, "Embodied Redemption: Past, Future and Acting in *Habima's The Golem*," *Reshit* 1 (2009): 281; Marvin Carlson, "Invisible Presences: Performance Intertextuality," *Theater Research International* 19, no. 2 (1994): 111–17.

20. Halpern Leivick, "The Golem," in *The Dybbuk and Other Great Yiddish Plays*, trans. and ed. Joseph C. Landis (New York: Bantam, 1966), 224.

21. Ibid., 225.

22. This scene also resonated with the dialogue between the Spirit and Faust:

> The Spirit: You have implored me to appear,
> make known my voice, reveal my face; . . .
> Where are you, Faust, whose voice pierced my domain?

In Johann Wolfgang von Goethe, *Goethe's Faust*, trans. and intro. Walter Kaufmann (New York: Anchor Books, 1963), 103.

23. Shimon Finkel explains that Meskin's voice sounded from the backstage with the escort of the choral voices. See Shimon Finkel, *Aharon Meskin and the Legend of The Golem* (Tel Aviv: Akad, 1980), 35. On screen scenes in general and specifically in *Hamlet*, see Freddie Rokem, "Meta Theatricality and Screen Scenes," in *Hamlet Handbuch,* ed., Peter W. Marx (Stuttgart: Verlag J. B Metzler, 2014), 53–58.

24. Leivick, "The Golem," 226.

25. Book of Samuel 1, 28:15.

26. On the parallel Christian theological debate regarding "truth" in the necromancy of the witch of Endor, see Connor, *Dumbstruck*, 75–101.

27. I thank Talia Trainin for pointing this out to me.

28. Leivick, "The Golem," 226–27.

29. Probing into the sematic development of the term *Figura,* Erich Auerbach connects the notions of "model," "copy," "figment," and "dream image"—as meanings that clung to the term *figura.* See Erich Auerbach, "Figura," in *Scenes from the Drama of European Literature* (Minneapolis: University of Minnesota Press, 1984), 11–79.

30. Stephen Greenblatt and Catherine Gallagher, *Practicing New Historicism* (Chicago: University of Chicago Press, 2000), 34. For an elaborate critical discussion on Erich Auerbach's theory of "Figura," see James I. Porter, "Disfigurations: Erich Auerbach's Theory of *Figura,*" *Critical Inquiry* 44, no. 1 (Autumn 2017): 80–113.

31. Greenblatt, *Cultural Mobility*, 13.

32. Auerbach, "Figura," 18.

33. Gershom Scholem, "The Golem of Prague and the Golem of Rehovot," in *The Messianic Idea in Judaism and Other Essays on Jewish Spirituality* (New York: Schocken, 1971), 338.

34. J. L. Austine, *How to Do Things with Words*, ed., J. O. Urmson and Marina Sbisà. Second ed. (Cambridge: Harvard University Press, 1975), 12.

35. On "The Golem" tradition in general, see Elaine L. Graham, "Body of Clay, Body of Glass," in *Representations of the Post/Human: Monsters, Aliens, and Others in Popular Culture* (Manchester: Manchester University Press, 2002), 84–108; Lewis Glinert, "Golem: The Making of a Modern Myth," *Symposium* 55 (2001): 78–94; Peter Schäfer, "The Magic of the Golem: The Early Development of the Golem Legend," *Journal of Jewish Studies* 46 (1995): 249–61; Emily D. Bilski, *Golem! Danger, Deliverance, and Art* (Albany: State University of New York Press, 1988); Gershom Scholem, "The Idea of the Golem," in *On the Kabbalah and Its Symbolism* (New York: Schocken, 1965), 158–204; Byron L. Sherwin, *The Golem Legend: Origins and Implications* (Lanham, MD: University Press of America, 1985); Frederic Thieberger, *The Great Rabbi Loew of Prague: His Life and Work and the Legend of the Golem* (London: Horovitz, 1965). On the Golem of Prague, see John Neubauer, "How Did the Golem Get to Prague?" in *History of the Literary Cultures of East-Central Europe: Junctures and Disjunctures in the 19th and 20th Centuries,* vol. 4, *Types and Stereotypes,* eds. M. Cornis-Pope and

J. Neubauer (Amsterdam: J Benjamins, 2010), 296–307; Vladimır Sadek, "Stories of the Golem and Their Relation to the Work of Rabbi Löw of Prague," *Judaica Bohemiae* 23 (1987): 85–91; Egon E. Kisch, "The Golem," in *Tales from Seven Ghettos* (London: Robert Anscombe, 1948), 153–65; On the Golem of Chelm, see Moshe Idel, *Golem: Jewish Magical and Mystical Traditions on the Artificial Anthropoid* (Albany: State University of New York Press, 1990), 207–12; Gershom Scholem, "The Idea of the Golem," 200–203; On Grimm Brothers' version of *The Golem*, see Cathy S. Gelbin, *The Golem Returns: From German Romantic Literature to Global Jewish Culture 1808–2008* (Ann Arbor: University of Michigan Press, 2011), 23–27.

36. Ron Kuzar uses the term "revivalism" to define the ideological traits of linguistic discourse from several periods'—pre-Zionist, Zionist, and Canaanite—political discourses. Revivalism, Kuzar explains, refers to the discourse framing that encodes the emergence of Hebrew in terms of a process of revitalization of ancient, or classical Hebrew. Up until the 1950s, Scholarship of Hebrew was conducted exclusively in historical linguistic terms within the framework of the revivalist perspective. The revivalist approach, according to Kuzar, considers the emergence of Hebrew as a singular occurrence, thereby perceiving it, or at least parts of it, as enigmatic and therefore un-analyzable. This scholarly restriction, according to Kuzar, forestalled any investigation that could challenge the revivalist premise. See Ron Kuzar, *Hebrew and Zionism*, 1–14.

37. Translated from German by Dr. Jan Kuehne. I learnt of this undated, previously unpublished fragment from Lina Barouch, "The Erasure and Endurance of Lament: Gershom Scholem's Early Critique of Zionism and Its Language," *Jewish Studies Quarterly* 21, no. 1 (2014): 22, n.35. I then located the full fragment in the Gershom Scholem archive at the National Library in Jerusalem. File number: ARC.4* 1599 08 277.1.56. Reprint permission granted by Suhrkamp Verlag, Berlin.

38. From Gershom Scholem's Letter to Franz Rosenzweig. Scholem (1926) is quoted from William Cutter, "Ghostly Hebrew, Ghastly Speech: Scholem to Rosenzweig, 1926," *Prooftexts: A Journal of Jewish Literary History* 10, no. 3 (1990): 431.

39. Ben-Yehuda barely spoke Hebrew and used hand gestures, or other languages, to express himself; his wife never learned Hebrew, and Itamar—often regarded as the first Hebrew-speaking child—was exposed to other languages than Hebrew. For more on Ben-Yehuda as the prophet of the Hebrew revival, see Robert St. John, *Tongue of the Prophets: The Life Story of Eliezer Ben Yehuda* (New York: Doubleday, 1952); Kuzar, *Hebrew and Zionism*, 111–12.

40. The prophetic image of Ben-Yehuda as a public figure is condensed into one paragraph in which Ben-Yehuda describes a vision he had in a dream:

> In the year 1810 of our exile [AD 1880], while I was then a student at the Russian high school in Dünaburg, as the Russians were fighting the Turks for the liberation of the Bulgarians . . . in those very day as if the heavens opened and a glistening light, bright and beaming, flashed before

my eyes, and a tremendous inner voice called upon my ears: The revival of Israel on the land of its forefathers!

in Ben-Yehuda, "Hamavo Hagadol [The Great Introduction]," Volume 1 of *Ben-Yehuda 1909–1959* (Jerusalem: Ben-Yehuda Publications, 1940), 1. Quoted in Kuzar, *Hebrew and Zionism*, 114.

41. Menachem Ribalow, *The Birth of Habima: Nachum Zemach,* ed. Yitzhak Norman (Jerusalem: Zionist Library Press, 1966), 352–53.

42. Boris Illich Vershilov (1893–1957) was the deputy artistic director of the Stanislavsky Opera studio-theater, and later the director of the Stanislavsky Opera Theater.

43. Ben-Ari, *Habima*, 118.

44. For more on Vakhtangov's method of fantastic realism, see Andrei Malaev-Babel, *The Vakhtangov Sourcebook*, 48–66; for Vakhtangov's writing on fantastic realism, see 125–58.

45. Ben-Ari, *Habima*, 120.

46. During 1951–52, Rosen launched a series of radio programs named "language processes" in the "language corner" of the Kol Yisrael radio. These programs were accompanied by an article published by Rosen in the French manuscript *Comptes-rendus du group linguistique d'études chamito-semitique* in March 1952. In this article, Rosen defines the Hebrew spoken in Israel as *Hebreu Israelien*, stating: "We need to reject the term 'Modern Hebrew,' which indicates merely normal linguistic evolution from classical Hebrew, and employ the term *Hebreu Israelien* "Israeli Hebrew." See Kuzar, *Hebrew and Zionism*, 157.

47. A selection of protocols from the meeting between "Kol Yisrael" staff and members of the Hebrew Language Academy on the standardization of Hebrew speech on the radio is gathered in A. Eithan and M. Madan, eds., "On the Hebrew Accent in 'Kol Yisrael,' in *Leshonenu La'am* (Jerusalem: The Scientific Secretary of the Hebrew Language Academy, 1964).

48. Ibid., 113.

49. Ze'ev Jabotinsky, *The Hebrew Pronunciation* (Tel Aviv: Ha-Sefer, 1930), 37–38. Quoted in Harshav, *Language in Time of Revolution*, 161.

50. Leivick, "The Golem," 334–35.

51. Chayim Bloch is quoted in Gershom Scholem, *On the Kabbalah and Its Symbolism*, 189; Jacques Derrida, *The Specters of Marx: The State of the Debt, the Work of Mourning, and the New International*, trans. Peggy Kamuf (New York: Routledge, 1994).

52. Wilhelm von Humboldt, *On Language: On the Diversity of Human Language Construction and Its Influence on the Mental Development of the Human Species*, ed. Michael Losonsky, trans. Peter Heath (Cambridge: Cambridge University Press, 1999). The concept *inner sprachform* guided Humboldt's work on languages, and condenses his thought on the differences between languages. This concept first appears as *Form der Sprach* in his essay "Uber die Verschiedenheit des Menschlichen Sprachbaues,"

written in 1827 and 1829, and then reformulated and refined as *innere Sprachform* in his essay *Über die Verschiedenheit des menschlichen Sprachbaues und ihren Einfluss auf die geistige Entwicklung des Menschengeschlechts*, written between 1830 and 1835 (published in 1936). See Anne-Marie Chabrolle-Cerretini and Savina Raynaud, "Humboldt's *innere Sprachform*: Its Contribution to the Lexicographical Description of Language Diversity," *Language & History* 58, no. 2 (2015): 95–110.

53. Joseph R. Roach, *The Players Passion: Studies in the Science of Acting* (Ann Arbor: The University of Michigan Press, 1993), 197, 214.

54. Konstantin Stanislavsky writes:

> Everything in our profession must become *habit* by which the new becomes part of my own being, second nature. Only then can we use the new, without thinking about the mechanics. This applied to the case in point. The *creative state* can only save an actor when it has become normal, natural, the only way for him. Otherwise, without knowing it, he will merely copy the externals of the leftist movement, without justifying it internally.

In Konstantin Stanislavsky, *My Life in Art*, ed. and trans. Jean Benedetti (New York: Routledge, 2008), 266. For an elaborate discussion on Stanislavsky's concept of "second nature," see Rose Whyman, "The Actor's Second Nature: Stanislavsky and William James," *New Theater Quarterly* 23 (2007): 115–23.

55. Sergey Volkonsky quoted in Rose Whyman, *The Stanislavsky System of Acting: Legacy and Influence in Modern Performance* (Cambridge: Cambridge University Press, 2008), 125.

56. Sergey Volkonsky, quoted in George Taylor and Rose Whyman, "Francois Delsarte, Prince Sergei Volkonsky, and Mikhail Chekhov," *Mime Journal* 23, Article 7 (2005): 102.

57. Emanuel Levy, *The Habima, Israel's National Theater, 1917–1977: A Study of Cultural Nationalism* (New York: Columbia University Press, 1979), 40.

58. *The New York Daily News*, may 17, 1948, written during *Habima*'s tour in United States in 1948. In this review, Jeanette Wilken refers to Shimon Finkel. Other actors that alternately played the Maharal are Baruch Chemerinsky and Shabtai Prudkin.

59. Shimon Finkel, *Aharon Meskin and the Legend of The Golem* (Tel Aviv: Akad Press, 1980), 37.

60. In this context, I choose to elaborate only on three *piyyutim*. Other *piyyutim* in the recording include: *Lechu Neranena*, and *Hashkivenu* prayer.

61. On Rabbi Elazar Ben Moshe Azikri (1533–1600), see Mordechai Pachter, "The Life and Personality of R. Elazar Azikri According to His Mystical Diary," *Shalem* 3 (1981): 127–47.

62. For an English translation of *"Yedid Nefesh"* (by T. Carmi) see *The Penguin Book of Hebrew Verse*, 471–72. On the language of love, and images of intimacy and unification with God in the *piyyut*, see Adena Tanenbaum, *The Contemplative Soul: Hebrew Poetry and Philosophical Theory in Medieval Spain* (Leiden: Brill, 2002), 234–36.

63. Visit https://www.ruthieabeliovich.com/possessed-voices to listen to Dvorah'le singing the *piyyut* "*Yedid Nefesh*."

64. Visit ibid. to listen to the *piyyut* "*Amar Adonay le Yaakov*" in *Habima's* audio recording.

65. Visit ibid. to listen this scene.

66. The question that arises here is, what is the vocalized sound of ruin? A possible answer to this interrogation can be found in the *Babylonian Talmud*, Tractate Berachot 3a: "[A]nd he said to me: My son, why did you go into this ruin? I replied: To pray. He said to me: You ought to have prayed on the road. I replied: I feared lest passers-by might interrupt me. He said to me: You ought to have said an abbreviated prayer . . . He further said to me: My son, what sound did you hear in this ruin? I replied: I heard a divine voice, cooing like a dove, and saying: Woe to the children, on account of whose sins I destroyed My house and burnt My temple and exiled them among the nations of the world!." Inside the ruins dwells an echo (in Hebrew: *Bat-Kol*) that transmits the voices of the dead. In Tanchum's lamentation, this echo cries the name of his dead son. I thank Ruth HaCohen for this reference.

67. I thank Edwin Seroussi for pointing out this interpretation to me.

68. Pierre Nora, "Between Memory and History: Les Lieux de Memoire," *Representations* 26 (1989): 7.

69. Eric Hobsbawm, "Inventing Traditions," in *The Invention of Tradition*, ed. Eric Hobsbawm and Terence O. Ranger (Cambridge: Cambridge University Press, 1983), 3.

70. Sinfree B. Makoni and Alastair Pennycook follow here the work of John E. Joseph, *Language and Identity: National, Ethnic, Religious* (Hampshire and New York: Palgrave Macmillan, 2004). See S. Makoni and A. Pennycook, *Disinventing and Reconstituting Languages, Multilingual Matters* (Clevedon, UK: Multilingual Matters, 2006), 7.

71. Friedrich A. Kittler, *Gramophone, Film, Typewriter*, trans. G. Winthrop-Young and M. Wutz (Stanford: Stanford University Press, 1999), 16.

72. Nora, "Between Memory and History," 8.

73. Svetlana Boym, *The Future of Nostalgia* (New York: Basic Books, 2001): 24–26.

74. For a discussion of these typological themes of Jewish messianism, see David Berger, "Three Typological Themes in Early Jewish Messianism: Messiah Son of Joseph, Rabbinic Calculations, and the Figure of Armilus," *AJS Review* 10, no. 2 (1985): 141–64.

75. Leivick, "The Golem," 256.

76. Raikin Ben-Ari, *Habima*, 123–24.

77. Maya Barzilai, *Golem: Modern Wars*, 107–108.

78. Ibid., 148.

79. Sixty-two sessions of the Eichmann trial were given over to witness testimony, by far eclipsing the thirty-three and one-half sessions in which Eichmann was on the stand. In the United States, the trial was watched almost live thanks to a contract with NBC, while ABC provided a daily hour-long summary. By contrast, few in Israel were actually able to watch the trial on TV—a fact that reinforces radio's status as the central news medium. For further reading, see Amit Pinchevski, Tamar

Liebes, and Ora Herman, "Eichmann on the Air: Radio and the Making of an Historic Trial," *Historical Journal of Film, Radio and Television* 27, no. 1 (2007): 1–25.

80. Shoshana Felman, *The Juridical Unconscious* (Cambridge: Harvard University Press, 2002), 113.

81. Joseph Landis, *The Great Jewish Plays* (New York: Avon Books, 1972), 220.

82. Tamar Liebes and Amit Pinchevski, "Severed Voices: Radio and the Mediation of Trauma in the Eichmann Trial," 267.

83. Jeffrey Shandler, *While America Watches: Televising the Holocaust* (Oxford: Oxford University Press, 1999), 81.

84. Felman, *The Juridical Unconscious*, 152.

85. Tamar Liebes, "Acoustic Space: The Role of Radio in Israeli Collective History," 72.

86. *The Trial of Adolf Eichmann: Record of the Proceedings in the District Court of Jerusalem* (Jerusalem, 1992) I:62. Session 6–8. See http://www.nizkor.org/hweb/people/e/eichmann-adolf/transcripts/.

87. Translated by Shoshana Felman, *The Juridical Unconscious*, 154.

88. Ibid., 163.

89. Ibid., 165.

90. Gregory Whitehead, "Who's There? Notes on the Materiality of Radio Art," *Art and Text* 31 (Dec.–Feb., 1989), 11.

91. Connor, *Dumbstruck*, 410–11; Connor, "Phonophobia: The Dumb Devil of Stammering," http://www.stevenconnor.com/phonophobia.

92. David Norman Smith points out that the metaphor of the Jew as a ghost is a recurrent theme in Heinrich Heine's writings, which appeared as early as his undated *Gedanken und Einfälle* ("The Jews—this ghost of a people that ineluctably stood guard over its treasure, the Bible!") and reappeared much later in his Confessions as well: "Like a ghost guarding a treasure that had once been entrusted to it—that is how this murdered people, this ghost of a people, sat in its dark ghetto guarding the Hebrew Bible." David Norman Smith, *The Seductiveness of Jewish Myth*, 148, fn.66.

93. Susan E. Shapiro, "The Uncanny Jew: A Brief History of an Image" *Judaism* 46, no. 1 (1997): 65.

94. Leo Pinsker, "Auto-Emancipation: An Appeal to His People by a Russian Jew," in *Modern Jewish History: A Source Reader*, ed. Robert Chazan and Marc Lee Raphael (New York: Schocken, 1974), 163.

95. For more on the Zionist body discourse, see David Biale, *Eros and the Jews* (Berkeley: University of California Press, 1997), 547–630.

96. Yair Lipshitz, *Embodied Tradition: Theatrical Performances of Jewish Texts.* Hekshrim Institute, Ben-Gurion University of the Negev and Kinneret, Zmora-Bitan (Dvir Publishing, 2016), 223–44.

97. Max Nordau writes that the "new muscle-Jew[s] . . . proudly affirm their national loyalty." See Max Nordau "Jewry of Muscle" (June 1903), in *The Jew in the Modern World: A Documentary History*, 3d. ed., ed. Paul Mendes-Flohr and Jehuda Reinharz (New York: Oxford University Press, 2011), 617.

98. Atay Citron provides a vivid description of the golem's appearance, see "Habima's *The Golem*," *TDR* 24, no. 3 (1980): 65.

99. David Biale's book *Eros and the Jews* provides an elaborate discussion on the Jewish model of the *Luftmenschen* and its transformation in modern Israel. See Biale, *Eros and the Jews*, 547–630.

Chapter Four. *Yaakov and Rachel*

1. New American Standard Bible (NASB), Genesis 12:1.

2. "Here in Our Beloved Fatherland" is a famous Zionist song written by Israel Dushman in 1912, as a reaction and antithesis to Moris Rosenfeld's Yiddish song "Diaspora March," which expresses the despair and fear of the wandering life of Jewish Diaspora. For further reading, including different variations of the song, see http://www.zemereshet.co.il/song.asp?id=150.

3. The story of Chaim Bezalel Panet's journey to Palestine was chronicled and published in a manuscript titled "The Journey to the Holy Land" (Cluz: Kadima press, 1921). Parts of this book were later published in a family book under the title: *"I will go there": C. B Panet Immigrates with his Family to Israel, 1922* (Jerusalem: Dudi Press, 1983).

4. C. B Panet's immigration story is not necessarily representative. As Gur Alroey argues, not all immigrants were driven to Palestine on account of Zionist ideology. Many sought to escape distressful conditions of life in Eastern Europe. See Gur Alroey, *An Unpromising Land: Jewish Migration to Palestine in the Early Twentieth Century* (Stanford: Stanford University Press, 2014).

5. The establishment of the *Ohel* theater was part of the Labor party's wide network which included libraries for workers, an organization for cultural events, an institute for workers' lectures, *Davar* daily newspaper, *Sifriat Hapoalim* publishing house. Ten years after its institutionalization as a drama studio, in 1935, it received the title "the workers' theater of Eretz Israel." More on the *Ohel* theater, see Dorit Yerushalmi "Toward A Balanced History: 'Ohel,' The 'Workers Theater of Eretz Yisrael' as a Cultural Alternative to *Habima* (1935-1946)," *Journal of Modern Jewish Studies* 13, no. 3 (2014): 340–59; Chaim Shoham, "From Moscow to Eretz Yisrael: Toward Creating a Genuine Workers' Culture," *Bama* 112 (1988): 36–37; Chaim Shoham, *The Histadrut and "Ohel": Toward the Formation of Workers' Theater* (Tel Aviv: Golda Meir Institute for Labour and Social Research, Tel Aviv University, 1989).

6. Regina Bendix, *In Search of Authenticity*, 25–26.

7. Yaacov Shavit and Mordechai Eran, *The Hebrew Bible Reborn: From Holy Scripture to the Book of Books*, trans. Chaya Naor (New York: Walter de Gruyter, 2007), 476–77.

8. Uzzi Ornan (1950) "The Ugarit Texts," *Alef* IV, no. 13. Quoted in Ron Kuzar, *Hebrew and Zionism*, 256.

9. Italics in the Original text. Benjamin Harshav, *Language in Time of Revolution* (Stanford: Stanford University Press, 1993), 111.

10. This translation appears in Yerushalmi "Toward a Balanced History," 345–46. This citation also appears (in Hebrew) in Chaim Shoham, "From Moscow to Eretz Yisrael: Toward Creating a Genuine Workers' Culture," 36.

11. Nikolai Krasheninnikov was initially published in 1910 in Russian, and once again in 1911 in German. See *Rahels Klage: ein tausendjähriges Märchen in drei Bildern mit einem Epilog* (Berlin: J. Ladyschnikow, 1911).

12. Moshe Halevy, *My Way on the Stage (Hebrew)*, 124.

13. David G. Roskies, "S. An-sky and the Paradigm of Return," in *The Uses of Tradition: Jewish Continuity in the Modern Era*, ed. Jack Wertheimer (New York: The Jewish Theological Seminary of America, 1992), 243.

14. Amnon Raz-Krakotzkin, "The Zionist Return to the West," in *Orientalism and the Jews*, ed. I. Kalmar and D. Pensler (Waltham, MA: Brandeis University Press, 2005), 168.

15. Johan Huizinga, quoted in Frank Ankersmit, *The Sublime Historical Experience* (Stanford: Stanford University Press, 2005).

16. Raymond Williams, *Keywords: A Vocabulary of Culture and Society* (London: Fontana, 1975), 126–27.

17. Ibid., 128.

18. The National Sound Archive is part of the National Library of Israel. See http://web.nli.org.il.

19. Arlette Farge, *The Allure of the Archives*, trans. Thomas Scott-Railton (New Haven: Yale University Press, 2013), 6. Helen Freshwater's essay "The Allure of the Archive" (which conspicuously bears the same title as Farge's book) may further provide a discussion of the materiality of the archive with specific relation to theater research. See Helen Freshwater, "The Allure of the Archive," *Poetics Today* 24, no. 4 (2003): 729–58.

20. Visit https://www.ruthieabeliovich.com/possessed-voices to listen to this recording.

21. *Song of Songs* 4:8.

22. On sympathetic musical models see Ruth HaCohen "The Music of Sympathy in the Arts of the Baroque; or, the Use of Difference to Overcome Indifference," *Poetics Today* 22, no. 3 (Fall 2001): 607–50.

23. On the Biblical figure of Rachel as the symbolic matriarchal figure, see Samuel Dresner, *Rachel* (Minneapolis: Fortress Press, 1994). On Rachel as a Zionist-Israeli symbol of the national matriarch, see Susan Starr Sered, "A Tale of Three Rachels, Or the Cultural Herstory of a Symbol," *Nashim: A Journal of Jewish Women's Studies and Gender Issues* No. 1 (Winter 1998): 5–41.

24. Walter Benjamin, "The Work of Art in the Age of Its Technological Reproducibility," in *Walter Benjamin: Selected Writings, vol. 4: 1938–1940* (3rd version), eds. Howard Eiland and Michael W. Jennings (Cambridge: Harvard University Press, 2006), 253, 271 n.4.

25. Walter Benjamin, "Work of Art," in *One-Way Street and Other Writings* (London: Verso, 1998), 254.

26. Greg Dening, "Performing the Beaches of the Mind: An Essay," *History and Theory* 41, no. 1 (Feb. 2002): 5.

27. Freddie Rokem and Yael Admoni, "Yaakov and Rachel at the *Ohel* and the Parody Yaakov and Leah at the Kumkum Theater" (unpublished paper), The Yisrael Gur Archive and Museum of Theater, Ohel Box no. 3.

28. Rebbeca Schneider, *Performance Remains: Art and War in Times of Theatrical Reenactment* (London: Routledge, 2011), 103.

29. Greg Dening, "Performing the Beaches of the Mind," 5.

30. Carolyn Steedman, "Something She Called Fever: Michelet, Derrida, and Dust," *American Historical Review* 106, no. 4 (Oct. 2001): 1171.

31. Deborah Kapchan, *Theorizing Sound Writing* (Middletown, CT: Wesleyan University Press, 2017), 4.

32. For further discussion on digital technologies and the archive, see Diana Taylor, "Save As: Knowledge and Transmission in the Age of Digital Technologies," *Imagining America,* Paper 7 (2010).

33. Diana Taylor, *The Archive and the Repertoire: Performing Cultural Memory in the Americas* (Durham and London: Duke University Press, 2003), 18–26.

34. For an elaborated discussion on voice and *stimmung,* see Giorgio Agamben, "Vocation and Voice," *Qui Parle* 10, no. 2 (1997): 89–100; Hans Ulrich Gumbrecht, *Atmosphere, Mood, Stimmung* (Stanford: Stanford University Press, 2012).

35. F. R Ankersmit, *The Sublime Historical Experience,* 109.

36. Krasheninnikov's play centers on Rachel's matrimonial episode. It lacks any depictions of Rachel as a matriarchal national model, and is not situated in the Canaanite landscape, but in Haran. For Halevy's description of Christian depictions in Krasheninnikov's biblical play, see Moshe Halevy, "Opening," in *Yaackov and Rachel in the Ohel* (Jerusalem: Pickovsky Press, 1931), unpaginated.

37. As Shavit and Eran note, the translation of biblical plays into Hebrew began in the seventeenth century. During the Haskala, this phenomenon began with the translation of Salomon Gessner's (1730–1788) play *Der Tos Abels* (1758), at first partially in Hame'asef in 1811, and later in full by Yehuda Witkowsky (Breslau 1816) and by Moshe Mendelsohn-Frankfurter of Hamburg; a translation in rhyme entitled *The Face of the Globe* (Amsterdam, 1972). Shavit and Eran, *The Hebrew Bible Reborn,* 503 n. 73.

38. Halevy quoted in Chaim Shoham, "*Yaakov and Rachel*—The Making of an Original Hebrew Theater and Culture in Israel," *Bama* 119 (1990): 67; my translation.

39. Moshe Halevy, "Opening," *Yaakov and Rachel in the Ohel* (Jerusalem: Pickovsky Press, 1931), unpaginated; my translation. (The Israeli Center for the Documentation of the Performing Arts at Tel Aviv University, file number 33.1.2.)

40. For an elaborate discussion on this topic, see Shavit and Eran, *The Hebrew Bible Reborn,* 483–89.

41. Shavit and Eran, *The Hebrew Bible Reborn,* 485. For more on Ben-Gurion and the Bible, see Benjamin Uffenheimer, "Ben-Gurion and the Bible," in *Ben-Gurion and the Bible—A People and Its Land,* ed. Morderchai Cogan (Beersheba: Ben-Gurion University Press, 1989), 45–96; Avraham Tziyon, "Like All the Nations and the Chosen People, Ben-Gurion's Bond to the Bible," *Shadmot: The Origin of the Kibbutz Movement* 107 (October 1988): 77–88.

42. David Ben-Gurion, "The Eternality of Israel," Government Annual, 1953; "Uniqueness and Destiny," in *Uniqueness and Destiny: On the Security of Israel*, vol. 1 (Tel Aviv: Maarachot Press, 1971), 108–135. Quoted in Shavit and Eran, *The Hebrew Bible Reborn*, 484.

43. Zeev Sternhell discusses the unique synthesis of nationalism and socialism formed by the central stream of the Labor movement in the process of nation building, arguing that socialism was renounced as an action plan of a humanistic, universalistic class struggle and equality, becoming a synonym for the bureaucratic government of the Histadrut. Zionist leaders of the Labor party, according to Sternhell, were guided by nationalist ideology of conquering the land by means of Jewish presence and Jewish labor. See Zeev Sternhell, *The Founding Myths of Israel: Nationalism, Socialism, and the Making of the Jewish State*, trans. David Maisel (Princeton: Princeton University Press, 1999).

44. For more on the Zionist "return" to the Bible, see Shavit and Eran, *The Hebrew Bible Reborn*, 18–22.

45. See, for example, performance reviews from *Haaretz*, Feb. 3, 1928 and Feb. 7, 1928.

46. Freddie Rokem and Yael Admoni, "Yaakov and Rachel at the *Ohel* and the Parody Yaakov and Leah at the *Kumkum* Theater," (unpublished paper) The Yisrael Gur Archive and Museum of Theater, The *Ohel* Box 3, 5.

47. Kuzar, *Hebrew and Zionism*, 256–64.

48. For a further elaboration of this idea, see Amnon Raz-Krakotzkin, *The Zionist Return to the West*, 167.

49. David L. Jeffrey, *A Dictionary of Biblical Tradition in English Literature* (Grand Rapids: Eerdmans, 1992), 710.

50. David Ben-Gurion, "The Bible Shines in Its Own Light," in Shavit and Eran, *The Hebrew Bible Reborn*, 479.

51. Shavit and Eran, *The Hebrew Bible Reborn*, 283.

52. All translations from Shlonsky's dramatic text of Yaakov and Rachel are mine.

53. Clifford Geertz, "Making Experiences, Authoring Selves," in *The Anthropology of Experience,* ed. Victor Turner and Edward Bruner (Urbana: University of Illinois Press, 1986), 380.

54. This position is contrary to the ideological position of the *Canaanite movement*, which instantiated an alternative to the dominant Zionist discourse. As Ron Kuzar explains, the Canaanites branched out of the radical right-wing revisionist movement, fostering a total rupture in Jewish existence, adopting a geographic, rather than ethnic, approach to Zionism including it its territory the areas of today's Israel, Jordan, Syria, and Iraq. They defined the Zionist homeland as "The Land of Kedem" (antiquity), "the Land of the Hebrews, or "the Land of Canaan." These designations frame the Canaanite homeland through its Hebrew autochthons, while disowning the Jews from this nationality as they are not the most of antiquity. For an elaborate discussion, see Kuzar, *Hebrew and Zionism*, 198–275.

55. Moshe Halevy; see *Yaackov and Rachel in the Ohel* (Jerusalem: Pickovsky Press, 1931), unpaginated.

56. Nathan Bristritzky, "Our Theater in the Land of Israel," quoted in Rokem and Admoni, 10.

57. Arieh Bruce Saposnik, "European Nineteenth-Century Fascination with 'The Orient,'" *The Historical Journal* 49, no. 4 (2006): 1105–23. For an elaboration on this internal Jewish categorization, see Steve Aschheim, *Brothers and Strangers: The East European Jew in Germany and German Jewish Consciousness 1800–1923* (Madison: University of Wisconsin Press, 1982). For a discussion of the transformations Eastern European Jews underwent in Western European cities, see Shelly Zer-Zion, "The Shaping of the *Ostjude*: Alexander Granach and Shimon Finkel in Berlin," in *Jews and The Making of Modern German Theater,* eds. Jeanette R. Malkin and Freddie Rokem (Iowa City: Iowa University Press, 2010), 176–96.

58. Yehuda Karni, *Hedim* I (1922), 37–38. Quoted in Jehoash Hirshberg, *Music in the Jewish Community of Palestine 1880–1948: A Social History* (Oxford: Oxford University Press, 1996), 254.

59. Marco Di Giulio, "Protecting the Jewish Throat: Hebrew Accent and Hygiene in the Yishuv," *Journal of Israel History* 35, no. 2 (2016): 153–75.

60. This article is discussed in Abraham Elmaliach "On Defects and Disruptions in The Language," *Do'ar ha-Yom* (January 9, 1925): 6.

61. Benjamine Harshav, *Language in Time of Revolution* (Stanford: Stanford University Press, 1993), 164.

62. On the depiction of the New Hebrew as an Arab, see Yael Zerubavel, "Memory, the Rebirth of the Native, and the 'Hebrew Bedouin' Identity," *Social Research* 75, no. 1 (2008); Israel Bartal parallels the figure of the Cossack—as image of a freedom fighter connected to his land—imported during the first two decades into Zionist culture, and the Bedouin Arabs as two models projected onto the Jewish pioneers in the land of Palestine. See Israel Bartal, *Cossack and Bedouin: Land and People in Jewish Nationalism* (Tel Aviv: Am Oved Publishers, 2007).

63. Moshe Halevy played the role of the Rabbi from Miropole in *Habima's* production of *The Dybbuk*, until he left the troupe in 1925.

64. Quoted in Regina Bendix, *In Search of Authenticity*, 40.

65. Sharon Aronson-Lehavi discusses Halevy's ethnographic excursion in relation to the Christian excursion initiated by theater director Christian Stückl, as preparation for leading actors in *The Oberammergau Passion Play* he directed in 1990, performed at the village of Oberammergau in Bavaria, Germany. See Sharon Aronson-Lehavi, *Identity and Alterity in Biblical Theater in Israel* (Jerusalem: The Israeli Democracy Institute, 2016), 42.

66. Al-Shabab is an Arabic word meaning "youth."

67. I use this word in the translation in order to keep accuracy with the original Hebrew text that uses the derogatory word «כושי».

68. Moshe Halevy, *My Way on the Stage* (Hebrew) (Tel Aviv: Masada Press, 1965), 127–28; my translation (RA).

69. Johann Gottfried von Herder, *Selected Early Works, 1764–1767,* ed. Ernest A. Menze and Karl Menges, trans. Ernest A. Menze and Michael Palma (University Park: Pennsylvania State University Press, 1992), 44. On Herder's natural poetry,

see Christa Kamenetsky, "The German Folklore Revival in the Eighteenth Century: Herder's Theory of Naturpoesie," *Journal of Popular Culture* 6, no. 4 (1973): 836–48.

70. Ella Shohat, "Sepharadim in Israel: Zionism from the Standpoint of Its Jewish Victims," in *Dangerous Liaisons: Gender, Nation, and Postcolonial Perspectives,* eds. Ella Shohat, Aamir Mufti, and Anne McClintoch (Minneapolis: University of Minnesota Press, 1997), 39–69.

71. Shohat, "Sepharadim in Israel," 50.

72. Halevy, *My Way on the Stage,* 125–26; my translation (RA).

73. J. G. Herder, *On Social and Political Culture,* ed. F. M. Barnard (Cambridge: Cambridge University Press, 1969), 186.

74. Shlomo Haramati, *The Pioneer Teachers in Eretz Israel* (Tel Aviv: The Ministry of Defence, 2000), 50–61.

75. Tamar Liebes and Zohar Kampf, "Hello! This Is Jerusalem Calling: The Revival of Spoken Hebrew on The Mandatory Radio (1936–1948)," *Journal of Israeli History,* 29, no. 2 (2010): 155, n.56.

76. Yitzhak Epstein, "The Accent in the Hebrew Theater," *Bama* A (1933): 31–40; *Bama* B (1933): 19–26; *Bama* D (1934): 19–26.

77. Yitzhak Epstein, "The Accent Question in the Hebrew Theater," *Bama* A: 33 (לג).

78. Yitzhak Epstein, "A Hidden Question," trans. G. Svirsky. *Ha-Shiloaḥ* 17, no. 97 (August 1907): 193–205.

79. Ze'ev Jabotinsky, *The Hebrew Accent* (Tel Aviv: Ha-Sefer, 1930).

80. For an elaborate discussion of Ze'ev Jabotinsky's language scheme, see Svetlana Natkovich, "Jabotinsky's Language Program: Between History and Myth, Between Grammar and Phoentics," *Bikoret Ve Parshanut* (Criticism and Interpretation) 45 (2017): 99–120.

81. Jabotinsky, *The Hebrew Accent*, 6–8. Quoted in Benjamin Harshav, *Language in Time of Revolution*, 160. For further discussion of Jabotinsky's work within the context of the revisionist fascination with Mediterranean culture, see Eran Kaplan, *The Jewish Radical Right: Revisionist Zionism and Its Ideological Legacy* (Madison: University of Wisconsin Press, 2005), 46–47.

82. Haiim B. Rosen, *Our Hebrew* (Tel Aviv: Am Oved, 1965), 123–24. Quoted in Kuzar, *Zionism and Hebrew*, 259.

83. The Hebrew language has an alphabetical orthography with twenty-two letters to stand for consonants and vowels, and an ancillary orthographic system of thirteen diacritic markers termed *nikud* (translated into English as *pointing*), originally designated to represent medieval Hebrew phonology. The *nikud* system has a consonantal functions, and they express phonological values. See Dorit Diskin Ravid, "The Hebrew Phonology-Orthography Interface," in *Spelling Morphology*, Literacy Studies (Perspectives from Cognitive Neurosciences, Linguistics, Psychology and Education), vol. 3 (Boston: Springer, 2012), 81–95.

84. The term *guttural* literally means "of the throat" (from Latin *guttur,* throat) and is applied by phoneticians to describe the Hebrew glottal [ʔ] (א) and [h] (ה), uvular [χ] (ח), and pharyngeal [ʕ] (ע).

85. Epstein, "The Accent in the Hebrew Theater," *Bama* D: 21.

86. Epstein, "Aesthetic Hebrew," *Teatron ve-Omanut* 1 (1925): 4–7.

87. Epstein, "The Hebrew Speech and Ways of Dispersing It" (Ha dibur ha-Ivri ve-darkei hafatzato), *Ha-Shiloaḥ* 12, no. 3 (1903): 326–31.

88. The Hebrew Language Council is the forerunner of today's Academy of the Hebrew Language. Marco Di Giulio, "Protecting the Jewish Throat: Hebrew Accent and Hygiene in the Yishuv," *Journal of Israeli History* 35, no. 2 (2016): 159.

89. Kuzar, *Hebrew and Zionism*, 259.

90. For more on this subject, see Di Giulio, "Protecting the Jewish Throat": 153–75.

91. Frida Yaffe, "Yaakov and Rachel in the *Ohel* Performance," *Theater and Art* (April 1928): 4–7.

92. Engel himself was affiliated with the *Ohel* theater. In April 1925 Engel accepted the position of the musical director of the *Ohel.*

93. Rosowsky articulated his artistic musical vision in *Yaakov and Rachel* in an article he wrote for a special pamphlet *the Ohel* produced. See *Yaakov and Rachel in the Ohel* (Jerusalem: Pickovsky Press, 1931), unpaginated (The Israeli Center for the Documentation of the Performing Arts at Tel Aviv University, 33.1.2).

94. Jehoash Hirshberg, "Music in Small Tel-Aviv," in *The First Twenty Years: Literature and Arts in Tel Aviv 1909–1929*, ed. A. B Yaffe (Tel-Aviv: Hakibbutz Hameuchad, 1980), 153.

95. Hillel Cohen, *1929: Year Zero of the Arab-Israeli Conflict*, translated by Haim Watzman (Boston: Brandeis University Press, 2015).

96. Derek J. Penslar, "Broadcasted Orientalism: Representations of Mizrahi Jewry in Israeli Radio 1948–1967," in *Orientalism and the Jews*, eds. Derek Jonathan Penslar and Ivan Davidson Kalmar (Boston: Brandeis University Press, 2005), 183.

97. Renato Rosaldo, "Imperialist Nostalgia," *Representations* 26 (1989): 108.

98. For an elaborate discussion on decontextualized historical experience, see Ankersmit, *The Sublime Historical Experience*, 143.

99. This sociopolitical phenomenon, as Alon Confino argues, is related to the establishment of nation-states, especially in times of war, colonization, and decolonization, and characterizes modernity. Other known, parallel instantiations are the forced immigrations of the Armenian people that turned into a genocide in the Ottoman Empire in 1915, and the expulsion of millions during the Greek-Turkish war in 1921–22. In Europe, the most extreme demographic changes took place between 1943 and 1948: approximately thirty million people—Polish, German, Ukrainian, Czech, and Hungarians—were displaced from their homes. In Israel 750,000 Palestinians were uprooted and expelled between 1947 and 1949. For further reading on this topic, see

Alon Confino, "Miracles and Snow in Palestine and Israel: Tantura, A Story of 1948," *Israel Studies* 17, no. 2 (Summer 2012): 25–61.

Epilogue

1. Hanoch Levin, "The Torments of Job," in *The Labor of Life,* trans. Barbara Harshav (Stanford: Stanford University Press, 2003), 81.

2. Friedrich A. Kittler, *Gramophone, Film, Typewriter,* trans. Geoffrey Winthrop-Young and Michael Wutz (Stanford: Stanford University Press, 1999), 13.

3. Thomas Elsaesser, "Freud as Media Theorist: Mystic Writing-Pads and the Matter of Memory," *Screen* 50, no. 1 (Spring 2009): 112.

4. Gershom Scholem and Ora Wiskind, "On Our Language: A Confession," *History and Memory* 2, no. 2 (1990): 97–99.

5. Jean-Luc Nancy, *Listening,* trans. Charlotte Mandell (New York: Fordham University Press, 2007), 40.

Bibliography

Adorno, Theodor. "The Curves of the Needle." Translated by Thomas Y. Levin. *October* 55 (1990): 48–55.

———, and Max Horkheimer. *Dialectic of Enlightenment: Philosophical Fragments.* Stanford: Stanford University Press, 2002.

Agamben, Giorgio. "Vocation and Voice." *Qui Parle* 10, no. 2 (1997): 89–100.

Alroey, Gur. *An Unpromising Land: Jewish Migration to Palestine in the Early Twentieth Century.* Stanford: Stanford University Press, 2014.

———. "Sexual Violence, Rape, and Pogroms, 1903–1920." *Jewish Culture and History* 18, no. 3 (2017): 313–30.

Ankersmit, Frank. *The Sublime Historical Experience.* Stanford: Stanford University Press, 2005.

An-sky, S. "*The Dybbuk*, Or between Two Worlds: A Dramatic Legend." In *The Dybbuk and Other Writings*, edited by David G. Roskies, translated by Golda Werman, 1–50. London and New Haven: Yale University Press, 2002.

Aronson-Lehavi, Sharon. *Identity and Alterity in Biblical Theater in Israel.* Jerusalem: The Israeli Democracy Institute, 2016.

Aschheim, Steve. *Brothers and Strangers: The East European Jew in Germany and German Jewish Consciousness 1800–1923.* Madison: University of Wisconsin Press, 1982.

Auerbach, Erich. "Figura." In *Scenes from the Drama of European Literature*, 11–79. Minneapolis: University of Minnesota Press, 1984.

Austin, J. L. *How to Do Things with Words.* Edited by J. O. Urmson and Marina Sbisà. Second Edition. Cambridge: Harvard University Press, 1975.

Back, Les, and Michael Bull, eds. *The Auditory Culture Reader.* Oxford: Berg, 2013.

Bartal, Israel. *Cossack and Bedouin: Land and People in Jewish Nationalism.* Tel Aviv: Am Oved Publishers, 2007.

Barouch, Lina. "The Erasure and Endurance of Lament: Gershom Scholem's Early Critique of Zionism and Its Language." *Jewish Studies Quarterly* 21, no. 1 (March 2014): 13–26.

Barzilai, Maya. *Golem: Modern Wars and Their Monsters.* New York: New York University Press, 2016.

Bell, Michael. *Literature, Modernism, and Myth: Belief and Responsibility in the Twentieth Century.* Cambridge: Cambridge University Press, 1997.

Ben-Ari, Raikin. *Habima*. Translated by A. H. Gross and I. Soref. New York: Thomas Yoseloff, 1957.

Bendix, Regina. *In Search of Authenticity: The Formation of Folklore Studies*. Madison: The University of Wisconsin Press, 1997.

———. "The Pleasure of the Ear: Toward an Ethnography of Listening." *Cultural Analysis* 1 (2000): 33–50.

Benjamin, Walter. "Goethe's Elective Affinities." In *Walter Benjamin: Selected Writings, vol. 1: 1913–1926*, edited by Marcus Bullock and Michael W. Jennings. Cambridge: Harvard University Press, 1996.

———. "Work of Art." In *One-Way Street and Other Writings*. London: Verso, 1998.

———. "The Work of Art in the Age of Its Technological Reproducibility." In *Walter Benjamin: Selected Writings, vol. 4: 1938–1940*, edited by Howard Eiland and Michael W. Jennings. Cambridge, MA: Belknap Press, 2006.

Ben-Yehuda, Eliezer. "Hamavo Hagadol [The Great Introduction]." *Volume 1 of Ben-Yehuda 1909–1959*. Jerusalem: Ben-Yehuda Publications, 1940.

Berger, David "Three Typological Themes in Early Jewish Messianism: Messiah Son of Joseph, Rabbinic Calculations, and the Figure of Armilus." *AJS Review* 10, no. 2 (1985): 141–64.

Bial, David. *Eros and the Jews: From Biblical Israel to Contemporary America*. Berkeley: University of California Press, 1997.

Bialik, Chaim Nachman. "Scroll of Fire." In *Songs from Bialik: Selected Poems of Hayim Nahman Bialik* [*sic*], edited and translated by Hadar Atari. Syracuse: Syracuse University Press, 2000.

Bijestfield, Karin, and José van Dijck, eds. *Sound Souvenirs: Audio Technologies, Memory and Cultural Practices*. Amsterdam: Amsterdam University Press, 2009.

Bijestfield, Karin, and Trevor Pinch, eds. *The Oxford Handbook for Sound Studies*. New York: Oxford University Press, 2012.

Bilu, Yoram, and Benjamin Beit-Hallahmi. "Dybbuk Possession as a Hysterical Symptom: Psychodynamic and Socio-cultural Factors." *Israel Journal of Psychiatry* 26, no. 3 (1989): 138–49.

———. "Dybbuk and Maggid: Two Cultural Patterns of Altered Consciousness in Judaism." *AJS Review* 21, no. 2 (1996): 341–66.

———. "The Taming of the Deviants and Beyond: An Analysis of Dybbuk Possession and Exorcism in Judaism." In *Spirit Possession in Judaism: Cases and Contexts from the Middle Ages to the Present*, edited by Matt Goldisht, 41–72. Detroit: Wayne State University Press, 2003.

Bloom, Gina. *Voice in Motion*. Philadelphia: University of Pennsylvania Press, 2007.

Boyarin, Jonathan. "The Other Within and the Other Without." In *The Other in Jewish Thought and History*, edited by Laurence J. Silberstein and Robert L. Cohn. New York: New York University Press, 1994.

Boym, Svetlana. *The Future of Nostalgia*. New York: Basic Books, 2001.

Caplan, Debra. "Nomadic Chutzpah: The Vilna Troupe's Transnational Yiddish Theater Paradigm, 1915–1935." *Theater Survey* 55, no. 3 (2014): 296–317.

———. *Yiddish Empire: The Vilna Troupe, Jewish Theater, and the Art of Itinerancy.* Ann Arbor: University of Michigan Press, 2018.

Carlson, Marvin. "Invisible Presences: Performance Intertextuality." *Theater Research International* 19, no. 2 (1994): 111–17.

Chabrolle-Cerretini, Anne-Marie, and Savina Raynaud. "Humboldt's *innere Sprachform*: Its Contribution to the Lexicographical Description of Language Diversity." *Language & History* 58, no. 2 (2015): 95–110.

Chion, Michel. *Audio-Vision: Sound on Screen.* Edited and translated by Claudia Gorbman. New York: Columbia University Press, 1994.

Citron, Atay. "Habima's *The Golem.*" *TDR* 24, no. 3 (1980): 59–68.

Cohen, Hillel. *1929: Year Zero of the Arab-Israeli Conflict.* Translated by Haim Watzman. Boston: Brandeis University Press, 2015.

Confino, Alon. "Miracles and Snow in Palestine and Israel: Tantura, a Story of 1948." *Israel Studies* 17, no. 2 (Summer 2012): 25–61.

Connor, Steven. *Dumbstruck: A Cultural History of Ventriloquism.* Oxford: Oxford University Press, 2000.

———. "Phonophobia: The Dumb Devil of Stammering." http://www.stevenconnor.com/phonophobia.

Cutter, William. "Ghostly Hebrew, Ghastly Speech: Scholem to Rosenzweig, 1926." *Prooftexts: A Journal of Jewish Literary History* 10, no. 3 (1990): 413–33.

Del Pilar Blanco, María, and Esther Peeren. *The Spectralities Reader: Ghosts and Haunting in Contemporary Cultural Theory.* London: Bloomsbury, 2013.

Dening, Greg. "Performing the Beaches of the mind: An Essay." *History and Theory* 41, no. 1 (February 2002): 1–24.

Derrida, Jacques. *The Specters of Marx: The State of the Debt, the Work of Mourning, and the New International.* Translated by Peggy Kamuf. New York: Routledge, 1994.

Deutsch, Nathaniel. "Thrice Born; or, Between Two Worlds: Reflexivity and Performance in An-sky's Jewish Ethnographic Expedition and Beyond." In *Going to the People: Jews and the Ethnographic Impulse,* edited by Jeffrey Veidlinger, 27–44. Bloomington and Indianapolis: Indiana University Press, 2016.

Di Giulio, Marco. "Protecting the Jewish Throat: Hebrew Accent and Hygiene in the Yishuv." *Journal of Israel History* 35, no. 2 (2016): 153–75.

Diskin Ravid, Dorit. "The Hebrew Phonology-Orthography Interface." In *Spelling Morphology.* Literacy Studies (Perspectives from Cognitive Neurosciences, Linguistics, Psychology, and Education), vol 3. Boston: Springer, 2012.

Dresner, Samuel. *Rachel.* Minneapolis: Fortress Press, 1994.

Eithan, A., and M. Madan, eds. "On the Hebrew Accent in "Kol Yisrael." In *Leshonenu La'am.* Jerusalem: The Scientific Secretary of the Hebrew Language Academy, 1964.

Elior, Rachel. *Dybbuks and Jewish Women in Social History, Mysticism, and Folklore.* Translated by Joel Linsider. Jerusalem: Urim Publication, 2011.

Elmaliach, Abraham. "Al ha-Likuyin ve-ha-Pegimut ba-lashon [On Defects and Disruptions in the Language]." *Do'ar ha-Yom* (January 9, 1925).

Epstein, Yitzhak. "The Hebrew Speech and Ways of Dispersing It [*Ha dibur ha-Ivri ve-darkei hafatzato*]." *Ha Shiloah* 12, no. 3 (1903): 326–31, 396–400.

———. "A Hidden Question [*Sheela Neelamah*]." *HaShiloah* 17, no. 97 (August 1907): 193–205.

———. "The Accent in the Hebrew Theater." *Bama* A (1933): 31–40; *Bama* B (1933): 19–26; *Bama* D (1934): 19–26.

Farge, Arlette. *The Allure of the Archives*. Translated by Thomas Scott-Railton. New Haven: Yale University Press, 2013.

Felman, Shoshana. *The Juridical Unconscious*. Cambridge: Harvard University Press, 2002.

Ferber, Ilit. "A Language of the Border: On Scholem's Theory of Lament." *Journal of Jewish Thought and Philosophy* 21, no. 2 (2013): 161–86.

Finkel, Shimon. *Aharon Meskin and the Legend of The Golem*. Tel Aviv: Akad, 1980.

———. *Hanna Rovina: A Memory Monograph*. Tel Aviv: Akad Press, 1978.

Fisch, Harold. "Elijah and the Wandering Jew." In *Rabbi Joseph H. Lookstein Memorial Volume*, edited by Leo Landman, 125–35. New York: Ktav, 1980.

Fischer-Lichte, Erika. *Theater, Sacrifice, Ritual: Exploring forms of Political Theater*. London and New York: Routledge, 2005.

Fishman, Pearl. "Vakhtangov's *The Dybbuk*." *The Drama Review* 24, no. 3 (1980): 43–58.

Fiske, Shanyn. "From Ritual to the Archaic in Modernism: Frazer, Harrison, Freud, and the Persistence of Myth." In *A Handbook for Modernism Studies*, edited by Jean-Michel Rabaté. John Wiley and Sons, 2013.

Foster, Hal, ed. *Vision and Visuality*. Seattle: Bay Press, 1988.

Freshwater, Helen. "The Allure of the Archive." *Poetics Today* 24, no. 4 (2003): 729–58.

Friedman, Ken. "Innovation by Translation: Yiddish and Hasidic Hebrew in Literary History." In *Arguing the Modern Jewish Canon: Essays on Literature and Culture in Honor of Ruth R. Wisse*, edited by Justin Daniel Cammy, Dara Horn, Alyssa Quint, and Rachel Rubinstein. Cambridge, MA: Centre for Jewish Studies and Harvard University Press, 2008.

Fülöp-Miller, René. *The Mind and Face of Bolshevism: An Examination of Cultural Life in Soviet Russia*. New York: A. A. Knopf, 1928.

———, and Joseph Gregor. *The Russian Theater: Its Character and History with Especial Reference to the Revolutionary Period*. New York: B. Blom, 1968; originally published by George G. Harrap, London, 1930.

Geertz, Clifford. "Making Experiences, Authoring Selves." In *The Anthropology of Experience*, edited by Victor Turner and Edward Bruner. Urbana: University of Illinois Press, 1986.

Gilboa, Yehoshua A. *A Language Silenced: The Suppression of Hebrew Literature and Culture in the Soviet Union*. Rutherford, NJ: Fairleigh Dickenson University Press, 1982.

Glatzer, N. Nahum. "Franz Rosenzweig: The Story of a Conversion" (1952). Reprinted as "Introduction," in *Franz Rosenzweig: Life and Thought*. New York: Schocken, 1953.

Gnessin, Menachem. *My Way with the Hebrew Theater*. Tel Aviv: Ha-Kibbutz Ha-MeUchad Press, 1946.

Gnessin, Mikhail. "*Habima* and Musical Opportunities Regarding Its Performances." In *The Birth of Habima: Nachum Zemach*, edited by Yitzhak Norman. Jerusalem: Zionist Library Press, 1966.

Goethe, Johann Wolfgang von. *Goethe's Faust*. Translated by Walter Kaufmann. New York: Anchor Books, 1963.

Goldberg, Sylvie-Anne. "Paradigmatic Times: An-sky's Two Worlds," In *The Worlds of S. An-sky: A Russian Jewish Intellectual at the Turn of the Century*, edited by Gabriella Safran and Steve J. Zipperstein, 44–52. Stanford: Stanford University Press, 2006.

Goska, Danusha V. "Golem as Gentile, Golem as Sabra: An Analysis of the Manipulation of Stereotypes of Self and Other in Literary Treatments of a Legendary Jewish Figure." *New York Folklore* 23 (1997): 1–4.

Greenblatt, Stephen, and Catherine Gallagher. *Practicing New Historicism*. Chicago: University of Chicago Press, 2000.

———. "Cultural Mobility: An Introduction." In *Cultural Mobility: A Manifesto*, edited by Stephen Greenblatt, Ines G. Županov, Reinhard Meyer-Kalkus, Heike Paul, Pál Nyíri, and Friederike Pannewick. Cambridge: Cambridge University Press, 2010.

Gumbrecht, Hans Ulrich. *Atmosphere, Mood, Stimmung*. Stanford: Stanford University Press, 2012.

———. *Our Broad Present: Time and Contemporary Culture*. New York: Columbia University Press, 2014.

Gur, Israel. *Playing the Pauper and the King: Masses on the Hebrew Actors*. Jerusalem: Theater Press, 1959.

Guy, Carmit *The Queen Took the Bus*. Tel Aviv: Am Oved, 1995.

HaCohen, Ruth. "The Music of Sympathy in the Arts of the Baroque; or, the Use of Difference to Overcome Indifference." *Poetics Today* 22, no. 3 (Fall 2001): 607–50.

———. *The Music Libel against the Jews*. New Haven: Yale University Press, 2011.

———. "The Birth and Demise of Vocal Communities." *AJS Perspectives: The Magazine for the Association for Jewish Studies*. The Sound Issue (Spring/Summer 2016). http://perspectives.ajsnet.org/sound-issue/the-birth-and-demise-of-vocal-communities.

———. "Vocal Communities in the Twilight: Real and Imagined Sonic Spaces in Central European Jewry at the Opening and Closing of the Gate." In *The Interpretive Imagination*, edited by Richard I. Cohen, Ruth HaCohen, Galit Hasan Rokem, Ilana Pardes. Jerusalem: Magnes Press, 2016.

Halevy, Moshe. *My Way on the Stage* (Hebrew). Tel Aviv: Massada, 1954.

Hasan-Rokem, Galit, and Alan Dundes, eds. *The Wandering Jew: Essays in the Interpretation of a Christian Legend*. Bloomington: Indiana University Press, 1986.

———. *Web of Life: Folklore and Midrash in Rabbinic Literature*. Stanford: Stanford University Press, 2000.

———. "Bodies Performing in Ruins: The Lamenting Mother in Ancient Hebrew Texts." In *Laments in Jewish Thought: Philosophical, Theological, and Literary Perspectives*, edited by Ilit Ferber and Paula Schwebel, 33–63. Berlin: De Gruyter, 2014.

Haramati, Shlomo. *The Pioneer Teachers in Eretz Israel*. Tel Aviv: The Ministry of Defence, 2000.

Harshav, Benjamin. *Language in Time of Revolution*. Stanford: Stanford University Press, 1993.

Herder, Johann Gottfried. *On Social and Political Culture*. Edited by F. M Barnard. Cambridge: Cambridge University Press, 1969.

———. *Selected Early Works, 1764–67*. Edited by Ernest A. Menze and Karl Menges, translated by Ernest A. Menze with Michael Palma. University Park: Pennsylvania State University Press, 1992.

Hilbrenner, Anke. "Simon Dubnov's Master Narrative and the Construction of a Jewish Collective Memory in the Russian Empire" [*sic*]. *Ab Imperio* 4 (2003): 143–64.

Hirshberg, Jehoash. "Music in Small Tel-Aviv." In *The First Twenty Years: Literature and Arts in Tel Aviv 1909–1929*, edited by A. B Yaffe. Tel Aviv: Hakibbutz Hameuchad Press, 1980.

———. *Music in the Jewish community of Palestine 1880–1948: A Social History*. Oxford: Oxford University Press, 1996.

Hobsbawm, Eric. "Inventing Traditions." In *The Invention of Tradition*, edited by Eric Hobsbawm and Terence O. Ranger. Cambridge: Cambridge University Press, 1983.

Holland, Peter. "Hearing the Dead: The Sound of David Garrick." In *Players, Playwrights, Playhouses: Investigating Performance, 1660–1800 (Redefining British Theater History)*, edited by Michael Cordner and Peter Holland. London: Palgrave Macmillan, 2007.

Humboldt, Wilhelm von. *On Language: On the Diversity of Human Language Construction and Its Influence on the Mental Development of the Human Species*. Edited by Michael Losonsky, translated by Peter Heath. Cambridge: Cambridge University Press, 1999.

Hymes, Dell. *Speech and Language on Inequality: Towards an Understanding of Voice*. London, UK, and Bristol, PA: Taylor and Francis, 1996.

Idelsohn, Avraham Tsvi. "He-hayah ve-hehoveh. Zikhronot 'al Herman Kohen." *Shay shel sifrut (Literary Supplement to the Palestine News)* 10, no. 7 (Aug. 23, 1918): 8–10.

Ivanov, Vladislav. *Russikiye Sezony Teatra "Gabima."* Moscow: Artist. Rezhissyor Teatre, 1999.

———. "An-sky, Evgeny Vakhtangov, and *The Dybbuk*" [*sic*]. Translated by Anne Eakin Moss. In *The Worlds of S. An-sky: A Russian Jewish Intellectual at the Turn of the Century*, edited by Gabriella Safran and Steve J. Zipperstein, 252–65. Stanford: Stanford University Press, 2006.

Jabotinsky, Ze'ev. *The Hebrew Pronunciation*. Tel Aviv: Ha-Sefer, 1930.

Jeffrey, David L. *A Dictionary of Biblical Tradition in English Literature*. Grand Rapids: Eerdmans, 1992.

Jessup, Lynda, ed. *Anti-Modernism and Artistic Experience: Policing the Boundaries of Modernity*. Toronto: University of Toronto Press, 2001.

Joseph, John E. *Language and Identity: National, Ethnic, Religious*. Hampshire and New York: Palgrave Macmillan, 2004.

Kafka, Franz. "The Animal in the Synagogue." In *Parables and Paradoxes*, edited by Nahum N. Glatzer, translated by Ernst Kaiser and Eithne Wilkins, 49–59. New York: Schocken, 1961 [1946].

Kahan-Newman, Zelda. "Yiddish Haunts: The Yiddish Underpinnings of Appelfeld's Laylah ve'od Laylah." *Mikan* 5 (2005): 81–90.

Kamenetsky, Christa. "The German Folklore Revival in the Eighteenth Century: Herder's Theory of Naturpoesie." *Journal of Popular Culture* 6, no. 4 (1973): 836–48.

Kapchan, Deborah A., ed. *Theorizing Sound Writing*. Middletown, CT: Wesleyan University Press, 2017.

Kaplan, Eran. *The Jewish Radical Right: Revisionist Zionism and Its Ideological Legacy*. Madison: University of Wisconsin Press, 2005.

Kaynar, Gad. "National Theater as Colonized Theater: The Paradox of *Habima*." *Theater Journal* 50, no. 1 (March 1998): 1–20.

———. "On Habima's Branding as a National Theater (1931–1958)." In *Habima: New Studies on National Theater*, edited by Gad Kaynar, Dorit Yerushalmi, and Shelly Zer-Zion, 83–104. Tel Aviv: Resling, 2017.

Kirby, E. T. "The Delsarte Method: 3 Frontiers of Actor Training." *The Drama Review: TDR* 16, no. 1 (1972): 55–69.

Kirshenblatt-Gimblett, Barbara. "The Corporeal Turn." *JQR* 95, no. 3 (Summer 2005): 447–61.

———. "Sounds of Sensibility." *Judaism: A Quarterly Journal of Jewish Life and Thought* 47, no. 1 (Winter 1998): 47–78.

Kittler, Friedrich A. *Gramophone, Film, Typewriter*. Translated by G. Winthrop-Young and M. Wutz. Stanford: Stanford University Press, 1999.

Kleberg, Lars. *Theater as Action: Soviet Russian Avant-garde Aesthetics*. Translated by Charles Rougle. Houndsmills, Basingstoke: Macmillan, 1993.

Krasney, Ariela. *The Badkhn*. Ramat Gan: Bar-Ilan University Press, 1998.

Krasheninnikov, Nikolai. *Rahels Klage: ein tausendjähriges Märchen in drei Bildern mit einem Epilog*. Berlin: J. Ladyschnikow, 1911.

Kuzar, Ron. *Hebrew and Zionism: A Discourse Analytic Cultural Study*. Berlin: Mount De Gruyter, 2001.

Landis, Joseph. *The Great Jewish Plays*. New York: Avon Books, 1972.

Lederhendler, Eli. *The Road to Modern Jewish Politics: Political Tradition and Political Reconstruction in the Jewish Community of Tsarist Russia*. New York: Oxford University Press, 1989.

Leivick, Halpern. "The Golem." In *The Dybbuk and Other Great Yiddish Plays*, edited and translated by Joseph C. Landis, 217–356. New York: Bantam Books, 1966.

Levy, Emanuel. *The Habima, Israel's National Theater, 1917–1977: A Study of Cultural Nationalism*. New York: Columbia University Press, 1979.

Levin, Hanoch. "The Torments of Job." In *The Labor of Life*, translated by Barbara Harshav. Stanford: Stanford University Press, 2003.

Liebes, Tamar. "Acoustic Space: The Role of Radio in Israeli Collective History." *Jewish History* 20 (2006): 69–90.

———, and Zohar Kampf. "Hello! This Is Jerusalem Calling: The Revival of Spoken Hebrew on The Mandatory Radio (1936–1948)." *Journal of Israeli History* 29, no. 2 (2010): 137–58.

Lipshitz, Yair. "The Dybbuk's Body: Traditions, Revolutions, Crises." In *"Do Not Chase Me Away": New Studies on The Dybbuk*, edited by Shimon Levy and Dorit Yerushalmi, 137–62. Tel-Aviv: Tel-Aviv University Press, 2009.

———. "Embodied Redemption: Past, Future, and Acting in Habima's *The Golem*." *Reshit* 1 (2009): 279–304.

———. *Embodied Tradition: Theatrical Performances of Jewish Texts*. Hekshrim Institute, Ben Gurion University of the Negev and Kinneret. Zmora-Bitan: Dvir, 2016.

Loeffler, James. "When Hermann Cohen Cried: Zionism, Culture, Emotions." In *Zionism as a Cultural Movement*, edited by Israel Bartal and Rachel Rojansky. Leiden: Brill, no date.

Loraux, Nicole. *The Mourning Voice: An Essay on Greek Tragedy*. Translated by Elizabeth Trapnell Rawlings. Ithaca: Cornell University Press, 2002.

Lukin, Benyamin. " 'An Academy Where Folklore Will Be Studied': An-sky and the Jewish Museum." In *Words of S. An-sky: A Russian Jewish Intellectual at the Turn of the Century*, edited by Gabriella Safran and Steven J. Zipperstein, 281–306. Stanford: Stanford University Press, 2006.

Macleish, Archibald. *Collected Poems 1917–1982*. Boston: Houghton Mifflin Harcourt, 1985.

Malaev-Babel, Andrei, ed. *The Vakhtangov Sourcebook*. New York: Routledge, 2011.

Mendes-Flohr, Paul. "Franz Rosenzweig and the German Philosophical Tradition." In *The Philosophy of Franz Rosenzweig*. London: University Press of New England for Brandeis University Press, 1988.

———. "Hebrew as Holy Tongue: Franz Rosenzweig and the Renewal of Hebrew." In *Hebrew in Ashkenaz: A Language in Exile*, edited by Lewis Glinert. Oxford: Oxford University Press, 1993.

Natkovich, Svetlana. "Jabotinsky's Language Program: Between History and Myth, Between Grammar and Phoentics." *Bikoret Ve Parshanut (Criticism and Interpretation)* 45 (2017): 99–120.

Nigal, Gedaliah. *Dybbuk Tales in Jewish Literature*. Jerusalem: Reuben Mass, 1983.

Nora, Pierre. "Between Memory and History: Les Lieux de Memoire." *Representations* 26 (1989).

Nordau, Max. "Jewry of Muscle" (June 1903). In *The Jew in the Modern World: A Documentary History*, 3rd ed., edited by Paul Mendes-Flohr and Jehuda Reinharz. New York: Oxford University Press, 2011.

Norman, Smith David. "Judeophobia, Myth, and Critique." In *The Seductiveness of Jewish Myth*, edited by Daniel S. Bleslauer. Albany: State University of New York Press, 1997.

Ornan, Uzzi. "The Ugarit Texts." *Alef* IV (1950): 13.

Palisca, Claude V. *Musica and Ideas in the Sixteenth and Seventeenth Centuries*. Urbana: University of Illinois Press, 2006.

Panet, Chaim Bezalel. *"I will go there": C. B Panet Immigrates with his Family to Israel, 1922*. Jerusalem: Dudi Press, 1983.

Pascoe, Judith. *The Sarah Siddons Audio Files: Romanticism and the Lost Voice*. Ann Arbor: University of Michigan Press, 2013.

Pedaya, Haviva. "The Wandering Messiah and the Wandering Jew: Judaism and Christianity as a Two-Headed Structure and the Myth of His Feet and Shoes." In *Religion und Politik*, edited by Gesine Palmer und Thomas Brose, 73–103. Tübingen: Mohr Siebeck, 2013.

Penslar, Derek Jonathan. "Transmitting Jewish Culture: Radio in Israel." *Jewish Social Studies* 10, no. 1 (Fall 2003): 1–29.

———. "Radio and the Shaping of Modern Israel 1936–1973." In *Zionism, Ethnicity, and National Mobilization*, edited by Michael Berkowitz, 60–82. Leiden: Brill, 2004.

———. "Broadcasted Orientalism: Representations of Mizrahi Jewry in Israeli Radio 1948–1967." In *Orientalism and the Jews*, edited by Derek Jonathan Penslar and Ivan Davidson Kalmar. Hanover, NH: Brandeis University Press, 2005.

Phelan, Peggy. *Unmarked: The Politics of Performance*. New York and London: Routledge, 1993.

Pinchevski, Amit, Tamar Liebes, and Ora Herman. "Eichmann on the Air: Radio and the Making of an Historic Trial." *Historical Journal of Film, Radio and Television* 27, no. 1 (2007), 1–25.

———, and Tamar Liebes. "Severed Voices: Radio and the Mediation of Trauma in the Eichmann Trial." *Public Culture* 22, no. 2 (2010): 265–91.

Pinsker, Leon. "Auto-Emancipation: An Appeal to His People by a Russian Jew." In *Modern Jewish History: A Source Reader*, edited by Robert Chazan and Marc Lee Raphael. New York: Schocken, 1974.

Pinski, David. "The Stranger." In *Six Plays of The Yiddish Theater: Second Series*. Boston: John W. Luce, 1918.

Plato. *The Symposium*. Translated by Robin Waterfield. Oxford: Oxford University Press, 1952.

Pollock, Benjamin. *Franz Rosenzweig's Conversions: World Denial and World Redemption*. Bloomington: Indiana University Press, 2014.

Porter, James I. "Disfigurations: Erich Auerbach's Theory of *Figura*." *Critical Inquiry* 44, no. 1 (Autumn 2017): 80–113.

Preston, Carrie J. Posing Modernism: Delsartism in Modern Dance and Silent Film." *Theater Journal* 61, no. 2 (2009): 213–33.

———. *Modernism's Mythical Pose: Gender, Genre, Solo Performance*. New York: Oxford University Press, 2011.

Raz-Krakotzkin, Amnon. "The Zionist Return to the West." In *Orientalism and the Jews*, edited by I. Kalmar and D. Pensler. Waltham, MA: Brandeis University Press, 2005.

Rivlov, Menachem. *The Birth of Habima: Nachum Zemach*. Edited by Yitzhak Norman. Jerusalem: Zionist Library Press, 1966.

Roach, Joseph R. *The Players Passion: Studies in the Science of Acting*. Ann Arbor: The University of Michigan Press, 1993.

Rokem, Freddie, and Yael Admoni. "Yaakov and Rachel at the *Ohel* and the Parody Yaakov and Leah at the Kumkum Theater." Undated and upublished paper, The Yisrael Gur Archive and Museum of Theater, The Hebrew University of Jerusalem, The Ohel Box no. 3.

————. "The Dybbuk on Haifa-Jeida Road: The First Performance of *The Dybbuk* in Israel." *Cathedra* 26 (1982): 186–93.

————. "Hebrew Theater from 1889 to 1948." In *Theater in Israel*, edited by Linda Ben Zvi, 51–84. Ann Arbor: The University of Michigan Press, 1996.

————. "*The Dybbuk* in Israel: Theater, Criticism, and the Establishment of Hebrew Culture." In *"Do Not Chase Me Away": New Studies on the Dybbuk*, edited by Shimon Levy and Dorit Yerushalmi. Tel-Aviv: Tel-Aviv University Press, 2009.

————. "Has This Thing Appeared Again Tonight? Deus ex Machina and Other Interventions of the Supernatural." In *Things: Religion and the Question of Materiality*, edited by Dick Houtman and Brigit Meyer. New York: Fordham University Press, 2012.

————. "Meta-Theatricality and Screen Scenes." In *Hamlet Handbuch*, edited by Peter W. Marx, 53–58. Stuttgart: Verlag J. B. Metzler, 2014.

Ronen, Diti. "Habima's recognition as a National Theater: Circumstances, Meanings, and Implications." In *Habima: New Studies on National Theater*, edited by Gad Kaynar, Dorit Yerushalmi, and Shelly Zer-Zion, 143–77. Tel Aviv: Resling, 2017.

Rosaldo, Renato. "Imperialist Nostalgia." *Representations* 26 (Spring 1989): 107–22.

Rosen, Haiim B. *Our Hebrew [Ha'Ivrit Shelanu]*. Tel Aviv: Am Oved, 1965.

Rosenstock-Huessy, Eugen. "Prologue/Epilogue to the Letters—Fifty Years Later." In *Judaism Despite Christianity: The "Letters on Christianity and Judaism." between Eugen Rosenstock-Huessy and Franz Rosenzweig*, edited by Eugen Rosenstock-Huessy. New York: Schocken, 1971.

Rosenzweig, Franz. "The Jewish People." In *Franz Rosenzweig: His Life and Thought*, edited by Nahum N. Glatzer, New York: Schocken, 1953.

————. "Classical and Modern Hebrew: A Review of a Translation into the Hebrew of Spinoza's Ethics." In *Franz Rosenzweig: His Life and Thought*, edited by Nahum N. Glatzer, 263–71. New York: Schocken, 1953.

————. "It Is Time: Concerning the Study of Judaism (1917)." In *Franz Rosenzweig: On Jewish Learning*, edited by Nahum N. Glatzer, 27–54. Madison: University of Wisconsin Press, 2002.

————. *The Star of Redemption*. Translated by Barbara E. Galli. Madison: The University of Wisconsin Press, 2005.

Roskies, David G. "S. An-sky and the Paradigm of Return." In *The Uses of Tradition: Jewish Continuity in the Modern Era*, edited by Jack Wertheimer. New York: The Jewish Theological Seminary of America, 1992.

Rosman, Moshe. "Hasidism as a Modern Phenomenon—The Paradox of Modernization without Secularization." In *Simon Dubnow Institute 2007 Yearbook: Early Modern Culture and Haskala—Reconsidering the Borderlines of Modern History*, edited by David B. Ruderman and Shmuel Feiner. 215–27. Leipzig: Vandenhoeck and Ruprecht, 2007.

Rotman, Diego. *The Stage as a Temporary Home: The Theater of Dzigen and Schumacher (1927–1980)*. Jerusalem: Magnes Press, 2018.

Rousseau, Jean-Jacques. *Oeuvres completes*. Edited by Bernard Gagnebin and Marcel Raymond. Vol. 55. Paris: NRF Edition de la Pléiade, 1969.

Saposnik, Arieh Bruce. "European Nineteenth-Century Fascination with 'The Orient.'" *The Historical Journal* 49, no. 4 (2006): 1105–23.

Safran, Gabriella. *Wandering Soul: The Dybbuk's Creator, S. An-sky*. Cambridge: Harvard University Press, 2010.

———. "Some Russian Jewish Writers in Switzerland and the Valorization of Jewish Argument Style." In *East European Jewish in Switzerland: New Perspectives on Modern Jewish History*, edited by Tamar Lewinsky and Sandrine Mayoraz, 77–96. Berlin: De Gruyter. 2013.

Safran, William. "Language, Ideology, and State Building: A Comparison of Policies in France, Israel, and the Soviet Union." *International Political Science Review* 13 (1992): 397–414.

Schafer, R. Murray. *Our Sonic Environment and the Soundscape: The Tuning of the World*. Rochester, VT: Destiny Books, 1994.

Schneider, Rebecca. *Performing Remains: Art and War in Times of Theatrical Reenactment*. New York and London: Routledge, 2011.

Scholem, Gershom. *On the Kabbalah and Its Symbolism*. Translated by Ralph Manheim, New York: Schocken, 1969.

———. "The Golem of Prague and the Golem of Rehovot." In *The Messianic Idea in Judaism and Other Essays on Jewish Spirituality*. New York: Schocken, 1971.

———. "On Lament and Lamentation." Translated by Paula Schwebel and Lina Barouch. *Jewish Studies Quarterly* 21, no. 1 (2014): 4–12.

Schmidt Camacho, Alicia. *Migrant Imaginaries: Latino Cultural Politics in the U.S.-Mexico Borderlands*. New York: New York University Press, 2008.

Sconce, Jeffrey. *Haunted Media: Electronic Presence from Telegraphy to Television*. Durham: Duke University Press, 2000.

Segal, Miryam. *A New Sound in Hebrew Poetry: Poetics, Politics, Accent*. Bloomington: Indiana University Press, 2010.

Seidman, Naomi. "The Ghosts of Queer Loves Past: An-sky's 'Dybbuk' and the Sexual Transformation of Ashkenaz." In *Queer Theory and the Jewish Question*, edited by Daniel Boyarin, Daniel Itzkovitz, and Ann Pellegrini. New York: Columbia University Press, 2003.

Seroussi, Edwin. "Nostalgic Zionist Soundscapes: The Future of the Israeli Nation's Sonic Past." *Israel Studies* 19, no. 2 (2014): 35–50.

Shahar, Galili. "The Sacred and the Unfamiliar: Gershom Scholem and the Anxieties of the New Hebrew." *The Germanic Review: Literature, Culture, Theory* 83, no. 4 (Fall 2008).

Shandler, Jeffrey. *While America Watches: Televising the Holocaust.* Oxford: Oxford University Press, 1999.

Shapiro, Susan E. "The Uncanny Jew: A Brief History of an Image." *Judaism,* 46, no. 1 (1997): 63–78.

Shavit, Yaacov, and Mordechai Eran. *The Hebrew Bible Reborn: From Holy Scripture to the Book of Books.* Translated by Chaya Naor. New York: Walter de Gruyter, 2007.

Shoham, Chaim. "From Moscow to Eretz Yisrael: Toward Creating a Genuine Workers' Culture." *Bama* 112 (1988): 36–37.

———. *The Histadrut and "Ohel": Toward the Formation of Workers' Theater.* Tel Aviv: Golda Meir Institute for Labour and Social Research, Tel Aviv University, 1989.

———. "*Yaakov and Rachel*—The Making of an Original Hebrew Theater and Culture in Israel." *Bama* 119 (1990).

Shohat, Ella. "Sepharadim in Israel: Zionism from the Standpoint of it Jewish Victims." In *Dangerous Liaisons: Gender, Nation, and Postcolonial Perspectives,* edited by Ella Shohat, Aamir Mufti, and Anne McClintoch. Minneapolis: University of Minnesota Press, 1997.

Simon, Julia. "Singing Democracy: Music and Politics in Jean Jacques Rousseau's Thought." *Journal of History of Ideas* 65 (July 2004): 433–54.

Sinfree, B. Makoni, and Alastair Pennycook. *Disinventing and Reconstituting Languages, Multilingual Matters.* England: Clevedon, 2006.

Smith, Bruce R. *The Acoustic World of Early Modern England: Attending to the O-Factor.* Chicago: University of Chicago Press, 1999.

Soffer, Oren. *Mass Communication in Israel: Nationalism, Globalization, and Segmentation.* Translated by Judith Yalon. Oxford: Beghahn Books, 2015.

Stanislavsky, Konstantin. *My Life in Art,* translated and edited by Jean Benedetti. New York: Routledge, 2008.

Starr Sered, Susan. "A Tale of Three Rachels, Or the Cultural Herstory of a Symbol." *Nashim: A Journal of Jewish Women's Studies and Gender Issues* 1 (Winter 1998), 5–41.

Steedman, Carolyn. "Something She Called Fever: Michelet, Derrida, and Dust." *American Historical Review* 106, no. 4 (October 2001): 1159–80.

Steidle, Hans. "Der Habima-Skandal in Würzburg 1930/31." *Mainfränkisches Jahrbuch,* Jg. 35, 1983, S. 152 bis 210, Zitat: S.161.

Sterne, Jonathan. *The Audible Past: Cultural Origins of Sound Reproduction.* London and Durham: Duke University Press, 2003.

———, ed. *The Sound Studies Reader.* New York: Routledge, 2012.

Sternhell, Zeev. *The Founding Myths of Israel: Nationalism, Socialism, and the Making of the Jewish State.* Translated by David Maisel. Princeton: Princeton University Press, 1999.

St. John, Robert. *Tongue of the Prophets: The life Story of Eliezer Ben Yehuda.* New York: Doubleday, 1952.

Tartakovsky, Elena. "Vakhtangov's *The Dybbuk*: Paradox of Preservation and Canonization." In *"Do Not Chase Me Away": New Studies on the Dybbuk*, edited by Shimon Levy and Dorit Yerushalmi, 163–78. Tel-Aviv: Tel-Aviv University Press, 2009.

———. *Habima: The Russian Heritage.* Tel Aviv: Safra, 2013.

Taylor, Diana. *The Archive and the Repertoire: Performing Cultural Memory in the Americas.* Durham and London: Duke University Press, 2003.

———. "Save As: Knowledge and Transmission in the Age of Digital Technologies." *Imagining America*, Paper 7 (2010): 2–17.

Taylor, George. "François Delsarte: A Codification of Nineteenth-Century Acting." *Theater Research International* 24 (1999): 71–82.

———, and Rose Whyman. "Francois Delsarte, Prince Sergei Volkonsky, and Mikhail Chekhov." *Mime Journal* 23, Article 7 (2005).

Truax, Barry. *Acoustic Communication.* Norwood, NJ: Ablex Publishing, 1984.

Turner, Victor. "Liminality and Communitas." In *The Ritual Process: Structure and Anti-Structure.* Ithaca: Cornell University Press, 1991.

Tziyon, Avraham. "Like All the Nations and the Chosen People, Ben Gurion's Bond to the Bible." *Shadmot: The Origin of the Kibbutz Movement* 107 (October 1988): 77–88.

Uffenheimer, Benjamin. "Ben Gurion and the Bible." In *Ben Gurion and the Bible— A People and Its Land*, edited by Morderchai Cogan, 45–96. Beersheba: Ben Gurion University Press, 1989.

Uritskaya, Liudmila. "Ashkenazi Jewish Collections of the State Ethnographic Museum in St. Petersburg." In *Tracing An-sky: Jewish Collections from the State Ethnographic Museum in St. Petersburg; Catalog of the Exhibition in Joods Historish Museum*, edited by Mariella Beuker and Renée Waale, 24–57. Zwolle, Netherlands: Waanders Uitgevers, 1992.

Vardi, David. *On My Path.* Tel-Aviv: Massada, 1950.

Volkonsky, Sergei. "On *The Dybbuk*." In *The Birth of Habima—Nachum Zemach in Vision and Deed*, edited by Yitzhak Norman. Jerusalem: The Zionist Library, 1966.

Walker, Julia A. "Voice: Oratory Expression and the Text/Performance Split." In *Expressionism and Modernism in the American Theater.* Cambridge: Cambridge University Press, 2005.

Weiss, Allen S. *Phantasmic Radio.* Durham and London: Duke University Press, 1995.

Weisser, Albert. *The Modern Renaissance of Jewish Music.* New York: Bloch, 1954.

Wertheimer, Jack, ed. *The Uses of Tradition: Jewish Continuity in the Modern Era.* Cambridge: Harvard University Press, 1992.

Whitehead, Gregory. "Who's There? Notes on the Materiality of Radio Art." *Art and Text* 31 (December-February, 1989).

Whyman, Rose. "The Actor's Second Nature: Stanislavsky and William James." *New Theater Quarterly* 23, no. 2 (May 2007): 115–23.

———. *The Stanislavsky System of Acting: Legacy and Influence in Modern Performance.* Cambridge: Cambridge University Press, 2008.

Wiedebach, Hartwig. "'Hebräisches Fühlen': Hermann Cohens Deutung des *Schma' Jisraël/ 'Höre Israel.'"* *Kalonymos. Beiträge zur deutsch-jüdischen Geschichte aus dem Salomon Ludwig Steinheim-Institut* 6, no. 2 (2003): 1–4.

Wiles, David. *Tragedy in Athens: Performance Space and Theatrical Meaning.* Cambridge: Cambridge University Press, 1997.

Williams, Raymond. *Keywords: A Vocabulary of Culture and Society.* London: Fontana, 1975.

———. *Marxism and Literature.* Oxford: Oxford University Press, 1977.

Wilson Kimber, Marian. "In a Woman's Voice: Musical Recitation and the Feminization of American Melodrama." In *Melodramatic Voices: Understanding Music Drama,* edited by Sarah Hibberd, 61–82. Aldershot: Ashgate, 2011.

Wolitz, Seth L. "Inscribing An-sky's Dybbuk in Russian and Jewish Letters." In *The Worlds of S. An-sky: A Russian Jewish Intellectual at the Turn of the Century,* edited by Gabriella Safran and Steve J. Zipperstein, 164–202. Stanford: Stanford University Press, 2006.

Yaffe, Frida. "*Yaakov and Rachel* in the *Ohel* Performance." *Theater and Art* (April 1928): 4–7.

Yair, Gad, and Michaela Soyer. *The Golem in German Social Theory.* Lanham, MD: Lexington Books, 2008.

Yerushalmi, Dorit. "In Hanna Rovina's Shadow." *Zmanim a Historical Quarterly* 99 (2007): 26–38.

———. "The Inter-relationship between Hebrew Theater and Yiddish Theater through the Work of Mandatory Palestine Directors." *Criticism and Interpretation* (Bar Ilan University Publishers) 41 (Winter 2009): 7–39.

———. "Toward a Balanced History: 'Ohel,' The 'Workers Theater of Eretz Yisrael' as a Cultural Alternative to *Habima* (1935–1946)." *Journal of Modern Jewish Studies* 13, no. 3 (2014): 340–59.

Young, James E. "When a Day Remembers: A Performative History of 'Yom Ha-Shoah.'" *History and Memory* 2, no. 2 (1990): 54–75.

Yzraely, Yosi. *Vakhtangov Directing the Dybbuk.* Unpublished PhD dissertation. Carnegie Mellon University, 1970.

Zemtsovsky, Izaly. "The Musical Strands of An-sky's Texts and Contexts." In *The Worlds of S. An-sky: A Russian Jewish Intellectual at the Turn of the Century,* edited by Gabriella Safran and Steve J. Zipperstein, 203–31. Stanford: Stanford University Press, 2006.

Zerubavel, Yael. "Memory, the Rebirth of the Native, and the 'Hebrew Bedouin' Identity." *Social Research* 75, no. 1 (Spring 2008): 315–52.

Zer-Zion, Shelly. "The Creation of New Sounds: Hebrew as a New Spoken Language on the Israeli Stage of the 1920's." In *Théâtre: Espace Visual,* edited by Christine Hamon-Sirejols and Anne Surgers, 359–63. Lyon: Presses Universitaires de Lyon, 2003.

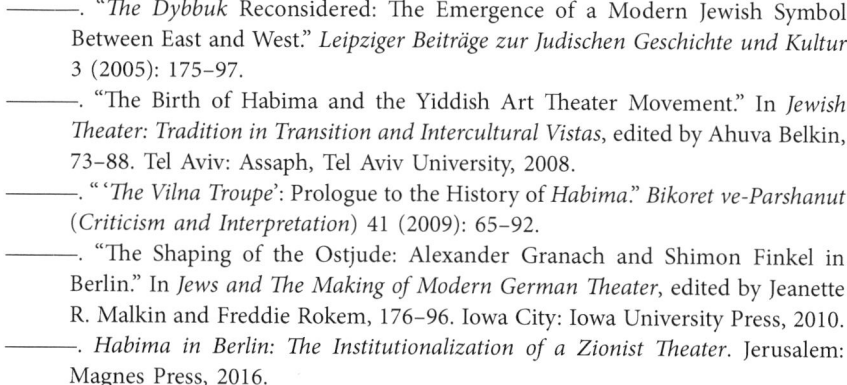

———. "*The Dybbuk* Reconsidered: The Emergence of a Modern Jewish Symbol Between East and West." *Leipziger Beiträge zur Jüdischen Geschichte und Kultur* 3 (2005): 175–97.

———. "The Birth of Habima and the Yiddish Art Theater Movement." In *Jewish Theater: Tradition in Transition and Intercultural Vistas*, edited by Ahuva Belkin, 73–88. Tel Aviv: Assaph, Tel Aviv University, 2008.

———. "'*The Vilna Troupe*': Prologue to the History of *Habima*." *Bikoret ve-Parshanut* (*Criticism and Interpretation*) 41 (2009): 65–92.

———. "The Shaping of the Ostjude: Alexander Granach and Shimon Finkel in Berlin." In *Jews and The Making of Modern German Theater*, edited by Jeanette R. Malkin and Freddie Rokem, 176–96. Iowa City: Iowa University Press, 2010.

———. *Habima in Berlin: The Institutionalization of a Zionist Theater*. Jerusalem: Magnes Press, 2016.

Zur, Muki. *Kehilatenu: 1922 Collection*. Jerusalem: Ben-Zvi Institute, 1988.

Index

accent, 4, 30, 86, 151–52. *See also*
Oriental aural sensibilities and
markers of language; Sephardic
accent
 Hebrew, 105, 126, 129, 149, 150, 152.
See also Hebrew pronunciation;
Semitic accent
 Oriental. *See* Oriental aural
sensibilities and markers of
language
acoustic (theater) community, defined,
80
Admoni, Yael, 132
Adorno, Theodor, 8, 13
"Aesthetic Hebrew" (Epstein), 152
"afterlife," 57, 58, 61, 76, 119
albums. *See* record albums; vinyl
records
Altman, Nathan, 50
"Amar Adonay le Yaakov" ("God said to
Yaa'kov"), 111
An-sky, S. (Shloyme-Zanvl Rappoport),
56, 61, 63–65, 145, 175n15. See
also *The Dybbuk*
 attempt to bring Jewish folklore onto
theater stage, 57
 death, 50
 ethnographic vision, 56
 Habima and, 65, 66
 Jewish Literature and Historical-
Ethnographic Society and, 66
 Moshe Halevy and, 145
 stage direction, 68

anachronism(s), 60, 144
 audio recording and, 60, 71, 75
 lingual, 138, 139
Anderson, Benedict, 81
"The Animal in the Synagogue" (Kafka),
xvii–xxi, 12
Ankersmit, Frank R., 134–35
anti-Semitism, 21, 66, 117, 168n4. *See
also* Arabs: relations between Jews
and
Arab fieldworkers (*Fellahin*), 148–50
Arab society
 indigenous, 144–46
 in Israel, 156
Arabic, 101, 127, 143, 148–51
Arabs
 Bedouin, 144–46, 147f, 154
 cultural similarities between Jews
and, 149–50
 relations between Jews and, 43, 117,
144, 150, 154. *See also* Palestinian
exodus of 1948
 speech, 155. *See also* Arabic
archival gesture. *See* "being there"
(archival) gesture
archival work and archival research, 133
archive(s), 132. See also under *The
Dybbuk*; ephemerality; *Yaakov and
Rachel*; *specific topics*
 "being" in the. *See* "being there"
(archival) gesture
Aronson-Lehavi, Sharon, 193n65
"Ars Poetica" (MacLeish), 7, 165n22

Printed in Great Britain
by Amazon

47200393R00151